P9-BYK-564

Praise for Dr. Mark Pettus's previous book, *The Savvy Patient: The Ultimate Advocate for Quality Health Care*

"Excellent. Contains the best advice I know on doctor-patient negotiations. In clear language it tells how a patient—by asking good questions—can improve the quality of a medical decision."

—Roger Fisher, director,
Harvard Negotiation Project; co-author, *Getting to Yes*

"Dr. Mark Pettus has done us all a magnificent favor. In *The Savvy Patient* he shares the insider's view of medicine we need to get the care we want—a vitally important book that every patient should keep by the bed side."

—Daniel Goleman, author, *Emotional Intelligence*

"An incredible source of information, which in the hands of an inspired patient, will help accomplish true healing."

—Bernie Siegel, MD, author, *Love, Medicine and Miracles;*
Help Me to Heal; and *365 Prescriptions for the Soul*

"Dr. Pettus empowers patients with the tools to overcome the complexities of an overwhelming and often isolating healthcare system. He offers practical advice to enable patients to expect not only excellence in quality of care, but also compassion and partnership. He reminds patients and healthcare professionals of the importance of paying attention to all dimensions of care—the body, mind, and spirit."

—Christina M. Puchalski, MD, director,
The George Washington Institute for Spirituality and Health,
The George Washington University

"*The Savvy Patient: The Ultimate Advocate for Quality Healthcare* by Mark Pettus, M.D., helps readers to understand how to navigate complicated health care systems."

—*Publishers Weekly*

"Doctors find it easier to write prescriptions than teach us new diets. Behavioral medicine, notes Pettus, author of *The Savvy Patient,* is a tough sell . . . Taking ownership of one's health is 'hard work,' says Pettus, but unlike drugs, 'it's not going to cost you a penny.'"

—*USA Today*

It's All in Your Head

Fondly!

Mark Pitton

Also by Mark C. Pettus, MD

The Savvy Patient: The Ultimate Advocate for Quality Healthcare

AVAILABLE IN CAPITAL'S SAVVY SERIES:

*Savvy Eating for the Whole Family: Whole Food,
Whole Family, Whole Life*
by Margaret McCullers Kocsis, MD

*The Savvy Consumer: How to Avoid Scams and Rip-offs
that Cost You Time and Money*
by Elisabeth Leamy, Good Morning
America's Consumer Correspondent

*The Savvy Part-Time Professional: How to Land,
Create, or Negotiate the Part-Time Job of Your Dreams*
by Lynn Berger, MA, EdM

The Savvy Patient: The Ultimate Advocate for Quality Healthcare
by Mark C. Pettus, MD

*The Savvy Woman Patient: How and
Why Sex Differences Affect Your Health*
edited by Phyllis Greenberger, MSW, and Jennifer Wider, MD,
The Society for Women's Health Research

Save 25% when you order any of these and other fine Capital titles from
our Web site: www.capital-books.com

CHANGE YOUR MIND—

It's All in Your Head

CHANGE YOUR HEALTH

Mark C. Pettus, MD

Foreword by Mark Liponis, MD
co-author, *Ultraprevention*

CAPITAL
BOOKS, INC.
Sterling, Virginia

Copyright © 2006 by author

All rights reserved. No part of this book may be reproduced or utilized in any form or by any means, electronic or mechanical, including photocopying, recording, or by any information storage and retrieval system, without permission in writing from the publisher. Inquiries should be addressed to:

Capital Books, Inc.
P.O. Box 605
Herndon, Virginia 20172-0605

ISBN 10: 1-933102-22-5 (alk. paper)
ISBN 13: 978-1-933102-22-1

Library of Congress Cataloging-in-Publication Data
Pettus, Mark C.
    It's all in your head : change your mind, change your health / Mark Pettus — 1st ed.
        p. cm.
    Includes index.
    ISBN 1-933102-22-5 (pbk. : alk. paper)
    1. Health—Psychological aspects.   2. Health behavior.   3. Health attitudes.   4. Mind and body..   I. Title.
    R726.5.P47   2006
    613—dc22

                                                                    2005032941

Printed in the United States of America on acid-free paper that meets the American National Standards Institute Z39-48 Standard.

First Edition

10   9   8   7   6   5   4   3   2   1

Dedication

To my good friend and colleague Alex Sabo who inspired more effective understanding and application of the principles that have formed the basis for this book. Also, to my incredible friends and colleagues in the Berkshire Hills of Western Massachusetts who lifted and sustained me for seventeen sweet years! You are what social connection, meaning-making, reward, and motivation are all about.

Acknowledgments

I am indebted to Martha Prescott for her impeccable assistance with comprehensive literature searches for many of the topics discussed in *It's All in Your Head*. I am also grateful for my wife Lee Ann's assistance with the preparation of the manuscript and to my many friends and colleagues gracious enough to review the content and provide helpful feedback.

Special thanks to Bruce McEwen, PhD, for his thoughtful review of the manuscript and for his valuable feedback. Lastly, I am grateful to Amy Fries for her superb editing expertise. This is a much better book because of her personalized attention to the manuscript.

Disclaimer

Open any publication that provides medical information and you will see, up front, a disclaimer. One important reason for the disclaimer is to make clear that any medical information must be interpreted on an individualized basis and discussed with your own physician prior to the application of this newfound knowledge. As there is no one-size-fits all approach to health, wellness, and disease management, I have tried to focus on generalizations that I believe most people will find extremely beneficial when applied to their lives and to their health care encounters. The second reason for the disclaimer is to protect the author from possible litigation if an adverse or negative event occurs as a consequence of the advice given.

We live in a litigious society. Many decisions are made, enormous sums of money are spent, and much energy is invested with the explicit purpose of minimizing medical legal risk; that is, avoiding a lawsuit. This has gotten way out of control in health care and in every other aspect of our social enterprise. With that said, the author will not assume responsibility for any adverse events that may occur as a consequence of your application of the wisdom to follow. I would be glad to assume, however, at least partial responsibility for any meaningful and positive outcomes that occur.

Contents

Foreword

Reading this book reminded me of a personal story. About three years ago my father became ill. His skin turned yellow, a condition known as jaundice, which results from a liver problem. His doctor told him this was serious and sent him for a CAT scan. The scan showed a tumor pushing on the liver and the pancreas. My mom and dad went to the doctor's office to learn what was wrong and the doctor said, "There's a tumor in your liver and pancreas. Most likely this is a cancerous tumor." My parents were distraught and asked the usual questions: "What can we do about it?," "Is there any treatment?," and "What's the prognosis?" The doctor was not optimistic and told them, correctly, that cancer of the liver and pancreas was not usually curable, and surgery could only relieve the blockage, not remove the cancer. Most patients would live only six months.

Six months to live. That was what my dad came home with. Six months. My parents were devastated. My dad was distraught. They asked me what I thought. I spoke with the doctor, who told me pretty much the same thing. They recommended surgery only to relieve the blockage and put in a shunt to drain the liver, and this was scheduled for the following week. Over the next few days, my parents became seriously woeful and depressed. The doctors recommended medication for depression and anxiety. I tried to cheer them up, and of course told them that the scan did not show cancer, it only showed a tumor. The scan couldn't tell if the tumor was cancerous. But the message stuck . . . six months to live.

The next week my dad went in for his surgery. The surgeons were surprised to find not cancer, but a large gallstone blocking the bile ducts that was causing the problem. They removed the gallstone and repaired the blocked ducts and the liver began to function again. My mom and I were overjoyed—the dire diagnosis and prognosis had been completely wrong. We were elated. When my father woke up from the anesthesia we explained the situation to him. He seemed to understand, but somehow did not seem relieved.

Over the next few days in the hospital we continued to explain to him that there was no tumor, only a gallstone. But somehow he couldn't get it out of his mind . . . six months to live. He had been so panicked by the doctor's premature prediction that it had become indelibly imprinted in his mind. Maybe he thought we were just trying to spare him the mental anguish, or perk up his spirits. But even the doctor himself could not convince him.

Despite our best efforts, we had little success in convincing Dad that he was OK. In his mind, he still had only six months to live. Before he became jaundiced, my dad was a charismatic, jovial, and talkative patriarch of our family—the driving force and "life of the party." From the moment after hearing that fateful prognostication, he changed completely. His personality was withdrawn, his mood depressed. His face became expressionless. He wouldn't smile. It completely changed his entire outlook. After the surgery his condition worsened. He became immobile and lost his balance. He could no longer navigate himself. He needed help walking and could no longer get out of a chair without assistance. His face showed a blank expressionless stare.

His condition continued to decline, and a few months later, he was diagnosed with Parkinson's disease. Now on several medications, he has never made the full "recovery" he should have. Of course it's been much longer than six months. He recognizes that the initial prediction was wrong. But he somehow never recovered. What should have been a fairly simple gallbladder operation became a major, irreversible decline in his overall health.

It is clear that one's own belief in their prognosis can have an important impact. What I really admire about this book is that Dr. Pettus has attached contemporary science and understanding to wisdom that is ancient and powerful. In doing so, he makes the reader more aware that the greatest gift of all is our capacity to adapt in marvelous ways! He opens the door to the most wonderful opportunity possible . . . the opportunity to make the most of life's most important gifts. As you read this vitally important book you will quickly appreciate the importance of self-care. Dr. Pettus makes accessible a

roadmap that will change your life. It is a roadmap that anyone motivated to
live a better life can assuredly navigate. His message is personal and clear:

The mind has a powerful effect on the body.

One of the greatest pleasures of being a physician is witnessing the miracles of life and the human body. The more science learns about the human
body, the more it seems we don't know. For every answer, more questions
arise. What's clear is there is still much we do not know, especially when it
comes to the myriad effects of our mind, emotions, and behaviors on our
health and wellness.

In this detailed examination of the science that informs our understanding of the power of mind over body, Dr. Mark Pettus reviews the research
that links anger, hostility, and stress with heart disease, high blood pressure,
and stroke. We are reminded that the quality of our relationships affects the
health of women and men with heart disease. Depression is linked with
osteoporosis and impaired immunity. Meditation enhances the healing of
many medical conditions. Stress reduction can improve most symptoms that
affect quality of life. Medical research is just beginning to identify the numerous linkages between various emotional states, personality types, and health
disorders. *It's All in Your Head* will awaken you to the importance of reducing stress and harmful emotions in your life while fostering compassion and
positive emotions that will improve health and longevity.

I am regularly reminded that our five senses of vision, hearing, taste,
touch, and smell provide us with only a rough interpretation of the world we
live in. My dogs are fully aware of an entire world that I have little sense of.
I'm quite sure they can smell or otherwise sense our emotions. Our perception is just a glimpse of our world, and science continues to make discover-
ies that improve our understanding of the miracles of the human body and
how our mind affects our health. *It's All in Your Head* is an elegant piece of
work that nicely ties the science of mind and body to experiences of everyday life.

Dr. Mark Pettus reminds us that we need to learn not to interfere with
those miracles, and to recognize and amplify the beneficial effects that the
mind can exert for improving the health and happiness of us all. As you will
soon see, your mind, emotions, and behaviors can transcend the most chal-

lenging of obstacles to optimal health. As an experienced and compassionate clinician and educator, Dr. Pettus has given us a thoughtful and inspiring story of hope.

Mark Liponis, MD
Corporate Medical Director
Canyon Ranch
Co-author *Ultraprevention: The 6-Week Plan*
That Will Make You Healthy for Life

Introduction

"Tell me and I'll forget.
Show me and I may not remember.
Involve me and I will understand."

Native American Proverb

My life has changed forever. I have lost some weight, and as I approach fifty, I take great pride in being able to comfortably wear the suit I wore at my wedding almost twenty years ago. I have gone from very little, if any, structured activity in my life to running twenty miles per week. I've been transformed from a sweets and refined-carbohydrate addict to one who craves green, leafy vegetables and tofu. I've been transformed from an individual who *thought* he had control over the tremendous burden of stress in his life to one who *actually has* more control over the tremendous burden of stress in his life. I meditate more. I pray more. I purposefully cultivate as many meaningful friendships in my life as possible. I have transformed the frustration of "not having time" to do the many things that I value to actually doing and experiencing the satisfaction of endeavors that I *value the most*. I no longer assume as a physician and as a human being that age-related decline in health and quality of life is an inevitability. I "passively accept" less and "consciously choose" more.

My family history is replete with health risks including diabetes, high blood pressure, kidney disease, depression, stroke, and premature death. The cards I was born with, in retrospect, were not that great for many of the age-related morbidities that many people confront. Five years ago, my trajectory of health and wellness was a path largely under the influence of inertia and passivity. My behavioral choices were undermining my health. I was confronting the need to take medications to control many of the risk factors I was genetically endowed with and behaviorally perpetuating.

Currently, my cholesterol and blood pressure have never been better. My mood, emotions, and concentration have never been better and more positive. My marital life has never felt more satisfying. I feel more accepting, trusting, open-minded, and resilient. And the only medications I take are supplements, e.g., fish oils and antioxidants. I have come to appreciate that I have much more control over my life trajectory than I ever thought imaginable! I am more mindful that while alive, it is never too late for meaningful change. Self-care is in fact a wonderful gift and opportunity!

This has also changed the way I care for others. The remarkable life transformation that I've experienced and the life transformations that many people I've cared for have experienced—combined with the scientific research that currently informs the health effects of behavioral and lifestyle change—have inspired me to write this book.

People who are in more control of their lives experience a lower burden of stress. People who are in more control of their lives are more resilient and better able to transcend setbacks and adversity.

More Control = Less Stress
Less Stress = Aging Well

Consider this sobering reality. Despite more than three decades of hammering home the health-promoting message of exercise and good nutrition, the best health advice is effectively heeded less than five percent of the time! It's simply not enough to have the knowledge of what is healthy and what isn't. That alone will not effectively influence behavioral change. There are formidable obstacles out there! Fast food and fast calories are readily available. Suburban sprawl has all but eliminated the option of walking and biking to complete errands and other daily tasks. Automation technology has increased the percentage of sedentary jobs that employ most Americans. The power of community and social capital, as the ultimate health-promoting enterprise, has not been creatively exploited. We are overworked, way too stressed out, and limited in our fun playtime, if we get any at all. This is an unhealthy constellation of trends. The pervasively negative biological effects as we respond to these behavioral patterns are referred to as **allostatic load.** This concept will come up throughout this book.

Our current systems of health care are designed primarily to put out the fires once they develop. This book is about reducing the likelihood of a fire ever occurring in the first place. You will need to take more control here. You may not be aware that the best path to health and wellness is within you and "low tech" by its very nature. We can easily take this for granted especially given the prevailing perception that any intervention has to be high-tech, sexy, and expensive to be effective. Nothing could be further from the truth. Health care as a product is not like buying an appliance. More expensive is not always better. For example, you may get a CAT scan that costs two thousand dollars that you didn't really need in the first place and not receive a five-cent-per-day aspirin that could add years to your life.

Low tech can be very sexy! You will not often get this message from traditional sources of health information.

We know that 50 percent of Americans are not realizing the potential benefits of good clinical evidence-based interventions, many of which, like aspirin, are inexpensive and low-tech. We know that the overwhelming majority of symptoms driving office visits in the primary care setting have an emotional and social component attached to them. In fact, it's estimated that as many as two out of three visits to primary care physicians have a primary component of stress as a contributor. We also know that the greatest impact on overall public health and quality of life can, more than anything, be significantly influenced by lifestyle and behavioral change. However, we also know that advice relating to lifestyle and behavioral change is usually not successfully applied. I should say it is not successfully applied most of the time. While my primary care provider is a terrific fellow, and I trust him wholeheartedly, my behavioral and lifestyle transformations had to come from within. In addition, we misinterpret feeling well with being in good health. The greatest threats to your longevity and quality of life, e.g., stress, high blood pressure, diabetes, high cholesterol, etc., are silent by their very nature until they strike.

In recent years, many behavioral health and other scientific disciplines like the neurosciences have converged on a new frontier of understanding as it relates to the relationship between thought, emotion, brain biology, behavior, and bodily function. A crystallization of complex interactions between nature and nurture is beginning to unveil itself as this fascinating research continues to unfold. As the veil of nature and nurture is lifted further, there appears to be far more overlap than once imagined. The misperceived boundaries of nature and nurture, mind and body, have all but broken down. This has major implications for how you perceive your potential for health and healing! And I can assure you, it will look different than you thought.

It's All in Your Head was written to open the curtain to your mind, revealing this masterpiece of auto-adaptation, the human brain, your body's CEO. I want to make more accessible to you an awareness of what is happening "behind the mind's curtain" when you think, feel, and behave in ways that are health promoting and perhaps in ways that are insidiously undermining your potential for optimal health and wellness. As the Wizard of Oz revealed after the curtain was pulled back, the greatest potential to find courage, heart, understanding, and home must come from within more than from some magical wand waved upon you.

We know that a complex cascade of intricately connected protein messengers in the brain referred to as neurotransmitters are delicately influenced by how we "see" the world we interact with and how we ultimately live our lives. These transmitters have a wide range of powerful influences on biological function throughout our body, e.g., immune function, blood pressure, vascular health, diabetes risk, metabolic rate, wound healing, cellular health, etc. What we experience emotionally—feelings of despair and anger vs. joy, love, or gratitude—are manifestations of subtle and very significant shifts in the symphony these neurotransmitters produce each and every moment. All elements of the orchestra need to be in harmony for joy and optimal immune function to be realized. If the brass section is slightly off, the harmony is disrupted in a manner that might allow fear and anxiety to overwhelm us or blood pressure and heart rate to become dangerously high.

In this context, anger and hostility are not just personality traits that you are predisposed to. They are emotional expressions of an underlying overdrive of your fight-flight stress response, which is squeezing cortisol out of your adrenal glands and revving up adrenaline and other neurotransmitters, all with negative health consequences. In this context, sustained or recurrent anger and hostility might be thought of, from a cardiovascular health perspective, as no less of a threat than smoking cigarettes. You get the picture. No longer can we accept the oversimplified separation of mind, emotion, and body. Just ask your CEO. The evidence is clear.

In this context, anger and hostility are not just personality traits that you are predisposed to. They are emotional expressions of an underlying overdrive of your fight-flight stress response, which is squeezing cortisol out of your adrenal glands and revving up adrenaline and other neurotransmitters, all with negative health consequences. In this context, sustained or recurrent anger and hostility might be thought of, from a cardiovascular health perspective, as no less of a threat than smoking cigarettes.

Mind is Brain. Brain is Body.
Mind is Body.

It's All in Your Head examines the health implications of how we interpret events in our lives and how we respond to those events. The experiences of your life will get into your head each and every time. There they interact with your brain. Your brain, the CEO of your body, distills the "data" of your experiences into recognizable patterns that set the agenda for how you feel, what you think, and how you behave. Unless you're a scarecrow, you've got a CEO too. And as you know, you can't just go out and get a new one from the Wizard. Your CEO is definitely worth getting to know. It is my goal to help you influence your CEO to more effectively assist in your journey of health.

The story is quite an extraordinary one. It is a story that is both ancient and intuitive and at the same time novel and fresh. It is a story that is both deeply rooted in human cultural behavior and in its infancy as a path to transforming our perceptions of health promotion and disease prevention. From an aerial view, this story is about greater understanding of how our thoughts, feelings, and behaviors influence a virtual orchestra of biological responses that can promote health and prevent disease. This is a symphony played by mind, emotion, brain, behavior, and body. I like to think of it as the ME-B^3 orchestra (figure 1).

The ME-B^3 orchestra, for example, can perform a symphony that alters perceptions of pain, mood, and cardiovascular risk. This interplay affects diabetes risk, inflammation, immune function, coping, symptom management, conflict management, behavioral management, and longevity. The ME-B^3

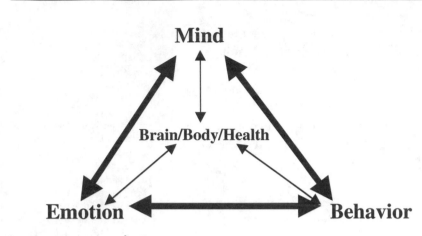

Figure 1.1   The ME-B³ orchestra

orchestra can work for you, and it can turn against you. Research points to the remarkable adaptability for change that is inherent in this incredible dance shared by mind-emotion-brain-behavior-body or ME-B³. This capacity is referred to as *plasticity*. Bridging the neurobiology of your thoughts, emotions, and behaviors to your conscious daily life, can and will change the way you conduct your orchestra and the symphony it produces.

I will attempt to make the case that you, as the conductor of this marvelous orchestra, have much greater influence over the symphony produced than ever imagined! Knowledge alone, however, is just a starting point. We all require some help with how to apply what we know. You may have a sense of what your destination is and no clue as how best to get there. You may know how to get there but feel stuck along the way. You may simply need more help. This is challenging and rewarding work. It forces you to reconsider who you are and what you are capable of.

In *It's All in Your Head*, I will provide you with the knowledge and tools to make success on your journey of health promotion and disease prevention more likely. You will begin to notice changes in how you feel, think, behave, and perform almost immediately. These powerful, low-tech interventions, some long recognized, now have more robust science to support them. Ideally they should be integrated with other aspects of your health care. See them as "trump cards" that can profoundly enhance the cards you're currently holding in your hand of life.

The challenge of moving forward with what I am about to share requires you to rebuild the house you are living in. You will have to take down the familiar perceptions that are framed and hanging on your walls and replace them. You will have to find the fuse box, turn a few off, and add a few more. You will have to be willing to accept the challenge of sanding, refinishing, and repainting the behavioral stains that you've been comfortable looking at and walking by each day for years and years. And you can. By applying yourself more thoughtfully and by reaching out to others who can help, you can.

It's All in Your Head is divided into three sections. The first will whet your appetite with some personal examples of how the house your brain resides in can be gutted and redesigned. My house looks and feels very different now than it did five years ago. I will give you some specific examples of how the applications of these neuroscience and mind-body principles have worked for me. I will provide you with some of the measurable benefits I have realized, e.g., lower blood pressure, cholesterol, weight, conflict management, etc., by more mindful integration and application of this knowledge in my life.

Over the last several years, I have become addicted to health. I simply had to take more effective charge of my life. So do you. I have come to appreciate that anxiety, impatience, anger, hostility, fear, and doubt are not just feelings that inevitably and randomly come and go with a life of their own. Joy, optimism, hope, confidence, and love are not just on the shelf of the lucky few who experience them. These are in fact physiological states that can be induced, understood, and managed. They are physiologic states that affect every dimension of our health and healing.

I have become attuned to using more of the orchestra I was born with. While I accept that some musicians in my mind's orchestra were genetically destined to be there, I no longer assume that they can only play their instruments in one particular style. Each musician can be trained to sound different and the orchestra, when taken full advantage of, can turn a dysfunctional cacophony into a resonating masterpiece.

I have come to appreciate that anxiety, impatience, anger, hostility, fear, and doubt are not just feelings that inevitably and randomly come and go with a life of their own. Joy, optimism, hope, confidence, and love are not just on the shelf of the lucky few who experience them. These are in fact physiological states that can be induced, understood, and managed. They are physiologic states that affect every dimension of our health and healing.

And it appears that the more you use it . . . the more you use it.

The second section will be a general overview of current research and understanding in the field of neuroscience, a sort of "neuroscience 101," if you will. I apologize in advance if some of this is a bit heavy on the technical side. Remember, there's no test afterwards. Hang in there. It's important that you not get too bogged down on the neurobiological vernacular. See this information as an interesting garden to walk through at a pace you feel most comfortable with. You can come back and revisit this information at any time. The rest will fall into place. This is the kind of stuff that's both ancient and new frontier, and from my unbiased perspective, quite sexy. Mention your amygdala over a glass of wine at a party and definitely be remembered by those in attendance. The third section will provide medical evidence and every day examples of how these powerful connections can more effectively be applied in your life.

I will review the best medical evidence currently available connecting lifestyle choices and practices with important health outcomes and how you can implement these choices and practices more effectively in your own life. From social relationships and interpersonal engagement to faith in its many expressions, you will see unfold a strategy for living that is hardly random but one that connects back to the orchestra within you and to the symphony it's capable of producing.

I will provide some everyday examples that can be immediately put to use. For example, observe the face of an individual maintaining a good pace while outdoors on a walk, and you will observe the reward response in action. Casually observe the smile of a person you are conversing with, and you will be able to distinguish the "airline hostess smile" from a smile that has genuine happiness beneath it. Try the relaxation response in the bottom of the ninth as your favorite baseball team is threatened with elimination from the World Series. It will save you a trip to your local emergency department or an unnecessary several hours of anger, anxiety, and frustration. Reduce a couple of otherwise inevitable surges of cortisol/adrenaline each day. That will add up to over 10,000 surges of cortisol/adrenaline reduced in just ten years! Exercise your prefrontal cortex control over your amygdala and improve the likelihood of more effectively navigating your way through the messiest of conflicts. There's no treatment I can prescribe as a double-board certified physician that can do that.

From managing conflict in your life to raising adolescent kids, your degree of physical, mental, emotional, and spiritual consumption or fulfillment can vary dramatically depending on how effectively you navigate. Greater awareness of the interactions of your thoughts, feelings, and behaviors will enable you to choose more consciously.

It is crucial to be more aware of when you are consciously driving your car and when you are a passenger in your own car, being driven by your subconscious. This is a very important distinction.

You will also acquire a greater awareness of what is happening behind the curtain of the minds of others.

Though we are all capable of expressing the turbulence beneath the surface of our lives as self-destructive ripples and dysfunctional waves, we are also capable of taking similar circumstances and cultivating a calm, serene, and beautifully balanced ecosystem. There is no reason to navigate from one storm to the next when the sailing can remain smooth even under the worst meteorological conditions.

Behaviors aligned with pursuit and fulfillment of that which carries the deepest meaning to you and satisfies that which you value most will activate primal brain circuitry that produces a biological response that pays handsomely. These responses when cultivated as a way of living can dramatically enhance health. A friend and colleague of mine refers to this as the "meaning-maker" capacity. Creating sources of meaning and value satisfaction in our lives elicits a brain-biological response, reinforcing the behaviors that created them in the first place. From a health promotion perspective, this is an important principle: The more meaning we have in our relationships, work, and play, the greater the odds of better health, wellness, and life satisfaction. We need to make choices that enhance positive "addictive" behaviors and diminish behaviors that serve us poorly. This leaves open the potential to transform interactions working in the opposite direction, perpetually undermining your health and wellness. The message here is:

**Where meaning exists in your work, love, and play sustain it.
Where it is missing, create it!**

While none of this can guarantee avoidance of bad health outcomes, it does liberate the potential for greater control over that within your influence. We are designed for survival. We are designed for resilience. We are designed for adaptation. We are designed to connect within ourselves and with others. No magic here. This is a lot of work. It can be overwhelming and intimidating. You have the potential to reinvent yourself, and I am going to give you some suggestions how. But I can only open the door. You will have to choose to walk through. It is within you. Believe in yourself. While you may not believe your circumstances are capable of change, the ride you are about to take will leave you transformed. The cost here is in time and commitment. No money necessary. There are NO side effects or adverse reactions. And if you are asking yourself, "Can I really succeed?" I would respond as Lennon and McCartney once did by saying, "You've got a ticket to ride." Strap yourself in and enjoy.

Mark C. Pettus, MD, FACP
www.savvypatient.com

Part I

Addicted to Health:
Getting Hooked

Chapter 1

Confessions of a Health Junkie: The Power of Plasticity

Before exploring some of the science that informs the extraordinary interplay of mind, emotion, body, and health, I thought it would help to see some everyday examples of where you can go with the mind and body you have.

I'm more addicted to health than ever before in my life. You can be too. As I have noted, my motivation for writing this book was largely influenced by the impact this stuff has had on my personal and professional life. I want to emphasize that seemingly small and trivial goal-reaching behaviors pay big dividends. The interest on these small deposits will be compounded over the weeks, months, and years. Trust me on this, not just because I'm a doctor, but because I have experienced the returns!

> I'm more addicted to health than ever before in my life. You can be too.

> I want to emphasize that seemingly small and trivial goal-reaching behaviors pay big dividends.

Several years ago, it would have never crossed my mind that I could practice medicine any other way than how I was trained to as an internist and nephrologist (kidney specialist) in an academic setting. After years of training, my dream was to develop a practice and then hope for a long, successful journey to retirement. This was the script. This was how my mentors and role models practiced. This was my expectation. This was what others expected of me. I didn't anticipate, many years later, having to reconcile growing tension between my values for patient care and my values for a successful marriage, parenting, and my own good health.

After more than fifteen years of being on call, I had lost my balance on the high-wire held in place by work, family, and self-care. I began to feel sucked into the illusion that the triad of work, family, and self could not easily coexist. Giving more to one would naturally take from the other. My perception was that the pie was fixed with only so many pieces to go around. My family needed more of me. My patients needed more of me. I needed more of me. I began to see these enormously important dimensions of my life as competitors with the flawed perceptual belief that one could not succeed if the other was to succeed.

That was then and this is now.

What appeared as an impossible choice eventually became a host of possibilities that enabled me to thrive professionally as a clinician-educator *and* to have more quality time for my family and me. The perception of win-lose was transformed into win-win with creation of options I did not hitherto realize existed.

We all reach crossroads in our lives where the signpost compels us to choose either A or B: relationship or job; work or play; love or loss. When A and B are both of value to us, it makes sense to explore options for allowing both A *and* B to prevail in some satisfactory fashion. The challenge for me was breaking free of the expectations I had of myself and that others had of me. The challenge was to consciously choose to navigate uncertain waters. The fear of walking an uncertain and unfamiliar path appeared more an obstacle than an open door.

That was then and this is now.

The doors of our lives most begging to be opened are often the doors we are likely to tiptoe by. This book, if anything, is about "showing you the door." If you choose to walk through it as I have, you're not likely to ever look back.

Years ago it would have never crossed my mind to go outside and run on a dark, frigid, February, New England evening. As a matter of fact, I wouldn't have thought to go outside and run on a perfect June evening (or morning, or midday, or late night). I hated running. Of course, I was well aware of the potential health benefits. But that wasn't enough. Running was boring, and it hurt my legs. I would drive my car down our neighborhood streets and see others running and think, "I sure wish I could get out there and do that." My perception was that running was an activity that only the chosen, with long smooth strides and perfect form, could truly enjoy and achieve. I could never imagine running in place on a treadmill, going nowhere in particular. Mark Pettus and running would have to remain a fantasy.

That was then and this is now.

Not long ago, I could not have imagined life without concentrated sweets and refined carbohydrates. My credo was drink two cans of Coke Classic each day, and I'll call you in the morning. That familiar red-and-white icon of carbonated, caffeine-enhanced, sugar-sweetened cola perfection was a perpetual extension of my right hand on most afternoons and evenings. It was like an old and trusted friend. It sharpened my mind, preparing me for the next interpersonal challenge. Its effervescent bubbles calmed me. Its caffeine and sugar lifted me from fatigue. Life without Coke Classic was yet another fantasy.

The thought of eating lunch and dinner without dessert was tantamount to unreasonable self-deprivation. Grazing on sweets late in the day was literally a no-brainer habit. By no-brainer, I would suggest that my behaviors, habitually driven, were largely occurring on a subconscious level. I lived for sweets. I would purposefully alter entrée selection to best prepare for the confectionary reward to follow. Not too long ago, I would have looked at the fellow sitting at the table next to me in our favorite restaurant eating a portabella mushroom and thought, "That could never be me." The thought of multiple small portions of colorful vegetables, sporadically scattered on an embellished dinner plate, did little to satisfy my carnivorous tendencies. After all, this was who I was and always had been. And I felt pretty good. My weight wasn't that bad. *C'mon Pettus, you look okay for someone old enough to have a colonoscopy!* No biggie.

That was then and this is now.

Several years ago while fully immersed in an every third night/weekend practice, I wouldn't have thought it possible that I could foster the time and energy to volunteer in my community, serve as a leader in my church, serve as an advocate for the developmentally disabled, write a book, learn to fly, and acquire an expertise in information technology. No way could enough time be garnered to cultivate these values in my life. I would've never thought I could be in a position of putting my kids on the bus, seeing and participating in more of their activities, coaching a team they played on, or serving my community more than I was. It simply was not possible. More fantasy.

The trajectory I was on, worthy and principled though it was, left me certain that what I thought, how I felt, how I behaved, and ultimately how healthy I was living were at the limit of my capacity to control. I had matured into a pretty good physician and enjoyed the challenge of practice. I'd become less attuned to the impact my very busy and stressful lifestyle was having on my effectiveness as a husband, father, and friend. I was unaware of the impact my choices and their consequences were having on my capacity for more effective self-care. The status quo was as comfortable as it was habitual. This can so easily become the theme of our lives, a familiar one indeed, with painfully predictable outcomes.

That was then and this is now.

My mind has always been a very busy place. I was always thinking, thinking, thinking. Rarely was my mind still enough to embrace the moment. While I have always generally connected well with others, my mind was usually looking forward, contemplating, speculating, and prognosticating. I was always several steps ahead of the moment I was in. That's one of the reasons, I looked forward to attending church as this seemed to be the one setting where I could become reacquainted with stillness. My mind and all its cognitive clutter raced forward with the perceptual illusion that less would be accomplished otherwise. I began to feel more anxious during interpersonal interactions to push my agenda, my thoughts, and my opinions. I felt pressured at times to say something to be heard—rather than to be still, to listen, and to be aware. I was acculturated to the mythical perception that being a good physician and leader meant knowing more than others and behaving in a manner consistent with that perception—having the last word, dominating a conversation, and dismissing uncertainty as a sign of vulnerability.

Well, that was then and this is now.

I made some significant changes in my professional life (a huge step indeed). I chose to leave a successful, thriving, academic nephrology practice. I left without a plan for what type of work would follow. I departed from a script that was all too familiar, habitual, comfortable, and predictable. While I chose a professional "free fall," my gut told me I would likely land on my feet. After this, I turned my attention to the value of self-care. I'd been good about getting regular physicals. In this respect, I walked the talk. My family history is impressively bad with a host of genetically influenced health issues. In addition, I knew enough to respect the silent nature of these beasts. I was also aware of the power of intervention to neutralize these risks and blessed to have the resources necessary to receive proper care. The health care system, by the way, is a critical partner in this dimension of your care. It's far from perfect, however, which underscores *the vital importance of cultivating a commitment to self-care.* You must take greater control and become the master of yourself.

> You must take greater control and become the master of yourself.

During a routine physical exam I had a few years back, I began to contemplate some of the good choices I'd made in an effort to redefine and improve the balance of values in my life. I could have easily accepted this place in my life as an ideal place to be. And I surely felt good about the positive momentum of change I had created. As I sat on the examining table looking very sharp in my paper, one-size-fits-all, tie-in-the-back exam "robe," my friend and physician colleague peered over the top of my medical record, took off his glasses, and looked into my eyes (very effective behavioral influence tool). His tone and body language were about to send a powerful message. Sensing this, my antennas were up as I thought to myself, "What he is about to say is really important."

In his focused and soft-spoken manner, he noted, "Mark, I was just noticing you've gained twelve pounds in the last few years. Your blood pressure has also shown some increasing trends (136/84–86, too high, particularly with my family history). And the blood work you had done yesterday shows your total cholesterol to be up to 260 and your LDL up to 170." Of course, I was listening and thinking, "I wonder if this is the same scale? Have I really put on twelve pounds? Perhaps I had more clothing on today than last year. (You know how heavy those ten-pound athletic socks can be?) Did I fast long enough before that blood work was drawn?" And yada, yada, yada, as I entered the land of rationalization.

All of these trends had developed over the last few years and were clearly connected to my poor dietary discretion and lack of exercise, resulting in the "obligatory two- to three-pound per year weight gain." Twelve-plus pounds; all fat, all adipose, all way too easy.

This was a wake up call! It was also the tip of an iceberg of other health markers that we hadn't specifically looked at like cortisol, insulin resistance, C-reactive protein (a marker of inflammation), aerobic capacity, musculoskeletal flexibility, and neurocognitive capacity, etc.

Well, that was then and this is now. I have since discovered that the "obligatory" weight gain associated with aging is not obligatory at all. It is instead a choice.

> I have since discovered that the "obligatory" weight gain associated with aging is not obligatory at all. It is instead a choice.

The strategy for moving forward, I knew from experience, would require hard work, risk-taking (necessary for behavioral change), commitment, and a willingness to be rendered vulnerable. *Prepare for vulnerability.* It's a necessary part of the journey. From the moment you choose to change, any behavior that's more effectively aligned with the pursuit of better health, becomes a source of fuel for motivating continued change.

> From the moment you choose to change, any behavior that's more effectively aligned with the pursuit of better health, becomes a source of fuel for motivating continued change.

The areas I chose to change I selected because they had personal meaning, they provided social connections, and they provided rewards in the form of better health and peace of mind. For example, as I have summarized in my "Four-Week Addicted to Health Program" in Chapter 2, I began to cut back on refined carbohydrates, eat more vegetables, and start a more structured aerobic and resistance exercise program. I bought some meditation tapes and books (see the Suggested Reading list at the end of the book) and began to practice a few days per week. I chose to volunteer my time with organizations that meant a lot to me—church, hospice care, and agencies that advocate for individuals with developmental disabilities.

All those "rewards," in turn, gave me the motivation to continue to change. I was trying to ignite the fires that would reward change and leave me wanting more. I will elaborate on these primal brain networks and how they can work better for you in Chapter 4: "Neuroscience 101." Trust me for now. They work wonders if you're willing to pay, and if you're willing to play.

RECONCILING VALUES

A logical place to start the process of effective behavioral change is taking inventory of what you value most. Our values emerge from an awareness of what is most important in our lives. The more deeply something means to you, the more you value it. As our behavior becomes driven by habitual patterns of thinking, feeling, and doing, we easily lose awareness of the disparity between what we value and how aligned our behaviors are with the ultimate goal of satisfying what we value.

> A logical place to start the process of effective behavioral change is taking inventory of what you value most.

It's an eye opener to hold our thoughts, feelings, and behaviors to the light for the purpose of illuminating how well they're serving us. The distance between where you are and where you desire to be may feel overwhelmingly far apart. The challenge is to reframe your perception of just how significant each step forward actually is. Your mind may be telling you that the steps are trivial and meaningless. However, the biology beneath the surface, the mechanisms that drive you, will be changing significantly in ways that are anything but trivial.

> It's an eye opener to hold our thoughts, feelings, and behaviors to the light for the purpose of illuminating how well they're serving us. The distance between where you are and where you desire to be may feel overwhelmingly far apart.

I would highly recommend some undivided time to think through and write down the aspects of your life that you value most. As you will see, the values that mean the most to you will begin to connect other values, and a value pyramid will begin to form. As connectors like equanimity, relationships, love, laughter rise to the top of your pyramid, take the top five to ten and write three goals that would better satisfy

> Your mind may be telling you that the steps are trivial and meaningless. However, the biology beneath the surface, the mechanisms that drive you, will be changing significantly in ways that are anything but trivial.

these values. For example, you may greatly value relationships. Three criteria to satisfy this value might include:

1. Make time for a weekly date with your significant other or work on a relationship that's in need of more attention.

2. Reconcile a deep wound from an unresolved conflict with a friend or family member.

3. Volunteer for a cause that means something to you.

It also helps to identify some thoughts, feelings, and behaviors that are not serving a value particularly well. In the case of fostering relationships, for example:

1. Feeling impatient with family or colleagues who "don't seem to get it."

2. Thinking you are without perceptual gaps in the interpretation of the events in your life.

3. Working too much and playing too little.

Now you may be thinking, "I don't have time for a mental exercise like this." I understand. I used to feel the same way. It was an eye-opener for me to do this task. Through this exercise, you will become aware that what you value most in life is left to chance. Through this short exercise, you will appreciate how easy it is to identify values that trump all others. You'll be able to compare your current trajectory with the satisfaction of your values and begin to develop strategies to get what you truly want out of life.

For me, values like inner peace, happiness, affirmation, contribution, fun, and influence ended up high on my list. Some values were more abstract—inner peace—compared to the more concrete values like contribution, which could easily be achieved by volunteering in the community. I began to look at exercise, nutrition, and volunteering as superb paths to satisfying my values for inner peace, happiness, contribution, fun, and health.

It was clear that many of my previous behaviors, actions, and choices were not well aligned with what I truly valued. While health and wellness were very high on my pyramid of values, I was not exercising in a purposeful way, and I was not eating as well I could be. I was drinking far too many sugary soft drinks and not eating enough fruits and vegetables. I was consuming far too many foods with a high glycemic index (as defined by the extent sugar is absorbed and elevated in the bloodstream after ingestion), putting out some serious insulin, and putting on two to three pounds a year around my mid section. I was on a classic trajectory of "lifestyle syndrome," a trajectory I shared with far too many others.

At the risk of sounding judgmental, inactivity and obesity have become epidemics in the U.S. Just because the club has a lot of members doesn't mean you should feel comfortable being part of the club. I've always valued physical activity and recreation, and yet I wasn't engaged in any regular aerobic or resistance activity. I valued my marriage and being a father, and yet I wasn't behaving in a manner consistent with a commitment to satisfying these values.

When you imagine who you could be in contrast to who you are, challenge becomes opportunity and fear becomes possibility. Behavioral change has to be a choice. Ultimately we act not because we must but because we can (Did someone famous once say that?).

The capacity for change and adaptation—called plasticity—is an inherent feature of our design as I will demonstrate throughout this book. Of course rationalization is a forte for most and nothing fuels inertia like rationalization. "So I put on the proverbial two to three pounds per year. That's not too bad. So I've become a bit more sedentary and get winded when walking up a hill in my neighborhood. I have vivid memories of playing baseball in college and having good hand-eye coordination. How far could I have drifted from such a clear vision of who I was twenty-five years ago? So my blood pressure and cholesterol are creeping up. That's my genetic legacy and therefore inevitable. I can take meds if I need to. There are a lot of pharmacological options out there."

> The capacity for change and adaptation—called plasticity—is an inherent feature of our design as I will demonstrate throughout this book.

I, too, had excellent ego-protecting, approval-seeking rationalizations. The paradox is that when it comes to our symphony of health, most of us think we're reasonable orchestra conductors. However, the symphonies we produce tend to sound better to us than they actually are. It's like singing in the shower. When the water temperature is just right, I'm certain I sound like Sting. Give me a soap-on-a-rope, and I'm *Starting Up A Brand New Day*. Of course, my wife would say I sound more like Bill Murray singing in the Lizard Lounge of a low-end hotel. In every aspect of our lives, we tend to be generous with our assessment of self. Prepare to reconfigure your perceptions!

UNDERSTAND YOUR STRENGTHS AND WEAKNESSES

Another good exercise is to make a list of your strengths and weaknesses. Getting feedback from a diverse group of constituents, friends, and family can provide additional "behavioral/performance data" to integrate into your assessment of self. While it's important to target areas that demonstrate the greatest room for improvement and return on the investment (ROI) of your time and energy, further developing areas of preexisting strength is also important.

You're also likely to feel more comfortable with the perceived risks of change when you are starting from a place of confidence. For example, I have some strengths in some interpersonal domains—empathy, communication, and active listening. I was also interested in developing more effective conflict management and leadership skills. These skills would allow me to build on my strengths and would serve many of my personal and professional values. I found myself more actively pursuing knowledge, skill, and experience in conflict management theory and practice. I took advantage of leadership opportunities. Heated conflicts that years ago I would have stayed clear of, I now had an interest in immersing myself in. I was drawn to the social sciences and how I could be more effective in my influence of others. These skills would come in handy on community task forces, boards, and committees. These skills would perhaps serve me better as my children approached adolescence. "Emotional Intelligence," I would soon recognize, was the *pièce de résistance* when integrated with knowledge and analytic reasoning.

The books on my reading list began to look different. In addition to the standard internal medicine and nephrology textbooks, I began reading for pleasure and self-development. This was a behavioral change closely aligned with my values for reading in a "non-professional" capacity.

This purposeful strategy of integrating mind-emotion-behavioral change would ultimately serve me better, serve my constituents better, and in the process, enhance my health by a natural tendency to reduce allostatic load (see figure 1.1). I would call this a win-win-win.

In committing to the development and application of emotional intelligence and principles of conflict resolution, I became more mindful of the interplay of thought, emotion, and behavior. I began to experience the adult-learning capacity of these competencies (old thought: empathy can't be learned).

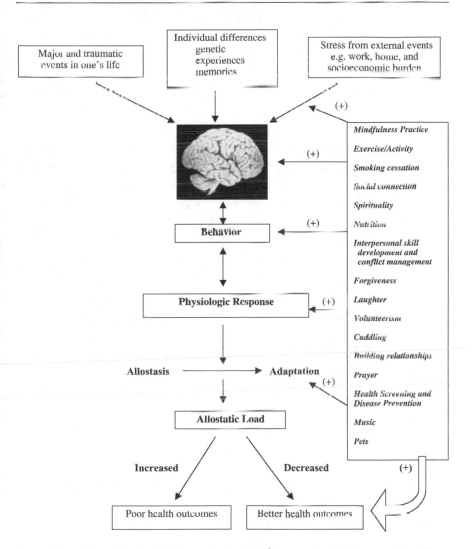

Figure 1.1 Allostatic Load and Opportunities for ME-B³ Intervention: (+) denotes positive effects

I became more attuned to the effects my old habitual patterns were having on my body and health, as well as the effects these patterns were having on my friends and colleagues.

I discovered there was an intriguing neurobiology that underpinned effective practice and application of interpersonal knowledge and skill. Helping friends and colleagues produced a feeling of connection, trust, and reward.

The more people trust you, the more they're willing to share. The more they share, the more you know. The more you know, the fewer your perceptual gaps. The fewer your perceptual gaps, the better you understand. Understanding leads to empathy. Empathy enhances rapport. Rapport builds trust. You get the picture.

I began to appreciate the positively reinforcing nature of these connections. I found that the potential unleashed with my new approach to conflict management would serve as a good framework for working on some of the other items on my long list of weaknesses. Five years ago, the Holy Grail of behavioral change as it related to exercise and better nutritional choices seemed an elusive fantasy.

That was then and this is now.

I am now fifteen pounds lighter and have probably added five pounds of muscle or lean body mass. Net effect: twenty pounds of pure life-sucking fat is gone. My blood pressure and cholesterol have never been better (sans medication); my interpersonal skill mix is deeper; my self-care is more effective; my social satisfaction and relationships with friends/family are more satisfying and meaningful. I am running. I am getting in regular resistance exercise. I am eating far fewer sweets and refined carbohydrates (lower glycemic index). I am eating more grains, vegetables, and fish. My reading list reflects a more curious value-satisfying intellect than it once did. Now do not get me wrong. Life is hardly perfect. It is what it is, a work in progress. While I could get struck by lightening tomorrow, I am stunned at the capacity that we have as humans for change, adaptation, and resilience.

Here is a short and significant inventory of changes in thought/perception, emotion, behavior, and the actual body/health benefits I've realized over the last five years and beyond.

Examples of:

Old Thoughts	**New Thoughts**
I can't run. My legs aren't made for running.	I don't know how I would get through the week without my runs.
I hate mushrooms.	Portabella please.
I would love to live near the ocean, but I could never move.	It's great living near the ocean.

I can't imagine life without Coke Classic.

I can't believe how sweet that tastes.

I can't imagine life without desserts/snacks.

Yogurt please.

I feel winded walking up this hill.

It was great running up that hill. I'm not even that winded.

I will probably soon need medication for my blood pressure and cholesterol.

My blood pressure and cholesterol have never been better and without medications.

I have never been one to openly share my feelings.

Let's talk.

It is important that I have something to say.

It is more important that I listen.

It is a sign of weakness to be uncertain.

It is a sign of strength to share vulnerability.

I am more likely to succeed by being understood.

I am more likely to succeed by understanding others.

If my team loses I'll be in a bad mood.

Once the game is over it is history.

Judge, judge, judge.

Reserve judgment.

Old Emotion

Futility

Anxiety/Fear

Overwhelmed

Jealousy

Grudge

Hostility

Sadness

Impatience

New Emotion

Confidence

Equanimity

Control

Gratitude

Forgiveness

Tolerance

Contentment

Patience

Old Behavior

Sedentary

Too much TV

New Behavior

Exercise 60 minutes/5 days per week

More reading, stretching

Mindless consumption of "empty" calories

Mental distraction

Thoughts racing

Sprinting forward

Retreat, not enough time

Blame

Talking

Avoidance of conflict

Comfortable with status quo

"No Coke, water please." "Dessert? No thanks."

Relaxation response, in the moment

Prayer. Meditation.

Pausing to savor the moment

Volunteer

Contribute

Listening

Problem-solving

Pushing edges. Living in the boundaries.

Body/Health (Old)

Increasing weight

Increasing waist-hip ratio

Increased body fat

Decreased lean body mass

Increased blood pressure

Increased cholesterol

Deconditioned

Decreased endurance

Increased cardiovascular risk

More pain and stiffness

Tense

Distracted

More fight-flight and less prefrontal cortex

Less laughter

Less physical contact

Body/Health (New)

15 lbs. lighter

Decreased waist-hip ratio

Decreased body fat

Increased muscle mass

Decreased blood pressure

Decreased cholesterol

Increased aerobic capacity

Increased endurance

Decreased cardiovascular risk

Less pain and more flexibility

Calm

Focused

More prefrontal cortex and less fight-flight

More laughter

More physical contact, e.g., hugging and cuddling

What these changes share in common are characteristics that foster *plasticity* and positive health-promoting behavioral reinforcement.

THE POWER OF PLASTICITY: CHANGING WITH THE TIMES

"The future ain't what it used to be."

Yogi Berra

Until recently, there had long been a consensus in the scientific community that after early childhood, our full complement of brain cells and their synapses (where our brain cells or neurons connect) were pretty much molded into place. This theory argued that in early childhood our mind's orchestra had a certain number of musicians, instruments, and a "fixed " repertoire of possible tunes to play. Traditional wisdom was that by early childhood, some people would have a good combination of musicians and play pretty good symphonies. Others would have musicians that performed less well. Conventional wisdom used to suggest that the "brain cards" you were handed in the game of life from an early age forward were the cards you were stuck with, the good, the bad, and the ugly. We know better now.

> Conventional wisdom used to suggest that the "brain cards" you were handed in the game of life from an early age forward were the cards you were stuck with, the good, the bad, and the ugly. We know better now.

While it continues to be true that we're all endowed with the genetic legacy of our extended family (the one we had from the start), the expression of this legacy as influenced by our experiences, memories, thoughts, feelings, and behaviors is not cast in stone in infancy and early childhood. It would be more apt to say that it is cast in clay, malleable clay. You, for example may have a strong history of high blood pressure and diabetes in your extended family, as I do. You may in fact have a genetically influenced trajectory that puts you at risk for high blood pressure from birth. But as we've discussed, positive behavioral modifications (becoming mindful, making friends, eating right, etc.) can powerfully influence the expression of that hereditary disposition.

> In the last two decades, research has fundamentally changed our knowledge and understanding of what happens in the brain as we get older. It's now becoming more clear that our brain never really stops changing and adjusting.

In the last two decades, research has fundamentally changed our knowledge and understanding of what happens in the brain as we get older. It's now becoming more clear that our brain never really stops changing and adjusting. While there may be times during our lives (like early childhood and adolescence) when changes and adaptation are moving with greater speed, some capacity for continual change continues throughout life. The capacity for change in the brain is what defines *plasticity* and is one of the key principles upon which this book is based. Each moment of our lives becomes imprinted in our brains, like a photograph on film or an object pressed into clay. While many aspects of brain development, cell structure, and connections (synapses) are well established in early childhood, new imprints and patterns continue to develop in our brains throughout life. The brain is a much more dynamic organ than once thought.

> The capacity for change in the brain is what defines *plasticity* and is one of the key principles upon which this book is based.

> The brain is a much more dynamic organ than once thought.

In the first few years, there's tremendous growth in the number of brain cells, synapses, and pathways as a new environment of sensory stimulation interacts with the brain of an infant-toddler. For example, at birth each neuron in the cerebral cortex or outer "gray matter" has approximately 2,500 synapses. By the time an infant is two- to three-years-old, there are approximately 15,000 synapses per neuron. An adult on average has about half that number, meaning we begin to prune the garden, eliminating weaker connections and holding on to the stronger connections. Experience determines which brain connections will be strengthened or pruned. Those we use with greater frequency are more likely to stick around compared to those we use less. The expression "use it or lose it" seems to hold true here. Another period of "brain growth" and pruning back occurs during puberty and adolescence.

> Experience determines which brain connections will be strengthened or pruned. Those we use with greater frequency are more likely to stick around compared to those we use less.

As it turns out, you have considerable influence over the musician, instruments, composition, and sheet music within your brain and thus are capable of producing a variety of symphonies throughout life. You can transform a garden from one that is stagnant and overgrown with weeds to one you would feel good sitting in, walking in, and sharing with your friends. You can take the cards you have been handed that may leave you feeling the temptation to fold and add a few additional trump cards, turning it into a full house. In effect, such change is made possible by processes that involve the pruning of some brain cells (neurons), the proliferation of other brain cells, and the numbers of synapses that connect neuron to neuron in complex networks that interconnect in structure and function.

I had a patient in his early fifties referred to me with severe, difficult to control high blood pressure. He was taking several different types of blood pressure medication and still struggling to find control. As part of his evaluation, he wore a continuous blood pressure monitoring device at home for twenty-four hours. Normally, blood pressure will run higher in the morning hours and reach its nadir during the night. This fellow had virtually no nocturnal dip in his pressure. In fact, it was at times accentuated, which is very unusual. When we reviewed the results together, he told me he had frequent night terrors. He served in Viet Nam as a "tunnel rat." His role was to crawl on his belly through narrow tunnels that the North Vietnamese had dug into underground areas where the "VC" hid, stored ammunition, and planned their next attacks on American soldiers. I was tense just listening to him describe this vivid replay of events that had occurred thirty years earlier. This fellow had heart disease, and at the time I attributed most of it to his obvious risk factors of high blood pressure and high cholesterol. I could not appreciate then, as I do now, the role his experiences/memories of Viet Nam were playing in their independent effects on fight-flight, physiological stress, and allostatic load.

Treatment for PTSD might include cognitive behavioral therapy, biofeedback, medication, support groups, prayer, and meditation, all attempts to reconfigure the sculpting of the replayed experience to one that enables greater control, calm, and reduced physiological and emotional stress. The desire is to help create the capacity to coexist with an indelible experience of tragic horror without it tormenting everyday life and activity. Though it can take some time and require a lot of work, brain plasticity makes this reconfiguration possible.

Transforming an experience of predictable anger, hostility, and defensiveness with a colleague at work, to an experience of patience, reservation of judgment, and value creation is another example of plasticity. What makes this transformation possible is the ability of the brain to adapt structure and function. It does so by proliferating cells, enhancing synapses or connections, strengthening networks, reconsolidating memories, adapting greater resilience to the effects of stress, and altering neurotransmitter messenger activity. It's this capacity for adapting thought, feeling, and behavior that becomes the premise for more conscious choosing of a healthier trajectory of life.

Plasticity also serves an important adaptive function to compensate for injury or loss. For example, it's long been recognized that the large area in the back of the brain known as the visual cortex processes information that is fed through our eyes and our retina. It is here that our images of the world are brought into clear development and focus. Interestingly, if one has a sudden loss of vision or loses vision in early childhood, this same region of the brain processes the reading of Braille as streams of information are sent from our fingertips. It's an adaptation of sight interpretation to touch interpretation. A remarkable study done by Alvaro Pascual-Leone of Harvard Medical School, using functional Magetic Resonance Imaging (fMRI), demonstrated this capacity within days after test subjects were blindfolded for one week and studied Braille.

Humans have developed the capacity to become lifelong learners. We're capable of acquiring new knowledge and skills, processes that require the brain to reorganize neural pathways. Functional and structural changes in the brain continue as a consequence of learning new skills and processing new memories.

> Functional and structural changes in the brain continue as a consequence of learning new skills and processing new memories.

At a recent meeting of the Society for Neuroscience, researchers presented results from an interesting study. As we age, it's harder for our brains to accurately distill and interpret speech. It gets harder to distinguish individual words and sounds. I find this now as I attempt to comprehend my adolescent daughter's "muffled" and rapid speech. Her friends, of course, understand her perfectly well. When elderly adults, age sixty to ninety, undergo several weeks of computer-based training to improve their brain's ability to discriminate the sounds of speech, remarkable improvements are seen compared to before the training. According to Michael Merzenich, from UCSF, "The majority improved 10 or more years in neurocognitive status. With more training, I expect we could get it to 25 years."

Evidence is now clear that the ability to change both structure and neurochemical events in the brain, such as creating more synapses and more integrated connections with other neurons, are the basis for plasticity, as seen with learning and memory. There's a great deal of interest in how "exercising" areas in the brain involved with memory and higher levels of reasoning may render our brains more resilient and resistant to the risks of memory loss and cognitive decline as we age. These structural and functional adaptive features of the brain would fit with those preliminary findings. Just as a conditioned athlete with good muscle tone, joint flexibility, and stability has a reduced risk of injuring themselves, an individual whose brain garden has been tended well will have less risk of losing vegetation over time.

There is growing evidence in animals and in humans that after a part of the brain has been damaged, there are adaptive changes that occur in surrounding preserved areas that attempt to compensate for the areas that are damaged. After paralysis from a stroke, for example, early and aggressive physical and occupational therapy stimulate and strengthen neighboring areas in the brain, enabling significant improvement to occur over time that might not otherwise be possible. Studies have shown an ability to adapt brain circuitry to better process language at any age. People with a reading disability like dyslexia have shown improvement with training techniques that rework failing language processing networks. Plasticity implies that you can teach an old brain, new tricks.

> Plasticity implies that you can teach an old brain new tricks.

It's important to reemphasize that mind, emotion, and behavior are linked to brain structure and function. This, in turn, has enormous influence on many dimensions of health and healing. Opportunity for meaningful change is therefore made possible by transformation of thought, feeling, and behaviors, all of which influence body and health. The current, deeply rooted and largely habitual footprints of brain structure and function are not only capable of change, they are designed for change.

> The current, deeply rooted and largely habitual footprints of brain structure and function are not only capable of change, they are designed for change.

Tapping into the processes that make plasticity possible, by the very nature of the design, becomes easier once the process begins to develop.

Convincing yourself of a fundamentally different perception from one you've held onto for many years—"The pain in my lower back and knees means I cannot be more active"—is not an easy task. It will hurt before it begins to feel better just as any beautiful garden takes perpetual work to develop and sustain itself. It will not be easy to contemplate forgiveness in response to a transgression that has hurt you. It will not be easy to alter the sweet bliss of a carbohydrate binge by choosing a raw vegetable instead. It will not be easy to manage your anger when your button is pushed.

It is very dangerous, however, to leave the sculpting of your brain and the adverse health consequences that may occur, on autopilot, as most of us tend to do. Taking full advantage of the power of plasticity, at its most basic and fundamental level, requires that you reexamine who you are and what you are capable of. This is first a journey inward that will later affect your journey outward. It is not magic. It is not hocus-pocus. It is not a gift for the fortunate few.

If you desire to hear a different symphony resonating from your mind's orchestra, the conductor's stand is all yours. If you are inspired to weed some aspects of your mind's garden and fertilize others, put on your gloves and tend away. If you are ready to add some powerful trump cards to the hand of life you are holding, there is hope.

MOVING FORWARD

Do not leave the inner workings of your brain to chance. If you are inspired to be the sculptor of you, grab your chisel and create the person you desire to be. The unfolding stories of the neurosciences and their implication for mind-body application are definitely worth keeping an eye on. Any information you come upon that connects thinking, feeling, and doing with health should get your attention. I'd recommend keeping a file on this topic. I have included a good reading list for your consideration. The more you know about who you are and how you work, the better off you'll be. This is ancient wisdom with a contemporary twist. We are living longer and more complicated lives, and so we need to put more thought and effort into taking care of ourselves.

> Do not leave the inner workings of your brain to chance. If you are inspired to be the sculptor of you, grab your chisel and create the person you desire to be.

There are a lot of lonely and sad people out there. You may be one. There is a lot of chronic disease out there. And there is an epidemic of lifestyle-related morbidity that will continue to declare itself as we baby boomers age. We've become increasingly dependent on a system of health care that can only give you so much. The rest is up to you. How will you respond?

A PERSONAL EPIPHANY

I had an experience recently that nicely captures the points I'm making in *It's All in Your Head*.

It was early on a crisp, autumn Sunday morning in the low country of South Carolina. It was one of the first days in weeks where the heat and humidity of summer had finally given way to the promise of a beautiful fall. I ventured out on my forty-five-minute run, iPod finely tuned. I was well-hydrated, well-caffeinated, and thankful to be alive another day. Soon, I would have a vigorous pace going in rhythm with my accompanying tunes, savoring the reward of being in the moment and doing something important for my health.

Predictably, about forty minutes into the run, I was beginning to feel fatigued, tight, and a bit dehydrated. Perceptually, I recognized that familiar story and saw, in my mind's eye, "the end" of the story quickly approaching as I rounded the corner for the home stretch. Emotionally, I felt calm, invigorated, and upbeat, and I felt resigned to call it quits and accept this level of satisfaction. The discomfort I started with in my lower back and left knee were no longer present as I began to slow my pace. The dopamine-endorphin dance of deep satisfaction was rewarding me for another effort. I thought to myself, "Nice work, feels good, ready for the day." I had reached what I thought was the familiar thinking, feeling, brain, behavior, and body limits on the outskirt of the Town of Exercise. The signposts were all there, familiar, welcoming, and affirming.

I could barely make out the silhouette in the distance as it slowly moved toward me. Moments later I recognized my son Alex, riding his bike, sitting bolt upright, and in total concentration as his path undulated side to side. There was great significance in this visual image for me. Alex has Down syndrome and until just a few days earlier, at the age of twelve and a half, could not ride his bike without the use of training wheels. As many kids with developmental disabilities get older, there are more noteworthy differences in many of the developmental milestones. All of Alex's friends had long abandoned their training wheels. They would sprint past him, popping wheelies, and jumping off small ramps as he labored to keep up with them and maintain his balance.

This is an example in my life where I must be more mindful of the need to consciously examine thought, feeling, and behavior. I can easily become distracted with where my son is developmentally instead of celebrating his marvelous and unique capacity to be perpetually in the moment, living life to its fullest. Alex harbors no grudges. He embraces life with an open and sincere authenticity. No frills. What you see is what you get. When my mind becomes cluttered with the many "what-ifs," I find myself easily drawn to a mindset of self-pity. No one is served by self-pity, especially my son.

So there is Alex, riding his bike, fully clothed (not always the case), helmet securely in place, smiling from ear to ear, eyes glowing with the freedom of the moment and his self-sustaining movement. No training wheels, no strings, just total contentment and a new experience of reward and meaning created with each rotation of his bicycle pedals.

Now Alex is moving in the opposite direction of me, starting out on the one-mile loop around our neighborhood. He approached me just as I was about to cross the finish line of my run, having just passed the ME-B^3 sign that read, "Congratulations, you're done for another day." Otherwise resigned to quit, I found myself doing a 180.

Alex waved me on to take the lead as I began to turn up the speed to run beside him. For the next mile, I would run faster, suck more air, and hit new perceptual, emotional, and behavioral/performance limits! Together, we were creating a new story. The signposts I had just passed moments earlier, before seeing him, were no longer on the landscape. I had such a deep feeling of love, pride, meaning, and value satisfaction as I watched Alex peddle with greater confidence and stability.

While the brain networks I was using earlier in my run had been well developed, firing and wiring together for the last five years, on this day and at this moment, the symphony inside my head and the symphony inside Alex's head had never sounded better. There was indeed a time not too long ago, when Alex and I would not have thought this moment possible. This was the poetry of plasticity in motion, changing and unfolding before us both. Now that's cause for celebration!

Chapter 2

Reprogram Your Brain: The Four-Week Addicted-to-Health Plan

The brain has the ability to adapt at any time in our lives to new behaviors and new conditions. Just as an addict is drawn to a substance like nicotine because of its potent biological "rewards," we can train our brain to respond with the same chemistry so that we become "addicted" to health-promoting behaviors like exercising, meditating, and eating right. In other words, we *can* cultivate the biological interactions that connect thought, feeling, and behavior so that we become "addicted" to choices that will make us healthier, happier people.

> Just as an addict is drawn to a substance like nicotine because of its potent biological "rewards," we can train our brain to respond with the same chemistry so that we become "addicted" to health-promoting behaviors like exercising, meditating, and eating right.

Current scientific evidence supports the idea that our primal mind-body systems are designed to adapt in ways that *reward* and *reinforce* positive emotions and thoughts and effective behavioral change. This means that even deeply rooted thoughts and behaviors that cause bad health can be "rewired" to promote better health and to reduce the risk of age-related disease.

The good news is that in as little as four weeks, these systems can be ignited to change your attitude, outlook, and life forever.

Current scientific evidence supports the idea that our primal mind-body systems are designed to adapt in ways that *reward* and *reinforce* positive emotions and thoughts and effective behavioral change. This means that even deeply rooted thoughts and behaviors that cause bad health can be "rewired" to promote better health and to reduce the risk of age-related disease.

The catch? This is challenging work. First you must believe that even small and "trivial" changes in your behavior start a cascade of life-enhancing changes deep inside you. For example, one hour of gardening per week could lower your risk of sudden cardiac death by as much as 66 percent. Walking one hour a week will significantly lower your risk of coronary artery disease. And while only four weeks are necessary to tip your mind-emotion-brain-body momentum in a positively reinforcing direction and to experience immediate results, you must ultimately redefine who you are and develop new healthier "addictions" and habits for the program to succeed in the long run.

But you and your brain are designed for just that. By choosing to put yourself into this four-week program, you are committing to redefining the thoughts, emotions, and behaviors that have defined your life to this point. The beauty of your new addiction will be that you'll feel too good to want to turn back. The more you do, the more you will do. The more you change, the more you will want to change.

Now that you've read in Chapter 1 about the strategies I've successfully applied in my own life, you're ready for an overview of the four-week plan that will set you on the path to feeling better, aging well, and living longer.

For this program, you'll be working in four areas of your life:

- Nutrition
- Activity and Movement
- Mindfulness and Meditation
- Social/Relationships and Positive Emotional States

Use the chart at the end of this chapter and the following guidelines to assess your current behavior in each category and for ideas on how to add small, doable, but meaningful and value-satisfying life changes each week. Some will look easy, but taking little steps will increase your capacity to get addicted to health! Remember, as you begin taking the small steps that will move you toward your ultimate four-week goals, you will consciously and subconsciously be transforming your thoughts, emotions, behaviors, and health.

Don't be discouraged if old thoughts and feelings attempt to sabotage your progress. Stay the course. This is your life. You deserve optimal health! Feel free to choose as many four-week goals as you feel comfortable pursuing and see this as a foundation to build upon. If you don't feel ready to take on the full program at once, commit to at least one or two goals in each of the four areas over the next four weeks. Then each month, you can add another goal in each area and pause to reflect on the progress you're making.

This is a lifetime challenge, a flame that you will ignite by committing yourself to successfully completing some of these goals over the next four weeks.

You must believe that you have within you the capacity for change and inner healing. You must see yourself as the ultimate agent of your own "self-care." Your greatest potential for health and happiness is in your hands. You must not overlook this gift and opportunity!

THE FOUR-WEEK ADDICTED-TO-HEALTH PLAN

Though your goals will need to be individualized, here are some general guidelines guaranteed to get you hooked. Please note that each of the "goals" and "action steps" for the program will be explained in much greater detail in the ensuing chapters. You should view these goals as cumulative—building upon what you achieved the week before. For example, by Week 4, if appropriate, a total of five sweets and five sugar-sweetened soft drinks should be eliminated from your diet.

NUTRITION: YOU ARE WHAT YOU EAT

Consider this: By more conscious selection of foods that result in a reduction of glycation and inflammation (see Chapter 9 for details), you will increase your odds of living longer and disease free. And in as little as four weeks, you will experience a dramatic reduction in your carbohydrate craving and the addictive drive to consume more. Imagine craving fresh cruciferous vegetables as much as you once craved potato chips! You'll lose weight, reduce your waistline, and reduce the risk of metabolic syndrome (high blood pressure, high triglycerides, insulin resistance or pre-diabetes, and diabetes). You will also look and feel better, and you'll experience greater control over your nutritional choices and health. This is more than just a pie-in-the-sky promise. This is a biologically induced adaptation, and with motivation, discipline, and strong commitment, you can adapt your mind and body in a short time frame. But it's up to you. Here we go.

Goals:

1. Reduce the number of high glycemic load calories you ingest, e.g., breads, pastries, desserts, bagels, potatoes, sugar-sweetened drinks, chips, pretzels, candy, etc.

2. Reduce your weight and reduce your risk of diabetes and cardiovascular disease, e.g., reverse the tendency toward lifestyle or metabolic syndrome.

3. Enhance your mood.

4. Reduce inflammation and formation of "oxygen free radicals," damaging byproducts of oxidation or metabolism of nutrients that are responsible for most age-related diseases.

5. Reduce your risk of age-related disease, enhancing greater wellness and vitality.

Action Steps:

Things to do daily:

- Eat breakfast within one hour of waking up.

- Eat 30 grams of fiber daily.

- Color your plate with fruits and vegetables for at least one meal.

- When cooking with oil, cook with extra virgin olive oil.

- Avoid going more than three hours without eating something of low glycemic index, e.g., one serving of nuts or raw vegetables, one serving of low-fat yogurt, or a boiled egg. Strive for variety and balance, in other words, don't eat four boiled eggs per day!

- Try Stevia as a natural sweetener.

- Increase consumption of healthy fats, e.g., omega-3's from such sources as walnuts, salmon, and flaxseed and reduce unhealthy hydrogenated and trans fats

- Eat more cruciferous vegetables, e.g., broccoli, kale, cauliflower, asparagus, green leafy varieties.

- Eat more soy products— tofu, tempah, soy milk—a good source of protein, vitamins, and disease-protective isoflavones.

Things to do per week of the plan:

Week 1

- *Eliminate* just *two* desserts and/or snacks per week (not per day, per week—you can do that!).

- *Substitute* water for *two* sugar-sweetened soft drinks per week (not per day, per week—you can do that!).

- *Substitute* whole-grain products for *two* servings of refined white flour/starches per week.

- *Limit* visits to fast-food restaurants to *once* per week maximum.

- *Add one more* fruit or vegetable portion to your daily diet.

- *Eat one* serving per week of foods high in omega-3 fatty acids, e.g., fatty fish (salmon, albacore tuna), tofu, walnuts, flaxseed, and soybeans.

- *Eat at least three portions per week* of cruciferous vegetables, e.g., broccoli, spinach, asparagus, and fruits like strawberries, blackberries, cherries, and blueberries, all of which are high in vitamins, minerals, phytonutrients, and anti-oxidants, and have a low glycemic load.

Week 2

- *Eliminate three* desserts and/or snacks per week.

- *Substitute* water for *three* sugar-sweetened soft drinks per week.

- *Substitute* whole-grain products for *three* portions of refined white flour/starches per week.

- *Quit* fast-food restaurants all together!

- *Add two more* fruits and vegetable portions to your daily diet.

- *Eat one to two* servings per week of foods high in omega-3 fatty acids, e.g., fatty fish (salmon or albacore tuna), tofu, walnuts, flaxseed, and soybeans.

- *Eat at least three or four* portions per week of cruciferous vegetables, e.g., broccoli, spinach, asparagus and fruits like strawberries, blackberries, cherries and blueberries.

Week 3

- *Eliminate four* desserts and/or snacks per week.

- *Substitute* water for *four* sugar-sweetened soft drinks per week.

- *Substitute* whole-grain products for *four* portions of refined white flour/starches per week.

- *Quit* fast-food restaurants all together!

- *Add three more* fruits and vegetable portions to your daily diet.

- *Eat one to two* servings per week of foods high in omega-3 fatty acids, e.g., fatty fish (salmon, albacore tuna), tofu, walnuts, flaxseed, and soybeans.

- *Eat at least four or five* portions per week of cruciferous vegetables, e.g., broccoli, spinach, asparagus, and fruits like strawberries, blackberries, cherries, and blueberries.

Week 4 and Beyond

- *Eliminate five* desserts and/or snacks per week.

- *Substitute* water for *five* sugar-sweetened soft drinks, and *limit* yourself to *no more than two* sugar-sweetened drinks per week.

- *Substitute* whole-grain products for *five* portions of refined white/ flour starches per week.

- *Drive past all "drive-in" restaurants.* Give up fast food.

- *Eat six to nine* portions per day of fruits and vegetables, including legumes, lentils, soy, etc.

- *Eat two servings* per week of foods high in omega-3 fatty acids, e.g., fatty fish (salmon or albacore tuna), tofu, tempah, walnuts, flaxseed, and soybeans.

- *Eat one portion daily* of cruciferous vegetables, e.g., broccoli, spinach, and asparagus and fruits like strawberries, blackberries, cherries, and blueberries.

ACTIVITY, EXERCISE, AND MOVEMENT: MOTION IS THE LOTION

Positive addictions, such as the reward-endorphin pleasure response that comes with exercise and movement, will take over in as little as four weeks.

Goals:
1. Improve physical, emotional, and mental health.
2. Reduce weight.
3. Reduce cardiovascular risk and risk of diabetes.
4. Enhance mood and energy level.
5. Enhance cognitive functioning, e.g., reasoning and memory.
6. Remember that small, seemingly insignificant increments of change will pay handsomely over time.
7. Reduce mediators of allostatic load, e.g., cortisol and insulin.
8. Moderate pain by enhancing dopamine and endorphin systems.

ACTION STEPS:

Things to do daily:
- Exercise your brain with reading, word puzzles, or journal writing.

Things to do at least once every week:
- Dance to the tunes you love while wearing your portable music player or listening on your home system.
- Participate in a relaxing recreational activity you love, like gardening or playing with your children or grandchildren.

Things to do per week of the plan in addition to the list above:

Week 1
- Get into motion with any physical aerobic activity appropriate for your current condition, e.g., walking, jogging, biking, etc., by exercising for *ten to fifteen minutes, three times per week.*

- Practice a resistance exercise (pushing to twelve repetitions with maximum effort) for *ten to fifteen minutes, once per week.*

Week 2
- *Increase* your aerobic exercise by *five minutes per session.*
- Practice a resistance exercise (pushing to twelve repetitions with maximum effort) for *ten to fifteen minutes, one to two times per week.*

Week 3
- Increase your aerobic exercise by *ten minutes per session.*
- Practice a resistance exercise (pushing to twelve repetitions with maximum effort) for *ten to fifteen minutes, two to three times per week.*

Week 4 and Beyond
- Target at least *twenty to thirty minutes* of aerobic exercise, *five times per week.* This can vary from brisk walking to running, biking, swimming, etc. Walking is effective and portable.
- Practice a resistance exercise (pushing to twelve repetitions with maximum effort) for *twenty minutes, three times per week.*

MINDFULNESS PRACTICE AND MEDITATION

In as little as four weeks, mindfulness practice will profoundly bring you into better balance with your parasympathetic (calm-protective) tone and your sympathetic (fight-flight stress response) tone. This balance will improve every dimension of your health and give you the basis for a long life.

Goals:
1. Reduce stress, as many illnesses are related to or exacerbated by excess stress.
2. Enhance clarity of thought and enhance moods and positive emotional states.
3. Enhance feelings of peace and equanimity.
4. Enhance experiences and interactions.
5. Improve your health via the cascade of positive mind-body effects created when you reduce stress through mindfulness practice and meditation.

6.   Reduce mediators of allostatic load, e.g., cortisol and the fight-flight stress response.

7.   Enhance parasympathetic (calm and protective) central nervous system tone.

Action Steps:

Things to do daily:

- Cultivate a stronger sense of "non-self" through altruism and compassion. Perform an act of kindness to yourself or others at least once a day. This could be saying hello to a stranger, opening the door for someone whose hands are full, offering assistance to someone who appears lost or overwhelmed, or forgiving yourself for a mistake.

- Start a gratitude journal and spend *five minutes* a day jotting down a few experiences or people you feel grateful for that could easily be taken for granted otherwise.

- Notice and appreciate nature.

Things to do at least once every week:

- Yoga is an excellent discipline for balance, mindfulness, and flexibility. Participating in one class per week with instruction or with the use of a home, self-guided tape will quickly leave you feeling more calm and satisfied.

- Worship, if appropriate, based on your values and preferences, religion or spirituality.

Week 1

- Cultivate a form of meditation that feels right to you: prayer, paced respirations, relaxation response, body scan, self-hypnosis, guided imagery, walking meditation, or Tai Chi, etc. See Chapter 17 for descriptions and how to get started performing these various forms of mindfulness practice. Perform one of these practices for *ten minutes, three times per week.*

- Spend some time outdoors experiencing nature—take a walk, ride a bike on a path, sit under at tree, watch a sunset—*once per week.*

- Avoiding thinking about or doing any work-related activities *one evening per week.*

Week 2
- Increase your mindfulness/meditation practice to *fifteen minutes, three times per week.*
- Spend time outdoors experiencing nature *twice per week.*
- Avoiding thinking about or doing any work-related activities *two evenings per week.*

Week 3
- Increase your mindfulness/meditation practice to *twenty minutes, three times per week.*
- Spend time outdoors experiencing nature *three times per week.*
- Avoid thinking about or doing any work-related activities *three evenings per week.*

Week 4
- Perform your mindfulness/meditation practice *twenty to thirty minutes, three times per week.*
- Spend time outdoors experiencing nature at least *four times per week.*
- Avoid thinking about or doing any work-related activities at least *four evenings per week* or make sure you have *one-day per week* completely work-free.

SOCIAL/RELATIONSHIPS AND POSITIVE EMOTIONAL STATES

Goals:
1. To reduce stress, enhance positive emotional states, and create feelings of satisfaction.
2. Build support and enhance resilience through bonding.
3. Leverage relationship capital to enhance fulfillment of values.
4. Develop more effective interpersonal connection, including conflict management, and satisfaction at work, love, and play.
5. Improve health by creating the many positive mind-body effects associated with positive social relationships.
6. Enhancement of bonding, reward, and positive emotion mediators, e.g., oxytocin, dopamine, endorphins, and serotonin.

Action Steps
Things to do daily:

* Tell your special friends and family how much you love them and/or appreciate them.

* Cuddle with someone you love—a significant other or a pet for no less than five minutes each day.

* Make a conscious effort to smile at someone . . . reciprocity is the natural rule here and will reinforce this socially connecting behavior.

Things to do at least once per month:

* Take part in an organized social outing—reading club, bridge club, etc.—at least once a month.

* Volunteer to help with a program or cause. Give generously. It can be in the form of time, talent, or treasure.

Week 1

* Commit to developing knowledge and skill in interpersonal management (see Chapters 10 and 13 on conflict management. Also refer to suggested reading list at the end of the book).

* Make a list of friends and family members with whom you've been out of touch.

* Think about someone who has wronged you, someone you haven't forgiven, and think about the potential heath benefits to you for forgiving them (see Chapter 12).

* Explore an opportunity to volunteer your time and talent to a cause that means a lot to you. Make a list of possible choices.

* Make a list of possible social groups you could join.

* Make a list of people who have touched your life.

* Think about ways to add more laughter into your life. Make a list of funny TV shows and DVDs. Investigate comedy clubs.

Week 2

* Consider the principles outlined in Chapter 10 on conflict management.

- Contact by phone, email, or snail mail at least one of the friends or family members with whom you've been out of touch.

- Forgive someone who has done a slight wrong to you.

- Narrow your list of volunteer opportunities. Contact them for more information.

- Narrow your list of social groups you could join and contact them for more information.

- Contact by phone, email, or snail mail, at least one person who's touched your life.

- Order a funny DVD or plan to watch a funny TV show or attend a comedy performance.

Week 3

- Take one step toward resolving a conflict.

- Contact another friend or family member with whom you've been out of touch.

- Write a list of the pros and cons of forgiving someone who has done a major wrong to you. Read Chapter 12 for information on how forgiving such a person benefits you, not the transgressor.

- Select one or two volunteer opportunities and visit the organization to get a better idea of the experience

- Select one or two social groups and plan an exploratory meeting/visit.

- Contact by phone, email, or snail mail another person who has touched your life.

- Watch a funny DVD or TV show for thirty minutes.

Week 4

- Commit to being aware of conflict management techniques and to practicing conflict management in your daily life.

- Stay aware of friends or family with whom you are out of touch, and consider re-starting or maintaining these friendships and relationships.

- Forgive someone who has done a major wrong to you. Practice forgiveness toward yourself and others.

- Join a volunteer group and commit to it. If it doesn't work out, commit to finding one that does.

- Join a social group. If it doesn't work out, keep looking until you find a good fit.

- Keep a mental or written list of people who touch your life in positive ways, and then contact them and let them know your appreciation when appropriate.

- Schedule time for laughter via a funny DVD or TV show (or outing) for thirty minutes, three times per week.

This is the plan to get you started with doable action steps that will build into your new addiction to healthy behavior. Don't try to jump ahead and make big changes all at once. The idea is that small changes are doable. Because they're doable, they're not overwhelming, therefore you'll keep doing them until they become a habit. As you move forward, you can increase the effort because by then you'll be getting a reward that fuels both the present effort and the motivation necessary to continue.

Throughout the book, I'll suggest other strategies for success as you move forward on your journey. As you add new positive behaviors each week, try to be consciously aware of how your thoughts, emotions, and behaviors are influenced by your successful pursuit of these goals and activities. Remember that there is a symphony of biological activity that underlies these transformations in your life. This symphony, often played beneath your conscious state, will continue to change your health for the better even when the changes seem subtle and insignificant to you. Changes over a lifetime will not appear as dramatic on a day-to-day basis unless you are more mindful of them. While your new growing addiction to health will not be as potent in the short term as a nicotine addiction, the subtle and sustaining effects over a lifetime will prove infinitely more powerful and sustaining as your body feels better and better.

The Four-Week Addicted-to-Health Plan Summary

	Nutrition	Activity and Movement	Mindfulness and Meditation	Social/Relationships and Positive Emotional States
Goals	☆ → glycation and glycemic load ☆ → insulin peaks/troughs ☆ → inflammatory burden ☆ ← intake of healthy fats and carbohydrates, fruits, vegetables, soy products	☆ ← conditioning ☆ ← strength/endurance ☆ ← weight reduction ☆ endorphins → cortisol ☆ → allostatic load	☆ → stress, cortisol ☆ → sympathetic (fight-flight) tone ☆ ← parasympathetic (calm) tone ☆ → stress (allostatic load) ☆ ← cognitive capacity	☆ ← relationship capital ☆ ← bonding ☆ ← leverage problem-solving, conflict management ☆ ← mood, positive emotions and support ☆ → stress (allostatic load)
Health Outcomes	☆ → cardiovascular risk ☆ → risk of diabetes and metabolic (lifestyle) syndrome ☆ → cancer risk ☆ → risk of neurodegenerative diseases ☆ → weight	☆ → cardiovascular risk ☆ → cancer risk ☆ → stress burden, pain ☆ ← mood, immune function ☆ ← concentration ☆ → risk of metabolic syndrome, diabetes	☆ → cardiovascular risk, e.g., blood pressure, pulse/respirations ☆ ← mood, resilience ☆ ← patience, tolerance, compassion ☆ ← symptom management	☆ ← enhanced longevity ☆ → symptoms of depression and anxiety ☆ ← resilience ☆ ← improved coping ☆ ← control, influence

The Four-Week Addicted-to-Health Plan Summary (Continued)

	Nutrition	Activity and Movement	Mindfulness and Meditation	Social/Relationships and Positive Emotional States
Action Steps to Target by Week 4	☆ minimal high glycemic load foods, e.g., bread, pastries, bagels, chips, pretzels, sugar-sweetened soft drinks	☆ aerobic, e.g., walking, running for 30 minutes, 5 days/week	☆ 20–30 minutes of meditation, 3 days/week, e.g., prayer, relaxation response, paced respirations, guided imagery, progressive muscle relaxation, etc.	☆ volunteer in a meaningful activity
	☆ substitute whole-grain products for white flour/starches	☆ resistance exercise, e.g., 12 reps for 20 minutes, 3 days/week	☆ yoga once per week	☆ join a social group
	☆ 6–9 servings per day of fruits/veggies, including legumes, lentils, soy products	☆ dance to the music that makes you feel great, 20 minutes, 3 days/week	☆ keep a gratitude journal	☆ resolve an important conflict
	☆ cruciferous vegetables, e.g., broccoli, asparagus, Brussels sprouts, kale, spinach, cauliflower		☆ spend time outdoors at least four times per week	☆ watch a humorous video for 30 minutes, 3 days/week
	☆ healthy fats, e.g., skinless chicken and turkey, salmon, fish, avocado, walnuts, flaxseed		☆ attend spiritual or religious worship, if so inclined, once a week	☆ forgive a prior transgression
	☆ avoid all trans and hydrogenated fats; minimize vegetable, safflower, corn oils		☆ avoid thinking about or doing work-related activities at least four evenings per week; strive for one work-free day per week	☆ cuddle with a significant other five minutes each day
	☆ avoid all fast food			☆ contact a person who has touched your life in a meaningful way to thank them

RETURN ON THE INVESTMENT (ROI) OF THE FOUR-WEEK ADDICTED-TO-HEALTH PLAN

- Improved physical conditioning
- Decreased weight
- Look better
- Improved self-esteem
- Enhanced mood, positive emotions
- Improved strength, endurance, flexibility, and balance
- Enhanced resilience
- Improved concentration
- Decreased illness/morbidity, age-related disease
- Reduced allostatic load or "stress response," including decrease risk for cardiovascular diseases, diabetes, metabolic syndrome, neuro-degenerative (Alzheimer's) diseases, and cancer
- Enhanced balance of parasympathetic systems (calm, protective) and sympathetic systems (fight-flight, stress-response)
- Improved immune function
- Longer life

TIME COMMITMENT FOR THE FOUR-WEEK ADDICTED-TO-HEALTH PLAN (PER WEEK, AT THE FOUR-WEEK MARK AND BEYOND)

Nutrition (variable if any)

Activity and Movement (270 minutes or 4.5 hours/week)

Mindfulness/Meditation (90 minutes or 1.5 hours/week)

Social/Relationship (variable: 120 minutes or 2 hours/week)

Total Time Commitment: 480 minutes or 8 hours/week (1 hour and 10 minutes per day)

Part II

Change Your Mind

Chapter 3

Hope and the Story of the Water Flea: You Are Not a Prisoner of Your DNA

"Life is what happens to you while you're busy making other plans."

John Lennon

Humans are complex organisms. We've long known that our health is influenced by our genetic endowment (nature), environmental-cultural factors (nurture), and that very important category called luck—that unsettling dimension in our lives that is tantamount to the proverbial "roll of the dice." For example, a person may fall tragic victim to an airline crash, to an act of terrorism, or to traumatic events for which there are no effective strategies for personal defense.

When it comes to nature and nurture, however, there's been a great deal of debate about which plays a more dominant role in our thinking, feeling, behaving, and health. On the nature front, molecular research tools have made possible the phenomenal capacity to encode our genome and examine life at its molecular roots. Elucidating the blueprint of our genetic endowment has and will surely continue to lead to fundamental breakthroughs in our understanding and treatment of diseases. It's increasingly clear, however, that a greater complexity defines the connection between gene and outcome. It isn't a simple matter of good gene/bad gene, or good gene/good outcome or bad gene/bad outcome.

It's become more and more apparent—as I will explain in this book—that our fate doesn't end with what our genes encode. Your genes have less control of you than the sum of experiences that define your life. This is the nurture part of the deal and the good news is—you are not a victim of your DNA.

> Your genes have less control of you than the sum of experiences that define your life. This is the nurture part of the deal and the good news is—you are not a victim of your DNA.

NATURE: THE IMPORTANCE OF FAMILY HISTORY ON HEALTH

You can tell an awful lot about the health trajectory you're on by knowing more about disease prevalence in your extended family. As an internist and kidney/blood pressure specialist, I deal largely with problems that run deep into the ancestral tree. Problems like high blood pressure, diabetes, high cholesterol, depression, and kidney disease, to name a few, are usually seen in the siblings, parents, grandparents, aunts, and uncles of the individuals I'm treating. Unfortunately, many of these problems are silent and unforgiving until more serious damage occurs, e.g., a heart attack, stroke, or need to be on dialysis.

The only clue you may have to the trajectory you're on is by knowing what has happened in your extended family. Unfortunately, too few people make the time and effort to find out about their family's health history. I suggest that you actively pursue information by questioning parents and grandparents or retrieving and reviewing the hospital records of family members. This is the best information available to examine the genetic cards you're holding.

If you learn of genetic risk in your family, use this knowledge to assertively pursue screening, disease prevention strategies, and treatment. If a close relative has or had high blood pressure and diabetes and subsequently died of a heart attack, this doesn't mean you're destined to the same fate no matter what you do. I find there's a tendency to assume that the genetic cards you hold are the cards you're stuck with, and that there's not much you can do about it.

Don't despair. Hope springs eternal when you understand that you do have significant control over the ultimate outcome, even if a genetic predisposition for prob-
lems like high blood pressure or high cholesterol
declare themselves. The emphasis then shifts
from the feeling of being stuck with bad genes to
figuring out how to best manage "what you're
stuck with." You have tremendous control over
the cards of health and healing you hold in your hands.

> You have tremendous con-
> trol over the cards of
> health and healing you
> hold in your hands.

NURTURE: THE POWER TO INFLUENCE NATURE

Research involving the study of identical twins in countries like Sweden and
Finland where national health databanks allow close tracking of health outcomes over long time intervals suggest that our genes, at most, contribute no
more than 30 to 50 percent of the final product.

Similarly, ten years ago, researcher David Lykhen, at the University of
Minnesota, published a paper examining genetic determinants of one's satis
faction with life using information he gathered from 4,000 sets of twins born
in Minnesota between1936 and 1955. He concluded that no more than
50 percent of one's satisfaction with life (personality traits of happiness, easy-
going personality, anxiety, etc.) had a clear genetic predisposition.

These are not easy attributes to quantify; however, my sense is that we
relinquish far too much of the big picture to our genes. The nature piece
is stunningly designed and provides the seeds necessary for a garden to
exist. The nurture piece has much more to say about how the garden is
cultivated.

Two points are worthy of emphasis here. The first is that in the ongoing
dialogue regarding nature vs. nurture, nurture is a more formidable contributor than once thought. The second is that na-
ture and its contribution in our lives, as enormous and significant as it may be, can often be
modified. A genetic predisposition to high cholesterol (nature) is not a life sentence; it can be
substantially lowered by changing your behavior
(nurture).

> A genetic predisposition to
> high cholesterol (nature) is
> not a life sentence; it can
> be substantially lowered by
> changing your behavior
> (nurture).

THE HUMBLE WATER FLEA

Sharon Begley, a science journalist for the *Wall Street Journal*, published a story recently that caught my eye as it affirmed other information I had gathered about genes and how they influence outcomes. It's the story of the water flea, a tiny crustacean that effortlessly skims across the surface of water.

The water flea can shift speed and direction along the surface of the water with great ease and precision. Interestingly, when one clones water fleas (cloning implies that the DNA or genetics of all the water fleas is identical) and divides them into two groups with different environments, something special happens. In one group, the scent of fish is added to the water. No actual fish are added, just the scent. As you might expect, fish are the arch nemesis of the water flea, capable of breaking the surface of the water at any time. With one voracious gulp, they turn the water flea into an instant snack.

In the other groups of genetically identical cloned water fleas, no fish scent is added to the water. In the group where scent is added to the water, the water flea acquires a tiny crust-like helmet. Fish find the tiny helmet unpalatable, kind of like chewing a nut that still has a hard shell attached. After swallowing a helmet-headed water flea, the fish promptly spits it back to the water's surface. How's that for a comeback . . . a snack one moment, back in the game the next. This life-saving helmet is not found on the water flea when scent is not added to the water they inhabit. So where are we going with this, Dr. Pettus?

This simple and elegant experiment suggests that our DNA, our genetic blueprint, is influenced by external or environmental factors. This is a good example of *plasticity* or the ability of the genetic code to express itself in a different way—one that can radically change the game, the deck, and the cards. The significance of what is innate begins to look different. The beauty of our genetic blueprint, it would appear, is its ability to adapt. What is innate is our capacity to adapt!

> The beauty of our genetic blueprint, it would appear, is its ability to adapt. What is innate is our capacity to adapt!

Similar examples have been seen in oak caterpillars. Despite an identical genetic endowment, their appearances vary considerably depending on when they hatch. Those that hatch in the spring look like flower blossoms and those that hatch in the summer look more like twigs.

HUMAN RESEARCH

Genetic research in humans also reveals the complexity of this dance shared by both nature and nurture. It's been long thought that analyzing and understanding our genetic code would reveal specific genes that could be used to predict with greater certainty, who is at risk for a particular problem and who isn't. This connection hasn't turned out to be so straight forward. For example, it's true that genes thought to contribute to aggressive and sociopathic behavior or depression have been found more commonly in families with histories of such problems. However, finding these genes in individuals did not predict aggressive behavior or depression in that specific individual. In other words, an individual with the "violence gene" when raised in loving, supportive, non-abusive homes behaves no differently than a person without the gene. In fact, individuals with the "depression gene," in the absence of deeply stressful life events, were no more likely to experience depression than those without the genes.

What this research suggests is that having a gene that increases the risk of a certain problem, e.g., depression or sociopathic behavior, is more likely to produce the problem if the environment the individual is in is unfavorable—hostile, abusive, unsupportive. A science historian and physicist, Evelyn Fox Keller, of the Massachusetts Institute of Technology, notes, "Historically, nature-nurture divided what was fixed for what could be changed. But what our biology gives us is our plasticity, our ability to respond to our experiences."

INSPIRING BEHAVIORAL CHANGE

I've been a practicing physician-educator for more than twenty years. My colleagues and I and those we serve struggle to make those behavioral changes we know to be of enormous health value like losing weight, exercising more, and quitting smoking. Our knowledge clearly informs us of the potential for a longer, healthier, and more satisfying life if we modify our choices. The challenge is less in the acquisition of knowledge and more in the execution of the knowledge we have.

Health care professionals know all too well that few things rival the challenge of influencing behavioral change. From the perspective of health promo-

tion and life satisfaction, behavioral change is the
Holy Grail. It's time for all of us to start accepting and understanding that. It's well worth it. It's
a big challenge, but it's doable. While medical
and surgical treatment options will continue to
change our lives, the key to health resides in self-
care. The goal of this book is to make the case
that we are designed for just that!

> From the perspective of health promotion and life satisfaction, behavioral change is the Holy Grail.

> While medical and surgical treatment options will continue to change our lives, the key to health resides in self-care. The goal of this book is to make the case that we are designed for just that!

YOU CAN DO IT!

This is a story about control and the vast array
of tools available to you. I am here to encourage
and inspire you to optimize control in your pursuit of health.

Let's look at stress, and more importantly, how we can ultimately control
or limit its damaging effects on our health. It's
long been known and universally accepted, for
example, that stress in our lives can wreak havoc
in every dimension of our physical, emotional,
mental, and spiritual wellness. We can all point
to the many sources of stress in our lives. Often
we feel overwhelmed by tension at work, pressure at home, stress in relationships, and trou-
bling events in the world. We tend to think of

> It's long been known and universally accepted, for example, that stress in our lives can wreak havoc in every dimension of our physical, emotional, mental, and spiritual wellness.

stress as the cumulative "fallout" of the complexity of our lives. It affects the
way we feel—sad vs. happy, impatient vs. patient, anxious vs. calm, out of
control vs. controlled. Stress can permeate our lives. We work more hours to
make ends meet, and as a result, our relationships become strained. Then we
become sleep deprived.

In this juggernaut of global communication technology, we're inundated
with one tragic event after another perpetually unfolding up close and personal in what was once the quiet sanctuary called home. I don't know about
you, but after watching the news, reading the paper, and gleaning world
events from the Internet, I could use a Prozac the size of a hockey puck.
There's no end to the unrelenting bombardment of marketing, advertise-
ment, and shear cognitive stimulation out there. All of this adds up to sur-

vival challenges that look very different today than what our hunter-gatherer ancestors on the African savannah experienced. Combine all this with the fact that we live longer, and we can see why we now confront an unprecedented "burden" of chronic disease.

As we are left navigating a perfect storm of time and energy consumption, the notion of effective self-care has become more of a fantasy than something readily achieved. With that said, I would like to challenge you to shift your perspective of stress from the cumulative impact that external events have on how you feel, to the biological and behavioral expressions of stress in your life.

Recent insights in the disciplines of neuroscience, behavioral science, medicine, and integrative health have converged, allowing a fundamentally different context for health and healing to emerge. As this story unfolds, you'll begin to recognize that the antidote to stress and its associated diseases is built into the design that is, in fact, you. To change your behavior in a positive way, it's essential to understand how behavior and biology interact. This is an important step in the direction of awakening you to the *power of your mind* to help you navigate life's complexities. This awakening leaves you more mindful of the influence you have on your thoughts, emotions, behaviors, and ultimately your health. It is in this awareness that transformation and better health is made possible.

> To change your behavior in a positive way, it's essential to understand how behavior and biology interact. This is an important step in the direction of awakening you to the *power of your mind* to help you navigate life's complexities.

THE ALLOSTATIC LOAD CONCEPT

In the late 1990s, Bruce McEwen, director of neurosciences at The Rockefeller Research Center, and his colleagues, in an attempt to more accurately conceptualize the connection between behavior and biology, came up with the concept referred to as ***allostatic load***.

Allostasis, first coined in 1988 by Sterling and Eyer, examined the cardiovascular system and how it adapted to change, e.g., from a resting state to exercise. It was known that many other "neurohormonal" patterns existed normally in response to change like diurnal rhythm. An example would be how the body adapts in transitioning from day to night, light to dark, or arousal to sleep. Hormones like cortisol and adrenaline were known to be central in response to these normal circadian changes. Homeostatic adjustment to change best characterized this concept.

Allostatic load was conceptualized to define the cumulative burden of physiological and biological response to change beyond that of normal diurnal rhythm, e.g., stress at work or traumatic events, or stress as a consequence of lower socioeconomic status. The concept here is to examine "stress" in a more quantitative, biological manner, based on growing insight into how external stress is translated, largely by our brain, our thoughts, our feelings, and ultimately the behaviors they collectively influence (Figure 1).

It's in this construct that we begin to get our arms around our response to the inevitable changes in life. Some changes promote health (good nutrition, exercise, and social connection), and some changes are devastating to our health (loss, conflict, smoking, and drug abuse). Allostatic load is the measurement or the physiological response of the body to both external input (environmental) and internal input (thoughts and feelings). Thus, the concept of allostatic load connects our experiences with our potential for health and resilience on one hand, and the risk for disease, morbidity, and mortality on the other.

DEALING WITH STRESS IS NO MONKEY BUSINESS

Let's briefly look at an example of allostatic load based on primate research, as it's not hard to extrapolate to the human experience. It's known that male dominance hierarchy in monkeys is a strong source of behavioral motivation. A monkey attempting to become more dominant in an unstable dominance hierarchy is noted to have higher blood pressure, higher cortisol, and higher adrenaline levels as a result of increased social confrontation. In turn, this stressed-out monkey is found to have increased atherosclerotic plaque formation. Conversely, the plaque build up is not seen in primates whose social behaviors like prolonged sitting and shared grooming are well cultivated. In fact scientists who have studied primate behavior for a generation will be quick to point out that social skills have no equal in the quest for survival and control.

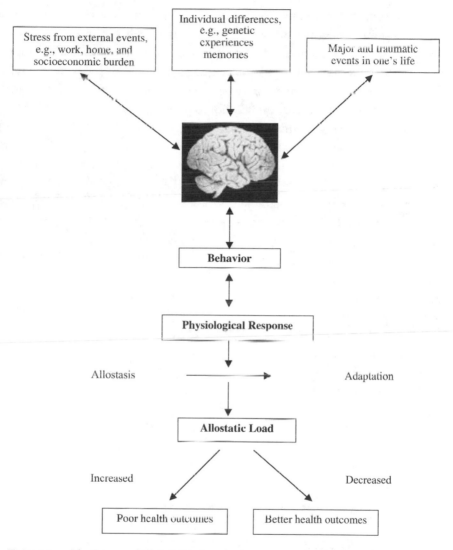

Figure 3.1   The Concept of Allostatic Load

GROWING BURDEN OF ADAPTATION

We're born to adapt to the changing world we live in. However, the pace of change in our environment is dramatically increasing. This places greater burden on our capacity to adapt. This growing burden for adaptation reveals in us a vulnerability that leaves us more susceptible to the effects of stress.

Allostasis, the process that enables adaptation to stress, is both necessary for survival and sometimes maladaptive if not managed with greater awareness and control. For example, allostasis, characterized by the cortisol-adrenaline fight-flight stress response to a potential and legitimate threat is lifesaving, e.g., jumping out of the way of an oncoming car. This is just how it assisted the hunter-gatherer in their quest first not to be eaten and second to eat. That response might look something like this:

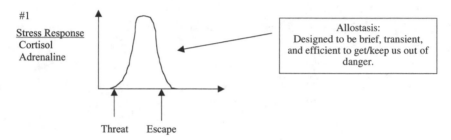

Contrast this adaptive response to an isolated threat with how a typical day at the office might appear.

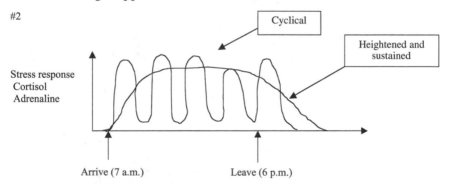

In the second example, the repetitive activation of physiological adaptation in response to the persistent stress of work, family, and dysfunctional relationships, added to maladaptive behavioral responses (eating more, moving less, smoking, poor conflict management, excessive alcohol, etc.) collectively create a substantial allostatic load. This increased and sustained beast of burden, over time, will manifest **bodily** in many deleterious ways:

- High blood pressure
- High blood lipids

- Increased heart rate
- Increased oxygen demand
- Increased cortisol
- Increased noradrenalin
- Increased cardiovascular risk
- Impaired immune function
- Impaired wound healing
- Depression
- Anxiety
- Altered sleep-wake patterns
- Lifestyle or metabolic syndrome
- Premature death, to name a few.

DON'T LEAVE YOUR HEALTH TO CHANCE WHEN YOU CAN CHANGE

It's certainly not difficult to appreciate the influence of allostatic load on health outcomes. As a result, we have two choices:

We can reduce our stress and thus age better and become more resilient, or we can continue raising our allostatic load and face greater health problems and risk premature death.

This biological response should and need not be left to chance. A system adapted for survival on the African savannah requires more effective management to survive the cacophony of modern living. A transient surge of cortisol to mobilize energy and send fat into storage in the event that a hunter-gatherer's next meal might not be quickly forthcoming looks profoundly different when perpetually "turned-up" due to traffic jams, job insecurity, communication overload, and fragile relationships. When cortisol and other mediators of the stress response are turned up, they raise insulin levels,

> When cortisol and other mediators of the stress response are turned up, they raise insulin levels, increase appetite, and *promote subsequent fat storage around the abdomen.*

increase appetite, and *promote subsequent fat storage around the abdomen.* These are the hallmark characteristics of "lifestyle syndrome," a public health epidemic in the U.S.

There's also a much higher risk of diabetes and cardiovascular complications like heart attack, stroke, and chronic kidney disease in individuals with lifestyle syndrome. Another feature of excessive allostatic burden is impairment of the immune function. You may notice a greater tendency for cold, respiratory, and gastrointestinal symptoms when confronting more stress in your life. In addition, the part of our immune system that "turns down" inflammation loses its effectiveness. As a consequence, individuals with stress overload have evidence of enhanced inflammation in their bodies. We're just beginning to appreciate the relationship between increased inflammatory load and vascular disease, cancer, and exacerbation of pre-existing inflammatory or autoimmune diseases like rheumatoid arthritis, lupus, multiple sclerosis, and fibromyalgia.

The good news is the brain is the Grand Central Station of sensory input and stress management. Therefore, we have both substantial control over our stress levels and a built-in capacity for change. No pills, no scalpel, no money needed—only the will to change.

Now allow me to introduce you to your CEO, your brain, which makes possible mind-emotion-brain-behavior-body (ME-B^3) interactions.

Chapter 4

Thinking Inside the Box: Neuroscience 101

"Reality is merely an illusion, albeit a persistent one."

Albert Einstein

"What lies behind us and what lies before us are
tiny matters compared to what lies within us."

Oliver Wendell Holmes

When is the last time you heard someone say, "C'mon, let's think outside the box. Let's get creative, and abandon the status quo! C'mon people, think outside the box!" It was probably not too long ago, and I suspect you may have heard it at work. The metaphor of thinking outside the box works well for those who perceive they are trapped. It's a good metaphor for breaking free of the habitual patterns of thinking, usually characterized by limited peripheral vision. I used to value thinking outside the box.

Though it's taken me a while, now I've come to appreciate the box I'm in. The problem isn't so much the need to think outside the box. The problem is we haven't explored enough of the box we feel trapped in. We're not aware of the available tools, options, and possibilities that are alive and well inside the box, in other words, in our mind. If we can make our habitual patterns of thinking positive, healthful, and creative, then the box works; and I'll stay inside mine, thank you. You won't believe the unexplored nooks and crannies inside your mind! There are quite a few areas of the mind that need better illumination. There are areas that are illuminated too long. And there are areas that I didn't even know existed.

In this chapter, my goal is to shine a light into your brain, with the goal of illuminating what is inside your box, my box, and all human boxes. Think of it as walking upstairs to the attic of your mind. Here you will discover gems that have long been waiting to be discovered. And here you will find some old demons you need to place outside for the trash pick up. Let's grab a light and explore your attic.

Let me introduce you to some of the key players in the orchestra performing behind your mind's curtain. They are seasoned players having practiced with evolutionary refinement in the minds of others for hundreds of millions of years. They can serve you incredibly well. They can also, at times, wreak havoc.

Some of this technical content may seem a bit overwhelming at first. That's okay. This is information that can serve as a reference to revisit, as you need. It's also a distilled composite of many complex fields of study. I appreciate that I assume some risk of oversimplifying this complex story, whose depths have yet to be fully explored. I'm scratching the surface of an area that will fundamentally shift the way we look at health promotion, disease prevention, and self-care. We're living in an era of extraordinary advances in the neurosciences. Many fields of research including genetics, behavioral science, pharmacology, and neuroimaging have converged to shed a glade of light on the biological imprints of how we think, feel, and behave. I've carefully tried to distill that which is most significant as this landscape unfolds. It's technical but important information that I will attempt to link back to daily life. While some of this information may seem overwhelming and slow to crystallize, my hope is for you to get a high-level feel for the general composition of the orchestra—your mind—that plays the symphony of your life.

My objectives in this chapter are as follows:

1.   To introduce key structures (see figure 1) in your brain that appear to play an important role in the biological basis for how you think, feel, and behave.

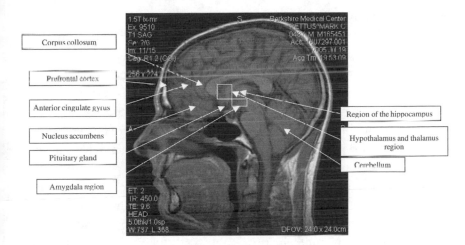

Corpus collosum

Prefrontal cortex

Anterior cingulate gyrus

Nucleus accumbens

Pituitary gland

Amygdala region

Region of the hippocampus

Hypothalamus and thalamus region

Cerebellum

Figure 4.1   Some Key Players Critical to the Mind-Emotion-Brain-Behavior-Body (ME-B^3) Orchestra

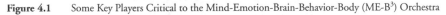

2. To introduce key neurotransmitters or messengers that work intricately with each other in your brain and in concert with many other physiological functions in your body.

3. To highlight four primal neurobiological systems that drive us, sometimes without our conscious knowledge of being driven. These include:

    -   Fight-flight or the stress response
    -   Reward-motivation system
    -   Fear conditioning
    -   Bonding and social attachment

4. To provide some common examples of how these systems, with greater awareness, can sometimes be brought into conscious control. As a consequence, you can significantly influence the trajectory of health and healing you are on.

THE FIGHT-FLIGHT AND STRESS RESPONSE

It's after dark and you're walking alone down a quiet wooded road. As you walk, you're moving more quickly, focused, acutely tuned in to sound and obscured images that line your path. You suddenly notice a shadow approaching. Is it a person? An animal? Your pupils are fully dilated. Fear and anxiety begin to mount as you feel your heart pounding in your chest, your throat goes dry, you're breathing faster and shallower. The craving you had an hour ago for Ben and Jerry's is long gone, replaced by a twinge of nausea. Your muscles have tensed, and you're poised to change direction and run fast if necessary. Every cell in your body is on "red alert" as the shadow approaches. As you begin to run, a person passes by on their bicycle, apologizing for almost hitting you due to the diminished visibility. You experience a deep sigh of relief with a slowing of your pace, heartbeat, breathing, and release of your muscle tension. Your anxiety will soon diminish.

You've just experienced your fight-flight mechanism or stress response in action. Walter Canon first described this phenomenon almost ninety years ago in a laboratory at Harvard. We continue to gain insight into the biological mechanisms that underpin this rapid, powerful, and largely "subconscious" system. From an evolutionary biological perspective the fight-flight response is critical for survival. When confronted with any external stimulus that poses a potential threat, it's advantageous to have a system that scans the landscape and quickly focuses our attention, senses, energy, and drive to avoid harm. No time to think here. Fight-flight is about reaction and action. This powerful "stress response" leaves little time for deliberate consideration of all the available options confronting you (I'll tell you why in a moment). If the building I am in is on fire, I want out. No time to reflect on what caused the fire or what possessions I should bring with me, except other people who may need help (more on altruism to come). When we need to jump into action to save ourselves or others, we have the flight-fight or stress response to thank for "driving us".

What is happening from a neurobiological perspective that makes this response possible? Imagine you're swimming in the ocean and a shark fin breaks the surface nearby. The visual stimulus of the shark fin makes its way from your eyes (retina) to the surface on the back of your brain where vision is processed, to your hippocampus, where memories and learning about the potential dangers of sharks have been stored. This is then given an emotional rocket-booster from your amygdala, a small almond-shaped structure in the center of our brain that serves as our 24/7 sentry for potential threats. Almost instantaneously a cascade of neurotransmitters or messengers is produced. A structure in your brain called the hypothalamus sets these messengers in motion by producing a hormone known as the corticotropin releasing hormone

(CRH). CRH is one of the most important mediators of the stress response—coordinating the adaptive behavioral and physiological changes that occur when we are stressed. CRH stimulates release of the adrenal corticotropic hormone (ACTH) from the pituitary gland. ACTH travels in the bloodstream to the adrenal glands, each of which sits atop your kidneys (see figures 2 and 3). The adrenal glands then produce cortisol, a powerful hormone with myriad effects throughout your body.

The amygdala accentuates feelings of fear and avoidance by its effects on these other structures, keeping continuous guard for any potential threat real or perceived. It works with stored memories that have a significant emotional dimension—for example, trauma, abuse, or experiences associated with feelings of shame, guilt, or humiliation.

The other key player in this response is the locus coerulus-norepinephrine system. Stress inducing stimuli activate the locus coerulus with input from the amygdala, stimulating release of adrenalin and accentuating the release of CRH from the hypothalamus and ACTH from the pituitary gland. This enhances the further release of cortisol.

> This is your very own 24/7 sentry for potential threat, scanning your landscape, and jumping you into survival mode. It can save your life, and it can increase your risk of heart disease.

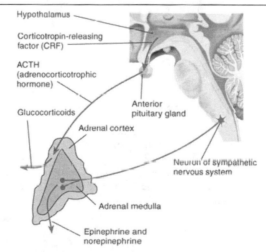

Figure 4.2   Brain Structures and "Messengers" Involved in the Fight-flight Response

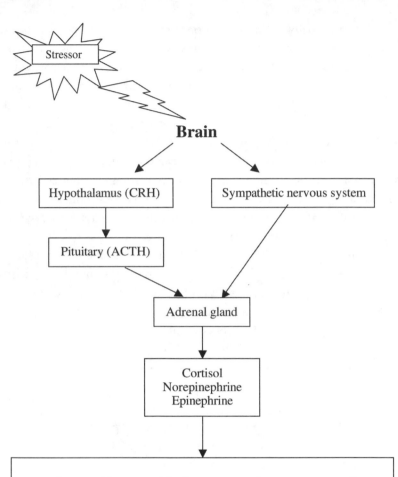

Figure 4.3   The Stress Response

This powerful boost of cortisol and adrenaline tend to inhibit higher levels of conscious thinking. Instead, you're rendered hyper-focused on a very specific target of concern. Potentially life-threatening emergencies undermine well-organized and deliberate thought and cognition. Have you ever wondered why it is hard to concentrate on anything when you're feeling stressed out?

However, recent evidence has identified some additional neurotransmitters that may offset the magnitude and duration of this response. This is consistent with the ying and yang of physiological checks and balances that define our homeostasis. We have within us many biological systems that enable balance or homeostasis to resume after a "peak" in activity in an effort to prevent perpetual overdrive. Current research is focusing on DHEA (dihydroepiandrosterone), neuropeptide Y and galanin. These are the "downers" of the response enabling us to regroup, apply higher levels of reasoning, and restore balance.

There is some evidence that these transmitters assist resilience in the setting of repeated stressful events in our lives. We all know people who somehow are able to remain calm under pressure. Higher levels of reasoning are not as easily highjacked during fight-flight in people who are "cool under pressure." Being cool under pressure is an important attribute for anyone who confronts crisis on a regular basis. It's a critical dimension to effective leadership. As an aside, I make the case that leaders are made, not born. People can become cool, calm, and focused even if that has not previously been a forte. That doesn't mean fear is not present. Firefighters, policemen, astronauts, professional athletes, physicians, etc., confronting very stressful situations will quickly admit to feeling fear. The difference is that activation of the stress response doesn't overwhelm the capacity to stay focused and to perform.

While on call one Sunday evening, I was paged by our local emergency department. The ED physician was evaluating a young man I knew who was on chronic hemodialysis because of kidney disease. He was brought into our ED because he was weak and having difficulty breathing. He was so weak that he had virtual paralysis of his legs. The fight-flight response of the evaluating physician was turned on. I could immediately sense this based on the rapid-fire words that came forth, the sense of urgency in his voice, and the high alert-state and urgency to act. The patient had a life-threatening, high level of potassium (8 meq/l), well beyond a level for certain death. Hearing the story, my fight-flight response was fully turned on as I quickly drove to the hospital, pupils dilated, thoughts racing, heart pounding, oblivious to other activities around me.

I called our dialysis nurse en route to save time, because getting the patient on a dialysis machine would be the only hope of helping him and possibly saving his life. His lungs were also filling with fluid and very soon he would need to be on a breathing machine. His shunt, as horrible luck would have it, was blocked and not useable. This is usually how we hook people up for dialysis treatments. We were all behind the proverbial eight-ball. Silently praying for calm, I had to place a special intravenous catheter into his neck for the purpose of emergency dialysis. He was becoming less conscious by the minute, and as I glanced at the heart monitor, I could see his heart rhythm widening and slowing, an ominous sign of incipient cardiac arrest. Together the nurse and I rode the wave of peak cortisol and adrenaline, staying focused and in control. There would be no room for error here. We placed the line, initiated dialysis, and within minutes things began to stabilize. He fully recovered and now has a transplant. The fight-flight stress response makes this type of emergency rescue possible; though without balance, fight-flight can overwhelm to the point of total paralysis.

There's a growing body of research to suggest that individuals with post-traumatic stress disorder (PSTD) and depression manifest symptoms that result from dysfunction in the regulation of the fight-flight system, resulting in a perpetual accentuation of despair, anxiety, and overwhelming feelings of stress in the course of daily experiences.

As Ray Kurzweil and Terry Grossman note in their book *Fantastic Voyage*, hormones like insulin and cortisol are your "passports to aging." Overstimulate them and age-related diseases will overcome you. Control them (see the Four-Week Addicted-to-Health Plan Summary in Chapter 2), and you're in the driver's seat.

TOO MUCH STRESS CAN KILL QUICKLY. . .

There have been reports of individuals dying or experiencing severe heart dysfunction after experiencing major trauma like sudden loss of a loved one or confronting overwhelming fear. The medical literature contains reports of people actually being frightened to death. These somewhat unusual, though well described cases, likely result from sudden "super-normal" surges of stress hormones and neurotransmitters, overwhelming even the healthiest of hearts. These cases are literal examples of how the stress response, fear, and emotional overload can "break" an otherwise healthy heart. Apparently, a "broken heart" is more than a metaphor for feelings of sadness and loss.

Ilan Wittstein, MD, and Hunter Champion, MD, cardiologists at Johns Hopkins University, have seen first hand the powerful physiological effects that the mind can have on the heart. In recent years, they and other cardiologists have reported individuals with dangerously poor heart function and yet no evidence of blockage in their coronary arteries. Many had recently experienced severe emotional trauma in their lives.

Remarkably, these severe heart changes have the potential to completely reverse themselves. Research involving neurotransmitters has led to a genuine illness referred to as "broken heart syndrome," in which massively elevated levels of adrenaline in certain individuals have the effect of "stunning" the heart and its ability to pump. Shakespeare understood this connection as he wrote in Macbeth, "Give sorrow words: the grief that does not speak . . . whispers the o'er-fraught heart, and bids it break."

If thoughts and feelings can break a heart, perhaps they can mend them as well.

AND TOO MUCH STRESS CAN KILL SLOWLY

We've seen that a sudden overload of stress can create a life-threatening health crisis. But too much stress can also create life-threatening situations over time. For example, cardiovascular disease and depression are the top two causes of disability in the industrialized world. As many as 5 percent of Americans are experiencing symptoms of depression at any point in time. High levels of cortisol are known to decrease serotonin receptors in our prefrontal cortex. Decreased serotonin activity in the brain is central to the feelings of despair and depression. Many current treatments work by reestablishing balance of this neurotransmitter and others.

Six percent of Americans are diabetic and perhaps many more "pre-diabetic," an epidemic in our country and around the world. Is there a connection between the perpetual stress response in our lives and the public health burden of chronic disease? The evidence for this is provocative as the mediators of the stress response produce many of the changes seen in "lifestyle syndrome" and diabetes.

Necessary for survival, the fight-flight stress response, well designed to save us from an oncoming truck, becomes a fault line when overstimulated from the unrelenting stress of our everyday lives.

WANT GOOD HEALTH? GET "PARA"

Many age-related diseases come as a consequence of overstimulation of our sympathetic nervous system, e.g., fight-flight. We have within us a built-in system to counter this response. It's called the *para*sympathetic system. This system, "turned on" by meditation and relaxation techniques, has a calming and protective effect, e.g., decreasing heart rate, metabolism, brain distraction, anxiety-provoking neurotransmitters, etc.

Cultivating behaviors that enhance parasympathetic tone—meditation, positive relationships, mindfulness, or listening to a beautiful piece of classical music—will serve as potent antidotes to sympathetic overdrive.

REWARD-MOTIVATION RESPONSE

In addition to fight-flight, we are also driven by another neurobiological system, often without our conscious knowledge, and that is the reward-motivation response. We can all look at our lives and point to experiences we would consider very rewarding—raising children, working through a relationship problem, graduating from college, completing a challenging project, or winning a championship, for example. It's hard to imagine getting through life without experiences that reward us in ways that satisfy what we value most, experiences that create meaning and motivation and inspire feelings of optimism, hope, and joy.

Resilient individuals (see Chapter 18) seem to have cultivated a reward system that is resistant to change despite setbacks, sometimes catastrophic, acute or chronic in nature. In other words, life's setbacks do not diminish their capacity to experience positive emotions. Individuals whose reward

Individuals whose reward response is dampened are less likely to experience pleasure in their lives and are more prone to states of anxiety and depression.

response is dampened are less likely to experience pleasure in their lives and are more prone to states of anxiety and depression. They're also less resilient.

Some studies have made note of differences in activity in the part of the brain that lies behind the forehead called the prefrontal cortex. As noted, this region integrates and distills information from many other areas in the brain. Some studies have shown that activation in these regions is associated with experiences of positive emotional states like bliss, love, joy, and contentment. The prefrontal cortex may, therefore, be an important player in the reward section of your brain's orchestra. The limbic system, including the hippocampus (memory), amygdala (emotional charge), hypothalamus, and the nucleus accumbens is the driving force in the reward orchestra.

Neurotransmitters of interest in the reward response include dopamine, glutamate, GABA (gamma amino butyric acid which facilitates a calming effect), and endorphins. The reward response is designed to seek reward in new and novel ways. Behavior that produces a satisfying outcome that is new or novel, or that exceeds expectations, will enable a more potent biological response. The memory of that behavior-response will be etched in a more indelible, accessible way. The result is a greater desire or motivation to repeat the behavior.

> Behavior that produces a satisfying outcome that is new or novel, or that exceeds expectations, will enable a more potent biological response. The memory of that behavior-response will be etched in a more indelible, accessible way. The result is a greater desire or motivation to repeat the behavior.

Dopamine, a big player here, is released in the prefrontal cortex and nucleus accumbens. Endorphins, our own manufactured opiates, are also central to this response. It's important to appreciate that a behavior that elicits a reward response is not always a health-promoting behavior. Dopamine, for example, rewards carbohydrate binging as it does exercise. It can reward cocaine as it does a romantic gaze. Endorphins act to lessen pain and to produce a high. A potent high, whether natural or artificial, is produced in a similar fashion, though drugs like heroin and cocaine produce more intense surges reinforcing their addictive nature.

These highs also have the amygdala adding a charge of emotional energy as if to say "ooooohhhhh that was sssooooooooo sweeeeeeeet. . . . I looooovvve that. Mooooore pleeeeeease." As the effects of these powerful messengers begin to diminish in minutes to hours, withdrawal or detachment manifestations motivate recall of the memory of how good it felt and the behavior repeats itself.

It's also noteworthy that studies using functional fMRI to image brains in individuals engaged in a deeply romantic gaze, or a new mother responding to her crying infant, or a cocaine abuser demonstrate similar areas of neurobiological activation. That speaks to the nasty biological power that some drugs have in controlling the victims they inflict. It also suggests that individuals who are ravaged by addiction have the potential to elicit some semblance of the same effects with aggressive multidimensional approaches like cognitive behavioral therapy (CBT), social supports, pharmacological protocols for better control of withdrawal symptoms and cravings, etc.

In researching and preparing this book, I found myself more attuned to what was happening inside my head as thoughts and feelings passed by. For example, I experienced what I determined was a small battle between my fight-flight response and my reward response.

I was out for a short jog, and I could see ominous black clouds quickly approaching. Thunder had begun to rumble in the distance. Limited meteorological knowledge and learned memory left me with the recollection that thunder equals lightening. I thought that soon I would be a running human lightening rod. My fight-flight response was working appropriately and appeared intact as my apprehension grew. At the same time, I was far enough into my run that the dopamine and endorphins had begun to kick in. *I was both frightened and high.* Do I stop in the spirit of self-preservation, or do I continue in a state of blissful health promotion, undaunted and controlled? My prefrontal cortex served as the arbiter, both analyzing the risk and promoting the reward. Anyone peering into the orchestra behind my mind's curtain would have seen the players vigorously churning away. The orchestra would have sounded like "stop you fool . . . keep going it feels too good . . . stop in the name of safety . . . run, run, run, you indestructible machine."

At this point, the rain had begun to fall harder and the thunder had grown louder. As I have tried to do with greater commitment in my life when confronting a difficult challenge, I quickly scanned my options for the choice that would best reconcile this conflict, mutually satisfying my needs for safety and reward—I ran for cover.

The point is—we must weigh the benefit of short-term rewards or highs against behaviors that undermine our health in the long term—carb binging and smoking—and learn to use natural highs to hook us into health promoting behaviors like exercise and meditation. As for sex, well I guess that depends on the context. The limbic-frontal reward dance in sex is so awesome that relationship-based trust that can take a lifetime to build can unravel in a heartbeat. In sexual affairs as in conflict management, be careful of leaving your prefrontal cortex at the door.

> The limbic-frontal reward dance in sex is so awesome that relationship based trust that can take a lifetime to build can unravel in a heartbeat. In sexual affairs as in conflict management, be careful of leaving your prefrontal cortex at the door.

The reward response like the flight-fight response can drive behaviors that bypass or diminish input from the prefrontal cortex, which is responsible for reasoning, judgment, and emotional control.

THE LURE OF ADDICTIVE DRUGS: REWARD TRUMPS LOGIC

The "artificial buzz" from drugs creates an intense waxing-waning high and low that creates the perception that one cannot feel pleasure without the drug. Addiction occurs because drugs co-opt the body's natural high by triggering this dopamine-endorphin response. Repeated exposure fools the brain into craving these substances more than food and sex. This says something about the magnitude of the dopamine-endorphin surge. Narcotics like heroin and oxycontin mimic opiod endorphins, diminishing pain and producing a feeling of euphoria. Cocaine produces a powerful high by triggering the release of dopamine in the nucleus accumbens. Alcohol and nicotine have multiple biological effects, which likely involve endorphins and dopamine to some extent.

> Addiction occurs because drugs co-opt the body's natural high by triggering this dopamine-endorphin response. Repeated exposure fools the brain into craving these substances more than food and sex. This says something about the magnitude of the dopamine-endorphin surge.

It's very scary to contemplate the fact that after just a few acts of indiscretion with a powerful substance, addiction follows. As the reward surge begins to subside, the brain begins to respond, manifesting a withdrawal syndrome. Common and nasty withdrawal symptoms include increased restlessness, anxiety, fear, insomnia, and nausea. Re-exposure to the drug lessons the symptoms of withdrawal, reinforcing the motivation to seek and ingest the drug again. Heroin addicts will point out that they often continue to take the drug more to offset the withdrawal symptoms than to elicit a high.

Like the fight-flight stress response, the reward response is primal and robust. It can serve us incredibly well. And it can burn us badly. The challenge is applying greater knowledge and awareness of what your mind's orchestra can do and how you can influence the symphony it plays. Behaviors like exercise, meditation, prayer, and satisfying value-based goals like modest weight loss or volunteering your talent are able to promote health *and* turn on your reward response.

> Behaviors like exercise, meditation, prayer, and satisfying value-based goals like modest weight loss or volunteering your talent are able to promote health *and* turn on your reward response.

The reward of better heath, mind, and emotion will make it more likely you'll repeat the health promoting behavior. In addition, exercise, prayer, meditation, social connection, forgiveness, relationship reconciliation, etc., serve to mitigate the magnitude and duration of the stress response. The suggestion is that people can actually be addicted to health-promoting behaviors!

FEAR CONDITIONING AND LEARNED HELPLESSNESS

Fear is a powerful and pervasive emotion in our lives. It can serve us well if the fear we feel helps us to avoid a potentially dangerous or risky situation. Too often, however, it influences the choices we make. As a formidable obstacle, fear can diminish our potential for change and growth. For example, a person might fear taking a particular medication because someone they know had a reaction to a similar prescription. Or a person may fear going to see their doctor or going to the emergency department because they fear "what might be found." As you confront an escalating conflict with another individual, particularly one you have had a prior negative experience with, your assumptions will likely reflect your worse fears. "I know he wants to show our boss that he's better than me," or "I'm sure she's looking to steal that important contract from me."

These kinds of assumptions are largely influenced by the amygdala's footprint, which is based on stored memories associated with a prior event or individual.

It's hard to imagine a more potent obstacle to greater understanding, growth, and value creation than that inspired by fear. What players in your mind-body orchestra are at play here? Is it possible to transform the fear response to obtain greater control in your life? Is it possible to influence the fine line between fear's important role as protector and its pervasive role as an obstacle? Can we find opportunity and possibility in the midst of fear? While it is not always easy to get there, the answer is a resounding yes.

As Frances Moore Lappé and Jeffrey Perkins note in their book, *You Have The Power: Choosing Courage in a Culture of Fear*, transforming fear requires reconstituting thoughts. "Old thoughts: Fear means I'm in danger. Something's wrong. I must escape and seek safety. New thoughts: Fear is pure energy. It's a signal. It might not mean stop, it could mean go."

Remember, what we think, how we feel, and how we behave are malleable or "plastic" neurobiological states. I'll attempt to address these questions initially from the perspective of the neurobiological fingerprints of fear. Throughout the remainder of the book, I'll offer suggestions for how this potent source of emotional paralysis can be transformed into opportunity.

HOW WE BECOME CONDITIONED TO FEAR

Pavlov's research in this area provided some of the earliest insight into the understanding of fear conditioning. An animal receiving an external neutral stimulus, for example, the ringing of a bell, subsequently received a non-neutral electric shock. After several repeated sequences of bell-shock-bell-shock, the mere sound of the bell, even if a shock does not follow, elicits a physiological reaction identical to the one produced when a shock is given. This is an example of classic fear conditioning or associative learning.

The fear response is elicited by a host of behavioral, neurobiological, and endocrine reactions that normally occur in the context of danger. Fear conditioning when appropriately adaptive enables us to accurately predict threat and react in the face of danger. This powerful biological response, however, does not always lead to effective behavioral adaptation.

Let me give you an example of how a traumatic event can imbue an emotional memory so significant it replays itself over a lifetime, eliciting fear and anxiety with an intensity that can take an old wound and reignite it to feel as real as actually being in the moment. In 1960 my mother, father, and I were involved in a serious automobile accident. I was only three at the time, and with the exception of a rare flashback, have no conscious recall of the event. My parents were seriously injured; my mother, in particular, sustained life-threatening injuries requiring immediate surgery. Her recovery took more than a year and was nothing less than miraculous. For the remainder of her life, riding as a passenger in a car would never be quite the same. She never learned how to drive. I recall many instances growing up when she carried the look of hypervigilance as my father drove us home from a social gathering. She feared any car that appeared too close or going too fast. Heart racing, breathing increased, pupils dilated (fight-flight stress response), her arms would often extend as if to support herself in the event of another collision. In my mother's example, the neutral conditioned stimulus, riding in an automobile, became linked to the traumatic event, thus eliciting the unconditioned response. The mechanisms imprinted with the initial traumatic event were aroused and reconsolidated with re-exposure to similar stimuli, even in a different context.

The limbic system, i.e., the hippocampus, thalamus, and amygdala, are involved with storage of the memory and the emotional tattoo associated with the memory (see figure 4). The amygdala, in particular, is the fear center. There is also a known link between the limbic system and the prefrontal cortex as has been described with the fight-flight and reward circuitry. As previously noted, the prefrontal cortex helps us put things in proper perspective. I think of the relationship between the prefrontal cortex and limbic system like a parent responding to the concerns of a child in the midst of a late-night thunderstorm. "It's okay, honey. That noise you hear is just thunder. It sounds scary, but it's further away than it sounds and is not dangerous. I'll lay with you for a while until it passes."

Individuals with PTSD struggle with replays of events, often remote traumatic events that reawaken a powerful fear and fight-flight response. These neurobiological imprints of prior emotionally traumatic events can easily be prompted by stimuli that, in some way, despite occurring in a totally different context, rekindle the original experience. A friend of mine who was seriously wounded in Viet Nam tells me to this day that hearing a helicopter, even with the knowledge that the helicopter is not a threat, reawakens the emotional trauma he experienced now almost forty years ago. Our prefrontal cortex helps us by producing GABA (gamma amino butyric acid)

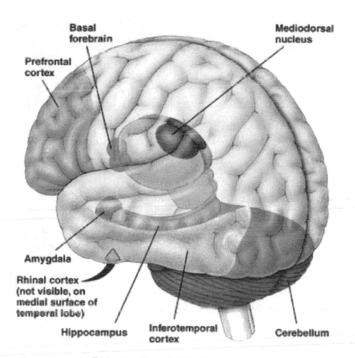

Figure 4.4 Structures of the Brain that Play a Role in Memory

serotonin, and other transmitters in an effort to keep this response in check. Its activity reassures and arbitrates, distinguishing a fear response requiring immediate action—an oncoming tornado—from one requiring reassurance—a distant thunderstorm.

Neurotransmitters like CRH, cortisol, norepinephrine, and NMDA (n-methyl, d-aspartate) are important in not only producing the emotional experience of fear but also in the deep storage or "consolidation" of the fear memory. People often have vivid recall of the fear of an experience more than they do a detail of the event itself. Each time a traumatic memory is retrieved, it's integrated into an ongoing perceptual and emotional experience and becomes part of a new memory. This phenomenon is referred to as *reconsolidation*.

There is much research in the behavioral sciences focused on helping individuals gain more control over the heightened fear response of the reconsolidation process, often seen in individuals with PTSD. Like many therapeutic approaches, these interventions integrate methods of cognitive behavioral therapy (CBT), a process that applies mind-body adaptation in a more health-promoting manner, sometimes with medications that can bring greater balance to the rational (prefrontal lobe) and emotional (limbic) sections of our brain.

For most people, repeated exposure to a neutral conditioned stimulus, riding in an automobile or hearing the chopping blades of a helicopter in flight, in the absence of an actual threat, leads to a reduction of fear that may have previously been consolidated in your memory bank. This phenomenon is referred to as *extinction*. If for example, an individual experiences fear each time they walk by a house that has a bold sign in the front yard that says "BEWARE OF DOG," and after repeated walk-bys never sees the dog, the fear is likely to be eventually extinguished.

This reminds me of a recent experience that falls into the category of neuroscience for every day living. My family and I recently moved from Massachusetts to Charleston, SC. We built a home in a developed community where many other new homes were complete or near complete. Our doorbell rang one afternoon, and a very nice fellow introduced himself as a salesperson for a reputable home security system company. He was installing systems for our neighbors (consensus is an important principle of influencing behavior—if the neighbors are putting in a security system, so should I), and of course he had a special deal that could save me a significant sum of money. He framed this as a one-time (creating the perception of scarcity . . . another effective method for influencing behavior) deal that would allow me to feel secure in the protection of my family (tapping into the emotional attachment of papa bear protecting his cubs). In a few short minutes, he had introduced three effective influences of behavior: consensus, scarcity, and fear.

He seemed very experienced and went on to mention his track record in our community and in our region (trust is critical in optimizing interpersonal effectiveness with others). "Thank you for the invitation," I quipped, a bit exhausted after a long day of unpacking. "I am curious. Can you provide me with any data on local crime statistics in this community, how they compare to regional benchmarks, and how families that have installed your security system fare as compared with those who don't?"

He had no answer and seemed somewhat defensive at the notion of having to answer questions he seemed unaccustomed to. By this time my front door had been open for a while and my exuberant lab-terrier came to the door, curious and suspicious. I then asked, prior to his departure, "Are you aware of any comparisons from the perspective of home security between systems like yours and a sign in a front yard that reads "BEWARE OF DOG" with an actual dog barking inside the house?" Though somewhat in jest, I gave this a little more thought after querying the salesman off my front porch. While there may actually be some data out there (I would welcome your forwarding it to me), I would speculate that a sign in front of a house reading "BEWARE OF DOG" (whether or not a dog actually lived there) would be a more effective deterrent to a prospective robber than a sign that reads "HOUSE PROTECTED BY ___." Assuming the robber can read (a big assumption, admittedly), it is likely that the image of a nasty, growling, salivating, carnivore and the fear-flight response attached to that image, powerfully reawakened in the hippocampus and further ignited by the amygdala of the perpetrator, would influence behavior more effectively than the security company's sign. Perhaps I can start my own home security system simply by printing "BEWARE OF DOG" signs and offering them for a few dollars each. But I digress.

The ability to overcome fear is a great example of the brain's inherent capacity for adaptation or **plasticity**, an ability to adapt response to the same stimulus in a fundamentally different way. Had I not been able to adapt to the fear I felt at the sight of blood, my professional life would have had a very different outcome. I went from predictable lightheaded wooziness at the

> The ability to overcome fear is a great example of the brain's inherent capacity for adaptation or *plasticity*, an ability to adapt response to the same stimulus in a fundamentally different way.

sight of blood (referred to as a vagal response) to putting large intravenous catheters in jugular veins to allow large volumes of blood to be circulated through an artificial kidney for dialysis, in a pretty short time. Thank God for plasticity!

The medial prefrontal cortex (see figure 4.1) again comes into play here. Individuals who function well after a fear-inducing experience exhibit greater prefrontal cortex control over the amygdala. The sophisticated work by Daniel Goleman, PhD, and others in the field of emotional intelligence emphasizes this same characteristic in people who more effectively manage their emotions and interpersonal skills in leadership, life, and in conflict resolution and negotiation (more of this in Chapter 13).

In contrast, individuals without an effective prefrontal cortex serving as the 24/7 emotional management sentry are at greater risk for depression, anxiety, fear, PTSD, dysfunctional relationships, and a lifetime of debilitating energy consumption. It is not my intent to be judgmental here. We all struggle with these issues as human beings. The point is that our mind-body integration makes effective change possible. The challenge is the application of this potential that enables transformation from victim to victory.

> The point is that our mind-body integration makes effective change possible. The challenge is the application of this potential that enables transformation from victim to victory.

SOCIAL BONDING AND ATTACHMENT

If there's one neurobiological system that brings together thought, feeling, behavior, and reward in facilitating effective survival and a greater likelihood of a longer and more satisfying life, it is the response that fosters attachment. Social connection and social satisfaction have both intuitive and scientifically proven benefits when it comes to stress reduction, health promotion, and disease prevention. When it comes to health and longevity, there is no substitute!

The bonding and attachment neurochemical system is an interesting story within a story. Our wiring for attachment has been referred to as "the separation cry." Approximately twenty years ago, Paul MacLean published observations based on years of work that examined distinguishing features between mammals and other living creatures. Combining comparative neuroanatomy (comparing mammalian brain structure with that of reptiles) and animal behavioral science, he developed his concept of the "mammalian triune brain" (see figure 4.5). It was sort of a neuroanatomical archeological dig that depicted neurobiological evolution from reptiles to higher-thinking Homo sapiens. The very core of the human brain in this analysis is not too different than what is found in reptiles and rodents. Hmmmm. . . maybe you're not off base in thinking your boss is a rat or your adversary a snake in the grass.

Above this reptilian core is a second or mid-layer of the brain. Here is what I have referred to as the limbic system. Recall that this area is central in placing an emotional charge (from fear to bliss) on our experiences. Memories both newly encoded and previously acquired and stored help us predict cause and effect, guiding our behavior, initiating fight-flight, and creating a subconscious drive to act in the cause of self-preservation and reward. Parts of

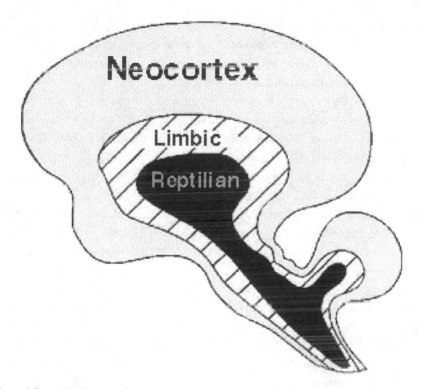

Figure 4.5   The Concept of the Triune Brain as Developed by Paul MacLean
Source: "The Stress Response and Separation Cry in Medical and Psychiatric Illness," by Alex Sabo, *Berkshire Medical Journal,* 1997 (4): 5-10.

this middle layer connect with the neocortex or early mammalian structures. It's in this increasingly sophisticated domain that we become more conscious thinkers, able to reason and judge. The neocortex also serves as an arbiter for mood, disposition, and the positive emotions of joy, love, bliss, meaning, and purpose.

When MacLean compared reptilian behavior with that of mammals, many patterns were shared with a few noteworthy exceptions. Mammals consistently displayed these distinguishing behaviors:

- Nursing and maternal care
- Communication for maintaining maternal-offspring control or "the separation cry"
- Cuddling and play

It would appear that mammals are wired to commit to a family-like social structure. This has intuitive survival advantages as the ability to adapt to change may be better leveraged over a socially connected group. Also, it takes much longer for baby mammals to reach an age where they can survive independently. A stronger maternal attachment is required to enable this development to successfully occur.

So what are the neurobiological correlates of this enormously important and primal response? The answer is elucidated when one compares the behaviors of the prairie and montane voles, of course! Though quite similar genetically, the prairie and montane vole vary greatly in their social behaviors. The prairie vole is quite social and outgoing, the Oprah Winfrey of the arid plains, forming long-lasting social bonds and attachments. The prairie vole is also monogamous. The montane voles tend to keep to themselves, social only when there is some mating involved.

The neurotransmitters currently understood to be involved with this drive for bonding and social attachment include oxytocin, dopamine (a familiar friend from the reward response), and endorphins (our internal opiates). The circuitry involves the nucleus accumbens and areas in the limbic system, especially the ventral pallidum in the limbic system. The medial frontal lobe cortex is also integral to this response. While I will elaborate on the health implications of this bonding-attachment response in more detail, I do wish to point out that when you embrace someone you love deeply, close your eyes, and feel awesome, the orchestra inside your mind is doing the following:

- Medial cortex of the frontal lobe increases serotonin responsiveness, enhancing mood, feelings of joy, and positive emotions
- Endorphins are turned up, modifying pain, enhancing comfort, and generating a "high"
- Your limbic system by enhancing dopamine and oxytocin creates feelings of bliss, love, and attachment
- Your hypothalamic-pituitary-adrenal axis (HPA) is downshifted, resulting in decreased cortisol production. This reduces the "stress response" and its health undermining tendencies, enhancing immune function, lowering blood pressure, reducing risk of diabetes, and enhancing resilience, etc.

- Your locus coeruleus decreases its production of norepinephrine or adrenalin, reducing heart rate, blood pressure, anxiety, and oxygen demand.

This circuitry when cultivated (like providing more water and sunlight to this part of your brain's secret garden) rewards cooperative social relationships and inhibits selfish impulse.

Nothing, and I mean nothing I can write on a prescription pad can reproduce this constellation of positive effects listed above.

This will also be a point revisited when we examine strategies for better health by way of more effective conflict management. The virtues of non-self perspectives are what define altruism. Altruism, extending kindness and compassion to others not because you have to but because you can, is a virtue identified in highly resilient children, adolescents, and adults.

Women tend to manage this response—the ultimate trump card of life, in my view—better than men. I would be a fool to speculate as to why this is except to note that childbearing and breastfeeding require robust activity of attachment-bonding-reward responses. When under increased stress or when confronting interpersonal conflict, women will tend to migrate toward a "tend and befriend" posture. Men are more inclined to "fend and defend."

Resilient individuals have often cultivated important supportive social networks and interpersonal attachments. Outstanding leadership and noteworthy acts of courage are often seen in individuals who value altruism, marked by unselfish concern for the welfare of others. All of this, not surprisingly, positively reinforces and motivates ongoing consistent behaviors. This is how the design appears to work. In other words, the more acts of non-self one engages in, the more acts of non-self one engages in. And in the end, the rewards to "self" are incredible—greater joy, happiness, contentment, meaning, and better health and longer life. Altruism and social connection are superb antidotes for stress and allostatic load. All of this and more and it don't cost a penny? Sign me up please!

> Altruism and social connection are superb antidotes for stress and allostatic load. All of this and more and it don't cost a penny? Sign me up please!

MEMORY: THE STORY OF YOUR LIFE

While necessary to examine (perhaps with greater portions than your appetite desired) an overview of the primal neurobiological systems underpinning stress, reward, fear, and attachment responses, it is also worth briefly reviewing current understanding about how we process old and new memories. As the narrator in Saul Bellow's *The Bellarosa Connection* reminds us, "Memory is life."

Memory is the basis of our expectations and defines our perceptions of the world. Our identities are attached to our memories. This is one of the difficult aspects of having a friend or family member with dementia, like Alzheimer's. It's painfully disturbing to observe someone you love, unable to recall your name and the countless memories that define your relationship.

Behavioral and neuroscientists make the distinction between two types of memory. One is referred to as procedural memory or subconscious memory. An example of this would be the memory of how to swing a baseball bat. Memory in this instance is linked with the process of learning in our prefrontal cortex. Declarative memories, on the other hand, allow us to recall past events like hitting a home run in a baseball game. In addition, declarative memories allow us to acquire general knowledge, also referred to as somatic memory. Knowing the capital of Spain would be such a memory. Much of our declarative memory is acquired, encoded, and recalled in areas connecting our hippocampus and our cerebral cortex (see figure 4.4). When we add to our memory, as previously noted, we reconstruct the story that may or may not accurately reflect what actually happened. I will come back to this point when we examine the implications and applications of these neurobiological responses in the management of conflict.

Sensory input from our eyes, ears, nose, and skin start in the cortex. They are assembled and encoded in the hippocampus and are essential to the process of learning. Research by Chantel Stern and Howard Eichenbaum, director of Boston University's Center for Memory and the Brain, suggests that the brain needs time to process a new stimulus before it can produce a memory, kind of like working memory. It can also take time to retrieve an old memory when trying to connect past with present. It may be that some of our most effective learning happens when our brain isn't responding to a stimulus. For example, often the best way to recall the name of someone you've unexpectedly run in to is not to try.

It's the amygdala that adds the emotional "spin" to the memory. Memories have the potential to reconfigure and strengthen as they are re-awakened, depending on the context in which they are rekindled. Our system of memory retrieval tends to be congruous with our mood. In other words, the memories we pull off the bookshelf of past events tend to be consistent with our current mood. So if your cup is half full, your brain will tend to add a bit to it. This can also work in reverse, a slippery slide indeed. Much of our emotional memory—the amygdala again—drives us in a powerful way as a motivator of behavior at a subconscious level. The greater the emotional attachment, the more likely we are to readily retrieve the details of the original experience. The neurochemical footprint that allows you to remember where you placed your sunglasses will look and feel very different than the footprint of a prior demeaning interpersonal encounter.

As many brain structures, networks, and neurotransmitters have been introduced in this chapter, I have summarized the primary players in your mind-body orchestra (table 1), their biological effects, and their health implications.

Table 1. Summary of Various Neurochemical Patterns

Fight-Flight Stress Response			
Neurochemical	Brain Region	Effects	Health Implications
cortisol	Prefrontal cortex Hippocampus, Amygdala, Hypothalamus	↑ Mobilize energy arousal, focused attention fear, memory formation	High blood pressure High blood sugar Insulin resistance High blood lipids Impaired immunity Depression Cardiovascular risk Osteoporosis
CRH	Prefrontal cortex Cingulated cortex, amygdala Nucleus accumbens, Locus coeruleus, Hippocampus, Hypothalamus	↑ Fear behaviors, arousal ↓ Reward expectations	May increase risk for depression and PTSD, chronic fear, anxiety, anhedonia
Locus coeruleus Norepinephrine	Prefrontal cortex, amygdala Hippocampus, Hypothalamus	Alarm for threat ↑ Fear, motor response Attention, fear memory	Chronic anxiety High blood pressure Hypervigilance Depression Panic disorder Intrusive memories

Table 1. (Continued)

Fight-Flight Stress Response

Neurochemical	Brain Region	Effects	Health Implications
Dopamine	Prefrontal cortex Nucleus accumbens Amygdala	High prefrontal cortex and Low nucleus accumbens Dopamine associated with helpless behavior, anhedonia	Impaired cognition Depression
Serotonin	Prefrontal cortex Amygdala Hippocampus	Low levels of anxiety and depression	Anxiety and depression
DHEA (dihydroepi- androsterone)	Hypothalamus	Positive mood Counteracts high cortisol	Low DHEA response increases effects of high cortisol
Testosterone	Hypothalamus	Reduced levels from stress, increase depression	Low levels of hormone enhance fatigue, associated with PTSD, depression
Estrogen	Hypothalamus Hippocampus	May dampen stress response	Uncertain
Neuropeptide Y	Amygdala Hippocampus Hypothalamus Locus coeruleus	Reduces stress response, ↓ anxiety	Low levels enhance risks of acute/chronic stress
Galanin	Prefrontal cortex Amygdala Hippocampus Hypothalamus Locus coerulus	Reduce stress response ↓ Anxiety	Low levels may increase vulnerability to stress

Reward, Fear, and Bonding-Attachment Systems

Neurochemical	Brain Region	Effects	Health Implications
Dopamine Glutamate NMDA ⇨ GABA Endorphins	Medial prefrontal cortex Nucleus accumbens Amygdala Hippocampus Hypothalamus	Pleasure, bliss Positive emotions Motivation Modulation of pain Euphoria	Reinforces (+) health- promoting behaviors Resilience ↓ Activation leads to hopelessness, anhedonia
Oxytocin Endorphins Dopamine ⇨ NMDA	Medial prefrontal cortex Nucleus accumbens Caudate nucleus Locus coeruleus	Love, pleasure Bonding Meaning Dampens stress response	↓ Allostatic burden Enhanced mood ↓ Anxiety Resilience
Norepinephrine Cortisol CRH ⇨ Glutamate Dopamine GABA/NMDA	Medial prefrontal cortex Amygdala Hippocampus Anterior cingulated	Fear Hypervigilance Fear memory Accentuation of stress response	Depression, anxiety, PTSD allostatic ↑ burden inertia to change

Chapter 5

A Day in the Life
of a Tibetan Monk

"Leave your mind unfabricated and free ... cutting through the
flow of inceptual thoughts ... old illnesses will disappear by
themselves and you remain unharmed by new ones."

Padmasumbkawa

Our mind has developed as a consequence of millions of years of evolutionary refinement, with characteristics selected for their survival advantages and
shared by all humans. Our thoughts and feelings are both shared and distinct, reflecting the nuances made possible by our unique experiences, memories, and genetic endowment. These experiences of mind and body can
elicit fear and emotional distress or they can resonate with happiness and
contentment.

In this chapter, I want to introduce you to an extreme example of how
the mind can influence bodily function. It is, in fact, a way of being. It
touches on the spiritual heart of Tibetan healing, one of many ways of examining health distinct from our Western models. Two of my close friends
and medical colleagues have been to Tibet, studied Tibetan spiritual culture,

and mastered meditation techniques. They have awakened me to a fundamentally different way of examining my relationship to life around me. They've also "shaken" the foundation upon which I've studied and understood disease prevention, treatment, and health promotion, with emphasis on more holistic perspectives that naturally integrate mind, body, and spirit. As I have learned more about Tibetan Buddhist philosophy and meditation, I have witnessed remarkable examples of the power to profoundly influence bodily function by greater awareness, mindfulness practice, and meditation. Needless to say, this was an awakening for a traditionally trained American physician.

Imagine this. A group of Tibetan monks sit quietly in a remote monastery located in northern India. They're scantily clad and the temperature is 40 degrees Fahrenheit. It's very cool, even by a native New Englander's standards. The monks then enter a state of deep meditation using a technique known as g-Tum-mo. Sheets, three-by-six feet, are then soaked in very cold water and placed over the meditating monk's shoulders. Now I have on occasion run in some cold, wet temperatures in the Berkshire Hills, with multiple layers of clothing, generating maximal body heat, and shaking like a leaf on a cold, windy New England day, just to stay warm. (This is what happens by the way when you become addicted to exercise.) Okay, back to Tibet. Despite sitting motionless, scantily clothed, in cold ambient conditions, with cold wet sheets on their backs, these monks enter more deeply into a meditative state. Soon steam begins to rise from the sheets as body heat is produced, and in about an hour, the sheets are totally dry! This is just slightly less efficient than my Maytag® dryer. Each monk proceeds to completely dry three sheets over a few hours while in a state of meditation.

Herbert Benson, MD, director of the Mind-Body Institute at Harvard has been studying these mind-body effects for more than thirty-five years. The developer of "the relaxation response," Benson appreciates the potential capacity for treating stress-related illness. Like most health care professionals who have trained in a disease-oriented model of understanding, I have been challenged to apply broader biopsychosocial contexts in response to what are many stress-related problems. We physicians are trained like fine-tuned Intel microprocessors to elicit the facts, reach a diagnosis, and eliminate the presenting physical symptom. Often there is no context that emerges in these encounters that addresses more global sources of contributing stress. As a consequence, an individual is likely to receive a prescription or more testing instead of a more appropriate treatment plan consisting of education and self-care. I discuss this in detail in my first book *The Savvy Patient: The Ultimate Advocate for Quality Health Care*. I now find myself spending more time emphasizing the importance of the physician-patient alliance as a partnership. I place much greater emphasis on the importance of self-care.

Benson and his research team have studied monks living in the Himalayan Mountains who were able, by g-Tum-mo meditation, to raise their body temperatures by as much as 17 degrees Fahrenheit! This is stunning. In addition, researchers have made measurements on practitioners of other forms of advanced meditation in Sikkam, India. These monks could lower their metabolic rate by as much as 64 percent. This, too, is stunning when one considers that metabolism and oxygen consumption drop only 10 to 15 percent during sleep. Simpler forms of meditation result in, on average, a 17 percent reduction. Significant drops in blood pressure, heart rate, and respiratory rate accompany these profound changes in metabolic rate. Traditional wisdom has always been that humans have little, if any control over these expressions of our "autonomic" central nervous system.

> Benson and his research team have studied monks living in the Himalayan Mountains who were able, by g-Tum-mo meditation, to raise their body temperatures by as much as 17 degrees Fahrenheit! This is stunning.

Tibetan monks have also been videotaped spending a winter night on a rocky ledge, 15,000 feet above sea level in the Himalayans. Imagine lying outside on a cold February night, almost three miles above sea level, where temperatures drop to zero degrees Fahrenheit or below. The monks are wearing only woolen or cotton shawls and promptly fall asleep. At dawn they awaken and return to their monastery to start another day, refreshed and rejuvenated. Had I learned these techniques years ago, I may never have left my New England roots for the warmer confines of the "low country" of southeastern South Carolina.

When monks are in a meditative state and imaged in a fMRI brain imaging machine, there is a sharp and sudden increase in activity of the left prefrontal cortex associated with a "dimming" or decreased activity of the parietal lobe located toward the back of the brain. The parietal lobe is important in our time-spatial orientation. This pattern of prefrontal enhancement of activity with diminished parietal activity is associated with an experience of intense focus, clarity of thought, calm, equanimity, and self-transcendence. A similar pattern has also been described when people are immersed in prayer, perhaps the most common form of meditation practiced around the world. Brain wave patterns (from studies using techniques of neurofeedback) demonstrate marked increases in theta wave activity, a manifestation of increased alertness and focus. The average Tibetan monk does not require Ritalin to achieve this.

As a traditionally trained physician with five years of post-doctoral training at Harvard Medical School, I would never have thought it possible that any human could induce such profound biological change by virtue of centering thought in a deep state of mindfulness or meditation. These monks, of course, have lived their lives in total commitment to the development of these mindfulness practices. They are ways of living. They are ways of being.

I bring these remarkable observations to your attention not with an expectation that anyone can achieve this level of control, but to point out an extreme example of the power of mind over body. There are no strings attached here. No magic here. It is an inducible state that allows the conductor of the orchestra to play a radically different symphony. It's the same musicians, same instruments, but a very different symphony.

In a simpler form, Benson's relaxation response involves two pieces. The first is sitting in a quiet place, silently repeating a word, phrase or short prayer (I use Psalm 118:24, "This is the day which the Lord hath made"). The second is to purposefully disregard all intrusive thoughts and return to your breathing and the silent repetition of your word or phrase. Choosing a word or phrase that represents a strong belief with meaning facilitates the relaxation response. It's easy to learn and with practice will have immediate and noteworthy effects on how you feel and how your body responds. The faith factor, which I will discuss in more detail in Chapter 12, is made possible by practices that combine deep and personal meaning with a meditative mind-body response.

From these examples of plasticity and others, I hope you can begin to appreciate how thoughtful integration of self-care with existing models of health care can create marvelous synergy. What's important to remember is that change of the magnitude sufficient to promote health requires full attention and awareness.

Successful change is more likely to endure when it is occurring at the "way-of-being" level; in other words, when the change becomes a habit in your life. To change a deeply rooted mind-body pattern, from a neurobiological perspective, is both doable and difficult. It is doable because the evidence is increasingly compelling that the brain's inherent plasticity forever allows areas of your garden to grow and thrive where minimal activity currently exists. Depending on the natural light and watering you provide, the garden can take on a more vigorous, adaptive, and colorful dynamic.

> Successful change is more likely to endure when it is occurring at the "way-of-being" level; in other words, when the change becomes a habit in your life.

Expect that on your way to a more beautiful garden you will encounter stumbling blocks: you may feel at times that plasticity can't be achieved, or it's not worth the effort. It will take time to acquire the trust needed to add more nutrients to your garden's soil, or in other words, to strengthen and expand your mind. You don't have to live the life of a Tibetan monk to realize the potential within you.

Small changes, as I will show, when examined from the perspective of a biological footprint, lead to shifts that will begin to draw you to the formation of an entirely new footprint. It's really quite cool. From my naïve perspective, you wouldn't meditate hours each day, live a simple life of thanks and gratitude, and experience self-transcendence (at very high altitudes and under harsh meteorological conditions) if it wasn't well worth it.

For behavioral change to result in a sustained health benefit, you should:

- Believe deeply in the value served by making the change
- Have deep meaning attached to the reasons for the change
- Make the change become a way of being and living

When the change becomes a way of living, you have effectively reconfigured the neurobiological default setting. Once in the default mode, you'll be able to sustain the change with less conscious effort, allowing you to move on to the next change. While your goals and practice will look different than that of a Tibetan monk, the tools available to you are essentially the same. Remember:

It can be done. And it is worth it.

ADDING SPIRIT TO MIND AND BODY:
THE EXAMPLE OF BUDDHISM

A mindset of selflessness largely defines the best path to health maintenance and disease prevention. As the Buddha once said,

"Commit not a single unwholesome action.
Cultivate a wealth of virtue.
We are what we think.
Speak or act with a pure mind
And happiness will follow you."

Buddhist practice embraces compassionate living and avoidance of attachment to material substances and avoidance of hatred and a closed mind. The medical evidence linking meditation practice with many positive health outcomes is unequivocal. The same is true for prayer.

Transcendence of self has health-promoting virtues. Buddhist practice attempts to displace negative mindset with cultivation of a more positive mindset. This, too, is an excellent health-promoting strategy, as I will show. The evidence linking negative emotional states/traits with poor health outcomes is clear. The evidence linking positive emotional states/traits with better health outcomes is clear. A Buddhist perspective would, without hesitation, acknowledge the capacity to transform negative states into positive states. As Herbert Benson has said, "Buddhists feel the reality we live in is not the ultimate one." The other reality is unattached to our emotions. Thinking and feeling in this manner reward (biologically) further pursuit of love, compassion, altruism, and empathy. A practice that has blended well with Western thinking is that of Tonglen or the practice of giving and taking. Tonglen practice diminishes the force of our attention-seeking ego while enhancing concern for others. Nyoshal Khen Rinpoche describes the spirit of Buddhist meditation as follows:

"Rest in Natural Great Peace
This exhausted mind
Beaten helpless by karma and neurotic thought,
Like the relentless fury of the pounding waves,
In the infinite ocean of samsara.
Rest in Natural Great Peace."

Chapter 6

The Placebo Response:
No Strings Attached

"The power over which a man's imagination has over his body to heal
it or make it sick is a force which none of us are born without.
The first man had it, the last one will possess it."

Mark Twain

As a medical subspecialist, I see many patients who are referred to me, usu-ally from primary care providers, or on occasion, from a local emergency department. As any professional in a service-oriented industry appreciates, a good reputation has no substitute in marketing one's services and assuring a steady flow of referrals. It takes time and commitment to develop a network of trusting relationships that become the underpinnings of success.

I have come to appreciate the power of reputation as more than just a for-midable marketing tool. As a healer, reputation is also a powerful therapeutic instrument. Fifteen years ago, an eighty-year-old fellow named Walter was re-ferred to me for further evaluation and treatment of severe high blood pres-sure. Walter's blood pressure was more challenging than most, requiring mul-tiple medications and resistant to any safe degree of control. As he also had other risk factors for heart and vascular disease, his health outlook was grim.

Resistant high blood pressure is typical of many referrals I receive. In addition to treating kidney problems, I am also trained to treat more complicated cases of high blood pressure. Walter had tried several medications under the guidance of his excellent primary care provider but to no avail. I had never met Walter prior to this visit. He had heard that "I was good" at treating this kind of problem, and he made immediate note of my reputation at this initial visit. He appeared vigorous, sharp, and slightly hunched from osteoporosis. He wore a light brown windbreaker and a Boston Red Sox cap, leaving the door wide open for instant rapport. I am a Yankee fan from the Boston area and appreciated the passion with which people in my community valued baseball and this great rivalry.

"What do you think of the Sox this year Mr. H.?" I asked. "Can they win the World Series again or is this it for another three generations?" Now I realized this might have the initial short-term effect of raising his blood pressure, however, my gut told me this rapport would have a much greater long-term salutary effect.

"I'm not getting my hopes up. These players get too much damn money to play a boy's game," he quipped. After a few minutes of connecting on a topic that had little to do with blood pressure, I could sense in Walter a connection, an avenue. We were eye-to-eye, talking baseball, and very much mutually in the moment.

As I mentioned, Walter had made note of my reputation. He was transparently entering this partnership with the expectation and strong belief that I would and could help him. In truth, the therapeutic benefits that would mutually pass between us began before we actually met. Walter was somewhat frustrated by prior lack of progress regarding control of his blood pressure, and he was poised for positive change. Behaving and performing in a manner that reinforced this mindset would render me more effective.

As you now better appreciate as a recent alumnus of the Pettus Neuroscience School of Mind-Body Control, Walter's brain was "lighting up" in areas that reward relationship and trust. The typical increase in anxiety that would ordinarily accompany a visit to a physician, especially a new physician, had long dissipated as the "flight-fright" mode was in check.

As you now better appreciate as a recent alumnus of the Pettus Neuroscience School of Mind-Body Control, Walter's brain was "lighting up" in areas that reward relationship and trust.

Our rapport reinforced a preexisting expectation for a positive outcome. We hadn't even discussed the substance of his medical problems and the healing was well under way. You can see how a good reputation is a major advantage to a provider of human service. The context within which the "consumer" experiences the service is primed for satisfaction. Good service on top of the preexisting expectation for quality will exponentially reinforce this perception. Borderline service, at least initially, may fall on the side of acceptable only because of the priming effect of reputation. However, reputation (regardless of how good it is) will ultimately fail if offset by repeatedly poor encounters.

Initial encounters—because of the magnitude of value the amygdala places on them—are remembered in great detail, particularly when they're consistent with what the reputation planted by way of expectation and belief. Thus, a good first impression does count!

Health care professionals, compassionate and caring though most are, often fail to recognize these critical moments of influence. I emphasize this often with resident physicians in training and with medical students. As we enter an experience with anyone, particularly for the first time, we enter into a spotlight that shines directly into the window of the mind of the person we are engaged with. We can leave an indelible footprint that will either serve as a foundation for the next encounter or quicksand that will doom a subsequent meeting. I would suggest that the biological consequences of hitting a home run while in the spotlight is profoundly more powerful than most pharmaceuticals we prescribe.

Back to Walter. After a detailed history and physical examination, we reviewed all available options for diagnosis and treatment of his high blood pressure. Together we agreed on a path best suited to his individual risk, benefit, wishes, and values. Over time and many visits and baseball seasons, we were able to achieve safe and effective blood pressure control with no unacceptable complications or side effects.

"You are the therapy, Dr. Pettus," Walter would graciously remind me with each and every visit for the subsequent fifteen years. And I believe Walter was right. Sure, he required plenty of medication. However, I feel our relationship and the positive context of our interactions likely contributed as much to his therapy as the complex polypharmaceuticals we employed in ultimately controlling his problem. That's because Walter took his drugs in the context of a firm belief that success would ensue. Walter believed in me. He would be compliant to the bitter end. Walter, unlike many of his age-matched peers, would not miss a dose of his multi-drug, complex regimen. Fifteen years after we first met, I can only be rewarded by the relationship we've shared. Belief makes compliance more likely, a serious result given that many poor health outcomes have non-compliance as a root cause. Again, this is no small matter as non-compliance with treatment plans is rampant in the U.S.

Walter, as many patients have done indirectly over the years, reminded me of the power of the placebo effect. An individual with a strong expectation connected to something of meaning—good health or a great reward like more energy—is already starting to feel better even before the actual intervention is applied. The relationship becomes the therapy. Bonding, relationships, attachment, and positive thoughts have powerful biological effects on reward, stress reduction, and mood enhancement, to name a few.

> Bonding, relationships, attachment, and positive thoughts have powerful biological effects on reward, stress reduction, and mood enhancement, to name a few.

THE PLACEBO RESPONSE

The placebo response is a well-described phenomenon that is worth exploring briefly as another context for appreciating the power of thought, experience, and emotion on a diverse spectrum of biological functions. The placebo response can be defined as a sense of benefit experienced by an individual that arises solely from the knowledge that treatment has been given. What the individual feels, experiences, and biologically expresses in response to a placebo cannot be distinguished by the individual experiencing the effect, or, in some cases, the researchers "blinded" to who received a placebo and who didn't.

Imagine this. You have a history of nasty allergic reactions to poison ivy. Even the subtlest exposure leaves your skin red, angry, weepy, and intensely itchy. Any place the resin of poison ivy touches your skin becomes a battlefield of angry mediators of inflammation and itch. Redness, blistering, and swelling just "take off." Now imagine you're participating in a research study and the investigator blindfolds you and says, "I'm going to rub poison ivy on

your left arm and the leaf of an innocuous birch tree on your right arm."
Soon your left arm is red and itchy beyond belief. Your right arm looks and
feels fine after the blindfold is removed. Predictable response, wouldn't you
say? The research investigator then drops a stunning surprise by informing
you that the poison ivy was actually rubbed on your right arm and the harmless birch leaf on your left. This is a rather striking and classic example of the
power of the placebo response.

Placebo comes from a Latin word meaning, "I shall please." In 1955,
Harvard researcher H.K. Beecher published "The Powerful Placebo" in the
Journal of the American Medical Association after careful analysis of twenty-six
studies comparing placebos or inert, inactive substances with actual biologically
active interventions. He found that on average 32 percent of individuals given
placebos had an effect indistinguishable from the actual intervention. Virtually
every good study of treatment published in the medical literature over the last
fifty years demonstrates similar findings. In fact, the medical community would
accept no investigational treatment of any kind unless it was demonstrated to be
more effective than the "background noise" of the placebo effect. The placebo
response has been observed to alter a diverse spectrum of biological responses
despite an absence of "active ingredients." Here are some examples of common
categories of health problems that when studied demonstrate a high prevalence
of a placebo response. When individuals with these health problems are enrolled
in studies and receive a placebo, they have a high likelihood of responding as if
they received a medication with an active ingredient:

- Depression disorder, 45 percent
- Irritable Bowel Disease, 40 percent
- Erectile dysfunction, 30 percent
- Migraine headache, 30 percent

Recently published studies with noteworthy placebo responses include:

- Sham orthopedic surgery for individuals with degenerative joint disease of the knees, responding similarly to individuals with actual surgical intervention.
- A small number of individuals (twenty) with Parkinson's disease received surgery in which human dopamine neurons were transplanted

in their brains. A similar number of individuals received "sham surgery." In other words, nothing was transplanted during the actual surgery. A "double-blind" method was used, meaning neither the patients nor the medical staff knew who got the dopamine neurons and who did not. At one year, there were similar numbers of patients improved from both groups, demonstrating higher dopamine brain responses and improved movement and mobility.

There is ongoing, active debate in the research community as to the validity, the cause, and the predisposition to the placebo response. I would suggest that the placebo response is a widely described, universally observed, and very real mind-body phenomenon. Recent neuroscientific insights are shedding a glade of light on yet another fascinating exchange between thought, perception, emotion, and ubiquitous physiological states. This is clearly not an act of self-deception beginning and ending in conscious thought. It remains unclear why some individuals, approximately 30 to 40 percent in most studies, seem predisposed to experience a placebo response and others do not.

> I would suggest that the placebo response is a widely described, universally observed, and very real mind-body phenomenon.

Some individuals given an inert intervention may have symptoms at the time that would have naturally and spontaneously improved anyway. The placebo gets the credit for an outcome that would soon have occurred under any circumstance. Some scientists speculate that in a formal research study, there is more medical attention paid to individuals who receive placebos than prior to the study, conditioning them for a beneficial response.

As we learn more about the health benefits of positive, supportive, and nurturing relationships on attachment-reward responses in the brain, we may see a nurturing dimension as to why people feel better in studies in which they receive placebos. The powerful effects placebos have on serotonin (which appears to play a role in mood), opiate/endorphins (pain), and oxytocin/dopamine (bliss and positive emotions like happiness and contentment) are all potential contributors to the placebo response.

I feel the placebo response gives construct and credence to the biologic and therapeutic potential manifest in the "art" of our shared encounters, like the one I had with Walter. Here I believe we really see the therapeutic art of medicine expressing itself.

THE NOCEBO EFFECT

Not surprisingly, when we examine the connection between negative thoughts and emotions and negative health outcomes, we see described the "nocebo effect." The nocebo effect would start with a trusted suggestion (by a doctor, for example) that certain side effects are common, e.g., nausea, headache, and fatigue after ingesting the pill (placebo) they've been given. A placebo pill without active ingredients results in these side effects for a good number of people. The strength of one's expectations and beliefs for the purported effect, at least for some individuals (though I believe, as Mark Twain notes, that we all experience this), is sufficient to elicit the physiology necessary to achieve the purported effect.

A few research studies published recently demonstrate some provocative findings. In one study done by Dr. Kenneth Casey, a professor at the University of Michigan, individuals were placed inside an fMRI brain-imaging machine. An electric shock was placed on their arm. As expected the parts of the brain that invoke sensation and pain became activated. The researchers then put a cream onto the skin, suggesting to the study participants that the pain of the shock would most likely be blocked. As it turns out the special "electric shock protecting cream" was an over the counter skin moisturizer. When the subjects were again shocked, 70 percent (yes, 70 percent!) noted the pain was much improved. While there was still activation of the cortical pain centers of the brain, there was also activation of the limbic system and prefrontal cortex not seen before the cream was applied. It was postulated that the thought of the cream being an anesthetic and expectation for relief (higher levels of reasoning, cause and effect, to be sure) resulted in greater prefrontal lobe activity. This, in turn, played a role in the limbic system's reward circuitry "lighting up," perhaps enhancing a dopamine/endorphin tilt and therefore augmenting the perception of pain. While this is a gross oversimplification, it makes the point.

In another study done by British researchers, sixteen couples were evaluated, again using an fMRI machine. When women were given a mild shock to the skin, beyond their view as they were inside the machine, the anticipated centers for sensing pain in the cerebral cortex and the emotional expression from the midbrain (amygdala, locus coeruleus) were again activated. If they observed their husbands receiving a shock, the same centers of emotional expression were activated without the pain sensors going off. While the women did not actually sense pain when their husbands received the shocks, they did "feel" the pain. This was vividly expressed as they debriefed after the testing. One might call this empathy in action.

COMPELLING EVIDENCE

Despite some limitations on the interpretations made possible by studies like this, the evidence is compelling that people who demonstrate the placebo effect have activation of their "pleasure or reward center." This fertile garden of pleasure allows the prefrontal (in particular the anterior cingulate gyrus) lobe's seeds of expectation to germinate and grow. The stronger one's expectations for a positive response, the greater the likelihood of experiencing the desired response.

Most importantly, the "human touch" made possible by trusting reassurance is what sets this cascade into motion. The power inherent in the art of the encounter between an individual and their healer is widely exposed here. A physician who is calm, reassuring, certain, and empathetic in their ability to create a positive context is more likely to enhance this response. The fascinating implication of the placebo response is that the effectiveness of a pill, for example, may be based more on the person prescribing than the pill itself.

HYPNOTHERAPY

More than twenty years ago, I became certified in hypnotherapy by the New England Society for Clinical Hypnosis. I was a medical intern at the time and was intrigued by the opportunity to learn more about this technique. I felt it would give me another tool to add to my repertoire in treating my patients, especially for common and challenging problems like cigarette smoking.

Like most people, I had many misconceptions about hypnosis. I would quickly learn that hypnosis is not an oblivious trance-like state where people act like zombies, unaware of the behaviors they're carrying out. This popular myth was perpetuated by Dr. Franz Mesmer in the eighteenth century, who performed hypnosis in a "show-like" display with lights, music, and theatre, where people came to be cured of their ills after experiencing a mesmerized state. In reality, all hypnosis is self-hypnosis, with people experiencing varying degrees of relaxation and deeper mindfulness. It is, in fact, a state of heightened awareness and attention.

Despite its origins as a poorly understood attempt to cure illness with an added entertainment value, hypnosis enabled, in some, an interaction of mind-body biology, perceptual change, and behavioral change. It has had a proven track record for assisting with pain management, anesthesia, smoking cessation, and weight loss. Research over the years has suggested, like the placebo response, that some people are "highly hypnotizable," approximately 10 to 20 percent. This may be as high as 75 to 80 percent in children under the age of twelve. Twenty-five percent of adults are not hyponizable at all and others fall somewhere in between.

Hypnosis involves a state of progressive relaxation like many forms of mindfulness meditation that heightens attentiveness to a particular suggestion or suggestions that are more likely to be accepted faithfully and uncritically, ideally resulting in a behavioral change that will become more successful, like eating less. Imagery is often used as a way to plant or shape the new suggestion. For example, during a hypnotic state for someone who wants to quit smoking, a therapist might suggest to the individual that they imagine placing their mouth around an exhaust pipe of an automobile instead of around a cigarette. You get the picture. Future attempts to smoke would then elicit this exhaust pipe image and the disgusting visceral response, making more powerful the likelihood of avoidance.

Michael Posner, an emeritus professor of neuroscience at the University of Oregon, has studied the brain biology that may be at play during hypnosis. As is true in the placebo response, altered perceptions and expectations have, in some instances, profound biological effects on the brain and body. Our brains process experiences by collecting information that is filtered and channeled from "outer-receiving" locations before being sent to higher levels for more sophisticated analysis. As an example, my wife and I enjoy feeding the birds that thrive in our local habitat. When a cardinal comes to feed, our brains take in the information and at a superficial level allow us to recognize that a bird is at our feeder. Channeling this information further adds the color red and then, at an even higher level, enables the appropriate labeling of cardinal as the type of bird. Neuroscientists refer to this as "bottom-up" or "feedforward" processing.

There is also an abundance of nerve fibers or circuits that run from the top-down. It's at the top that higher levels of consciousness reside and ultimately shape the reality we exist in. The implication is that a powerful belief or expectation "planted" at the top has the potential to override the information being processed at lower levels. In this construct, the experience of smoking a cigarette becomes the experience of sucking in auto exhaust. Or the experience of an innocuous skin moisturizer becomes the experience of anesthesia. Hypnosis, like the placebo response, taps into these higher levels of consciousness and, in some instances, overrides the circuitry of past experiences, perceptions, emotions, and behaviors, producing a more desirable outcome.

Research suggests that what we see, hear, and touch is what defines our reality. The brain then takes what we see, hear, and touch, and "constructs" our reality based on our past experiences. Dr. David Spiegel, a psychiatrist at Stanford who has studied hypnosis, notes that for some people in some instances, "what we imagine to be different, is different" despite what our prior experiences would lead us to believe. This perceptual modification in fact has the potential to change the reality of our experiences.

THE PARTNERSHIP EFFECT

Physicians don't routinely use placebo pills in non-research settings. Despite what would likely be widespread and significant responses that perhaps would decrease or eliminate the need for more toxic pharmaceuticals, there are ethical issues of free will and informed consent. Individuals in their exercise of free will need to know what they are putting into their bodies. There is no place for deception in the covenant shared between physician and patient. There is, however, enormous potential for health care professionals to more effectively leverage the biologic and therapeutic potential through their words, humility, compassion, and behaviors. As I stress in my first book, *The Savvy Patient: The Ultimate Advocate for Quality Health Care*, relationships are everything.

Despite the legacy of paternalistic approaches in health care that may have acculturated you to be passive and accepting of the disease-oriented approach to health and wellness, partnerships that openly share and communicate work best. These effects are not limited to the experiences between a health care professional and a patient. They're just as powerful, significant, and applicable to relationships you have with your friends, family, and colleagues. If those you serve believe you, have faith in you, and know what to expect from you, you're much more likely to serve well and be served well. Perhaps instead of calling it the placebo effect, we should call it the partnership effect.

A recurrent theme in the reduction of allostatic load, health promotion, and age management is the creation of meaning in your life, social support, empathy, understanding, faith, and the expectation of better things to come. This is the quintessential carrot on the end of the stick of life.

> A recurrent theme in the reduction of allostatic load, health promotion, and age management is the creation of meaning in your life, social support, empathy, understanding, faith, and the expectation of better things to come.

Part III

Change Your Health

Chapter 7

Mind-Body Medicine: An Overview

"Direct your eye inward, and you'll find
a thousand regions in your mind
yet undiscovered. Travel them and be
expert in home-cosmography."

Henry David Thoreau

AN OVERVIEW OF MIND-BODY MEDICINE

Mind-body medicine encompasses practices that see optimal health as an interaction of mind, brain, behavior, and other body systems. These practices are based on the overriding principle that mind-brain-body-behavior are naturally integrated. Mind-body medicine recognizes that these forces in their emotional, cognitive, social, and spiritual effects powerfully influence health and wellness. It's the interaction of mind and brain on other body systems that ultimately influence behavior and health outcomes (see figure 7.1). The overriding principle of healing, in this construct, is that you need to tap into your own sources of natural healing.

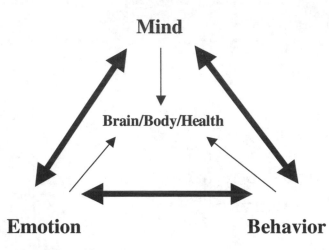

Mind

Brain/Body/Health

Emotion   **Behavior**

Figure 7.1   Mind-Body-Health Interactions

This principle of self-care has never been more important as we can expect to live longer, and in doing so, possibly confront a higher burden of chronic disease. Diminishing the effects of disease burden and enhancing resilience and coping are widely recognized benefits of mind-body practices. I've never prescribed any medications capable of doing this for a lifetime. The techniques that I'll briefly touch on demonstrate approaches that emphasize and enhance an individual's capacity for self-knowledge and self-care. Many go back to ancient times. When these techniques are employed, symptom relief and quality of life are often considerably improved.

While traditional models of health care in Western medicine tend to be more disease-oriented, mind-body techniques tend to place more emphasis on the person with the disease, not the disease in the person. Illness from a mind-body perspective is seen as opportunity for personal growth and transformation.

It's true there have been considerable shifts in how health care professionals think about healing and the limitations of modern medicine in meeting the complex needs of patients. Today, traditional models of care use some mind-body techniques, for example, support groups, biofeedback, and cognitive behavioral therapy (CBT). The National Institute of Health now has a separate complementary and alternative medicine (CAM) division that's promoting more vigorous research and education in the field. Still, there's a relative lack of routine integration of these approaches. That pendulum is gradually moving from a disease-symptom-oriented paradigm to one that embraces many integrative aspects of healing. But there's much more we can do as consumers of health care and as health care professionals to take advantage of integrated strategies for healing.

If practicing medicine has taught me anything, it is that human beings are marvelous and complex tapestries, with extraordinary potential to heal. The acculturation most physicians and I have experienced has been limited in terms of helping us understand the many dimensions of the human encounter. Our wounds as human beings are clearly not just physical. Biology is not the only language that expresses our aches and pains. It's not surprising that more than 50 percent of Americans spend billions on CAM therapies, some of which include common mind-body techniques. However, such practices as meditation and yoga shouldn't be seen as merely "complementary," but rather integral to health and recovery.

> Our wounds as human beings are clearly not just physical. Biology is not the only language that expresses our aches and pains.

An example of a common medical syndrome that's poorly understood (and therefore often thought of as a "head problem") that does much better with an integrative approach is fibromyalgia. Individuals with symptoms of fibromyalgia note changes in clarity of thought, impairment of memory, restorative sleep, and exquisite pain in various parts of the body that show no outward sign of inflammation—redness, swelling, and warmth. However, patients can experience increased quality of life through integrated approaches to pain and mood management such as exercise, meditation, yoga, B-complex, S-methyl methionine (SamE), music, massage, Reiki, prayer, modulating pharmaceuticals, and good nutritional food choices.

Examples of commonly applied and effective mind-body interventions include but are not limited to meditation, yoga, visual imagery, relaxation techniques, tai chi, qi gong, and prayer. I will elaborate on some of these techniques in more detail in this and other chapters.

Recent data suggests that 40 percent of the U.S. population uses relaxation techniques, imagery, biofeedback, and hypnosis. If you include regular prayer, that number increases to almost 65 percent!

Ayurvedic and traditional Chinese medicine date back more than two- to three-thousand years. In 400 BC, Hippocrates recognized the multi-dimensional nature of disease and healing, emphasizing mind, environment, and natural remedies. All ancient worldviews from the monotheistic traditions to Hinduism, Buddhism, and American Indian and Shamanic traditions see healing occurring naturally at the intersection of body and spirit.

> All ancient worldviews from the monotheistic traditions to Hinduism, Buddhism, and American Indian and Shamanic traditions see healing occurring naturally at the intersection of body and spirit.

Western traditions in the sixteenth and seventeenth centuries began to examine health and disease by separating spirit and emotion from the physical body. Technological advances like the microscope introduced life at the level of the cell. This was a world far removed from emotion, mind, and spirit. Microbiology, a field that made possible the recognition of bacteria as pathogens, led to the recognition of diseases that could be subsequently eradicated. More sophisticated research tools, methods, and treatments that made understanding disease more refined and mechanistic than ever, further accentuated this separation of mind, body, and spirit. Diseases or symptoms that could not be empirically studied, understood, and treated were considered diseases of the mind, not "real" in the absence of biochemical and physiological underpinnings.

Walter Cannon, in the 1920s, documented the relationship between stress and the neuroendocrine response in animals. He reported the "primitive reflexes" of nervous system and adrenal gland activation in response to perceived danger and exposure to extremes of temperature. This phenomenon he described as the "fight or flight" response. In 1956, Hans Selye described in *The Stress of Life* the health-undermining effects of excessive stress.

Henry Beecher, MD, who coined the term "the placebo effect," described belief and its impact on health. On the beaches of Anzio in World War II, wounded soldiers were given saline injections as supplies of morphine ran out. Much of their pain was relieved with the saline. At the time Beecher noted that 35 percent of individuals receiving placebos in the published literature demonstrated a similar effect. The placebo response has been seen, widely recognized, and published in a similar 30 to 40 percent of individuals studied over the last fifty years.

Meditation and prayer are the most commonly practiced mind-body techniques. Meditation in its various practices results in conscious induction of a cascade of physiological changes referred to as the relaxation response. In recent

> Meditation and prayer are the most commonly practiced mind-body techniques.

years, functional fMRI (magnetic resonance imaging) has been applied as a tool to examine in more detail what regions in the brains of people who are meditating demonstrate more or less activity. Areas of the brain that are involved with attention (prefrontal cortex) and "autonomic" control like heart rate and blood pressure, demonstrate enhanced activity. Increased activity in the left prefrontal cortex, a region associated with positive emotional states, is enhanced in mindfulness meditative states.

For the last thirty-five years, there's been a growing body of evidence to support the efficacy of biofeedback, hypnosis, and cognitive behavioral therapy. The physiological effects that form the basis of these treatments are now being elucidated with greater clarity.

The NIH has a comprehensive database of current research examining the efficacy of some of these approaches. I will briefly summarize what this information reveals, and I will provide a brief overview of the interventions themselves.

- *Stress* as a risk factor for coronary artery disease has been well described over the last thirty years. Mind-body techniques are known to be effective techniques for reducing stress. When these techniques are integrated with other approaches like cardiac rehabilitation, medication, balloon angioplasty, etc., they have an independent effect on reducing further complications and mortality.

- *Pain management.* Mind body techniques have also been studied as adjuncts to traditional approaches to pain management. They've been shown to be effective for the management of arthritis and other forms of acute and chronic pain, e.g., headache and back pain. Many studies that include various types of individuals with cancer show many areas of improvement using mind-body techniques. Improvements in mood, coping, quality of life, nausea, vomiting, and pain have been widely reported and reproduced.

- *Infection.* It's long been recognized that stress levels and emotional states influence susceptibility to infection. In laboratory studies, individuals with subjective reporting of high stress and depressed moods were more likely to develop severe illness when exposed to a respiratory virus. Individuals reporting more positive emotional states were less affected. Other studies support this mind-body interaction. Likewise, meditation has been associated with a more robust antibody response to influenza vaccine.

- *Parkinson disease.* In the chapter on the placebo response, a study of patients with Parkinson's disease using PET scanning of the brain reveals an increase in activity of the area of the brain that produces dopamine. Dopamine production is deficient in these individuals. This response was seen after receiving an inert substance. Other imaging studies demonstrate increased patterns of brain activity in the prefrontal cortex and in the reward-opiate regions of the limbic system when experiencing a placebo response. These interesting responses appear to be both cognitive (thought, belief, and expectation) and conditioned (learned wellness).

- *Wounds.* A common and challenging problem to treat in health care is a poorly healing wound. From diabetes, poor circulation, and chronic debilitation, poorly healing wounds are a growing source of morbidity, mortality, prolonged hospitalization, and need for skilled nursing. Mind-body research is demonstrating the connection between emotional and physical stress, depressed mood, and poor wound healing. Activation of the hypothalamic-pituitary-adrenal (HPA) and sympathetic-adrenal systems (remember the fight-flight, stress response?) appears to affect inflammatory "cytokines" and immunity that interfere with normal tissue healing.

- *Surgical preparation.* In individuals preparing for surgery, clinical studies have examined the effects of mind-body techniques like music, guided imagery, and the relaxation response. These techniques improved recovery and resulted in fewer hospital days. Improvements in pain management and nausea have also been reported.

WHOLE MEDICAL SYSTEMS

Whole medical systems is a term that refers to complete systems of theory and practice that have evolved separately from Western allopathic systems. Many of these systems have been practiced throughout the world by individual cultures. Examples that I will review briefly include traditional Chinese medicine and Ayurvedic medicine, a system of medicine in India. Other well-described systems include homeopathy and naturopathy, as well as the health practices and beliefs of Native American, African, Middle Eastern, Tibetan, and Central and South American cultures.

TRADITIONAL CHINESE MEDICINE (TCM)

TCM dates back to 200 BC in written form. It's a complete system of healing. In the TCM system, the body is delicately balanced by two opposing and inseparable forces: yin and yang. Yin represents the cold, passive principle, and yang represents the hot, excited, and active principle. Health is viewed as a balanced state between yin and yang. Disease represents an internal imbalance. Any imbalance leads to blockage of vital energy or "qi" (pronounced "chee") along well-defined pathways known as meridians. TCM practitioners use acupuncture, herbs, and massage to help unblock qi and restore blood and vital energy as harmony and wellness are brought back into balance. Therapeutic interventions include:

- Acupuncture
- Moxibustion—the application of heat from the burning of the herb moxa at the acupuncture point
- Chinese herbs
- Massage and manipulation

These approaches are usually combined in the treatment of individuals. While explaining the mechanism of action from a traditional Western scientific perspective is still unclear, acupuncture has had clinical value for nausea, vomiting, pain, movement disorders, and insomnia.

AYURVEDIC MEDICINE

Ayurveda literally translated means "the science of life." Its origins come from India's ancient healers who originated meditation and yoga thousands of years ago. Healing is seen as restoring innate harmony in an individual with equal emphasis placed on body, mind, and spirit. Meditation, herbs, diet, exercise, massage, and controlled breathing are dimensions to Ayurvedic treatment. In India, various diseases like diabetes, neurologic disorders, and cardiovascular conditions have specific Ayurvedic approaches.

HOMEOPATHY

Homeopathic medicine is based on the principle that administration of minute, highly diluted concentrations of substances—which ordinarily would, in much higher concentrations, cause similar symptoms to what a person is experiencing—allows the body to respond in a curative fashion.

NATUROPATHY

Naturopathic medicine involves varied approaches, including dietary, acupuncture, and massage, which facilitate natural healing forces in the body. Disease is seen as a manifestation of alterations in the processes by which the body naturally heals itself. Naturopathy originated in Europe. Its principles include:

- The healing power of nature
- Identification and treatment of the cause of disease
- The concept of "first do no harm"
- The doctor as teacher
- Treatment of the whole person
- Prevention

While clinical studies demonstrating the efficacy of these systems varies or is lacking, they each share the belief that the body has the power to heal itself. Healing often involves combining approaches that respect the integrative dimensions of mind, body, and spirit.

MANIPULATIVE AND BODY-BASED THERAPIES

These therapies are based on movement or manipulation of the body. Chiropractic techniques have proven successful for many varieties of medical illness and for health maintenance. Chiropractors use manipulation, usually of the spine, to improve balance between body structure and function, a basis for preservation and restoration of health. I've found chiropractic intervention particularly helpful for individuals with acute back strain and lumbo-sacral (lower back) pain, in addition to its many other utilities.

ENERGY THERAPIES

Ancient wisdom and healing practices have long recognized the role of life energy or divine energy that defines the essence of who we are. These energy fields surround and penetrate the human body and connect us with all life. Disease stems from an alteration in this energy, which manifests itself in a biological manner. Hindu wisdom, for example, recognizes seven chakras or divine truths that are energy centers whose balance and imbalance alters biological function and overall health. Some examples of energy therapy include:

- **Reiki** (pronounced "ray-key") is of Japanese origin. It also recognizes a universal life energy that's channeled through and around us. A Reiki master and friend demonstrates this energy in the following way. Close your eyes and rub your hands together briskly. Now separate your hands and slowly bring them toward each other, palm facing palm. Before they actually touch, you'll sense the energy and heat present in the space between. When this energy or life force is channeled through a Reiki practitioner, the individual's balance and flow of energy is restored and healing is facilitated. This, in turn, heals the physical body. I have personally tried Reiki therapy for migraine headaches and found it to be incredibly effective. Reiki is also very relaxing and calming.

- **Qi Gong** (pronounced "chee gung") is based on traditional Chinese medicine. It combines meditation with mind-centered breathing to enhance the flow of energy or qi, improving bodily function and allowing one to enter a deeper connection with a "higher source."

- **Therapeutic touch** is an ancient technique of the laying on of hands. The principle again is that of a healing energy force transferred from the healer to the recipient. Balance and unimpeded flow of energy promote healing.

BIOFEEDBACK

One of the more widely used and tested forms of "traditional" mind-body therapy is biofeedback. Biofeedback is best described as a simple loop. At the center of the loop is an individual who is motivated to gain more control over a challenging health concern. Using simple skin transducers placed on areas such as the forehead and face, a signal representing muscle contraction can be seen on a computer screen. For example, in an intervention to assist with headaches, an individual, usually with a biofeedback-trained therapist, looks at ways to gain self-control over muscle tension. Using such techniques as the relaxation response, deep breathing, and progressive muscle relaxation, the individual is able to see measurable change in muscle tension depicted on the screen. The loop is completed only when the individual uses the information to facilitate greater mastery over biological change. Other signs like blood pressure and respiratory rate can be measured and monitored. Biofeedback is used in many different settings, including schools, to assist with concentration, to help with stress management, and to optimize sports performance.

The Applied Psychophysiology and Biofeedback Society (AAPB) is an international organization that provides education and research on biofeedback and related mind-body interactions. Neurofeedback applies similar principles, but instead of focusing on muscle contractions, the process examines recorded brain waves (alpha-theta brainwave feedback), often in the evaluation and treatment of a host of behavioral health disorders. Increased alpha and beta wave states are seen with intense cognitive focus and minimal distraction: you might observe this as Tiger Woods approaches the 18 green at Augusta in a close match at The Masters or as Lance Armstrong races the final leg of the Tour de France. Or you would see this pattern in a monk meditating. Increased theta-wave activity is consistent with easy distractibility as might be seen in ADD. Some examples of proven clinical studies applying biofeedback techniques for common health problems include:

- **Alcohol and substance abuse:** Many studies have demonstrated some relief of depression and poor self-esteem in individuals with alcohol and substance abuse problems.
- **Anxiety:** A very common problem; biofeedback helps people with anxiety gain greater control over their breathing patterns and a more effective relaxation response. Individuals are made more aware of their physiological responses as they become anxious and gain greater control with use of behavioral techniques.
- **Arthritis:** Thermal (measuring changes in skin temperature) and EMG (measuring muscle contraction) biofeedback techniques have been shown to assist with pain management
- **Asthma:** Biofeedback techniques in asthmatics have focused on abnormal breathing patterns, particularly as an attack begins. Asthmatics can be taught to recognize and correct abnormal patterns and reduce symptoms of anxiety. Ideally, these techniques are used with other evidence-based treatments such as bronchodilator inhalers.

- **High Blood Pressure:** Many high-quality studies of individuals with stress-induced fluctuations in hypertension have demonstrated the benefits of biofeedback. As the causes and magnitude of blood pressure vary, so does the individual response to biofeedback techniques. This population can also gain improvements with other integrated mind-body interventions like dieting, exercise, stress reduction, meditation, etc.

- **Headaches:** As noted, biofeedback and biothermal feedback have been proven very effective in clinical trials to improve headache symptoms from migraine to tension or muscular headaches.

- **Incontinence:** This is a common problem, particularly in women who have experienced childbirth. The muscles of the pelvic floor are often fine but weakened, unable to resist the tension of a filling bladder. It's not easy to effectively train sphincter muscle tone without biofeedback sensors. These sensors can be placed into the vaginal canal and women can learn to train sphincter tone by relating to changes on the display associated with body sensations.

MASSAGE AND OSTEOPATHIC MEDICINE

Massage therapy can facilitate relaxation, blood flow, and restoration of health to muscles and soft tissues. Osteopathic medicine involves a hands-on manipulative approach with techniques to alleviate pain, restore function, and promote health. The idea is that symptoms arising from bone, muscle, and connective tissue are integrated with our body's organ systems. Disturbance of this balance may affect function and health.

I will explore the mind-body health implications of prayer, religion, and spiritual practices in Chapter 12. Mindfulness practice and meditation will also be examined in more detail in Chapter 17.

Chapter 8

Lifestyle and Behavioral Change: The Holy Grail of Health Promotion

Improving your mental and physical health through lifestyle change is where the mind-body message gets really exciting; it's where the mind's rubber meets the body's road, so to speak. This is also where it gets more challenging.

In Part I, I've given you an overview of current thinking as it relates to mind-body interactions, including a system that rewards even small degrees of change. We examined reward's role in motivating us to take our thoughts, emotions, and behaviors to another level. While the experience of a Tibetan monk serves as a striking example of the power of intentional mindfulness on bodily function, we're reminded that this power is universal and accessible to each of us. I introduced you to the phenomenon of *plasticity*, the process by which we're all capable, throughout life, of re-sculpting the clay that shapes our thoughts, feelings, and behaviors that often leave us trapped in the domain of sedentary living. In essence, I have attempted to open a window to your mind, allowing some light to reach dark, dusty, and forgotten places.

As I have noted, the majority of health concerns can be connected to lifestyle and behavioral issues. The epidemic of excessive caloric consumption, inactivity, high blood pressure, diabetes, and high cholesterol, even under clear genetic influences, can be dramatically altered by lifestyle. For more than thirty years, countless public health efforts have promoted nutritional and exercise strategies for healthier living. Unfortunately, these efforts haven't been successful as more Americans than ever confront these health risks. And of even greater concern, we're seeing this epidemic of lifestyle syndrome emerging in our children, adolescents, and young adults.

All of this begs the question, "Why is it we can understand what we need to do and yet seem unable to get it done effectively, even knowing the stakes are so high?" What are the forces that drive this growing wedge between what we know and how we apply it?

What is clear, however, is that these trends are getting dramatically worse. Less than 5 percent of Americans are able to heed the advice of their health care professionals when it comes to diet and exercise. It's increasingly clear that formidable forces are out there working against us. For example:

- If your quality of life is acceptable to you and you feel okay, there may be little incentive for change. For some it just may not matter much.
- Social trends make fast food, fast calories, and inactivity too easy. We no longer walk or bike to school, work, or to run errands. We can serve our daily needs and be entertained with a modicum of activity and with easy availability of calories to fuel our needs, and then some.
- These challenges require wholesale changes in our communities— schools, workplace, governance, and faith communities. We need an infrastructure that supports healthier behaviors at every turn.
- The biologic forces that drive our lifestyle behaviors are formidable and not easy to overcome.

This last bullet point is where I will be focusing. While communities are essential elements to fostering healthy behaviors through education, supportive resources, bike and walking paths, employer incentives for healthier workplaces, faith-health coalitions, and the like, when all is said and done, you can only be certain of your own behavior and actions. Not everyone is near a bike path or works for an employer who values health promotion in the workplace. Fast food is not going to disappear. Schools will continue to be forced to apply limited resources to growing educational needs. Municipalities will continue to confront budgetary constraints. In truth, the environment we live and work in is working against us in our individual mission to promote optimal health.

It's necessary to take matters into your own hands. What I wish to point out in this chapter is the following:

- We are designed to successfully navigate change.
- Small changes are doable and the reward-response motivates continued change.
- Your strategy is one that should reflect a lifetime of long-term goals.
- Your perceptions, emotions, behaviors, and ultimately your health are influenced by powerful biological systems working behind the scenes. The ultimate goal of change must have an impact at this level.
- Plasticity makes possible change that is successful, rewarding, and enduring.
- In a culture that will forever tempt negative behaviors, your best strategy is to reinvent how you live your life.

> In a culture that will forever tempt negative behaviors, your best strategy is to reinvent how you live your life.

MAINTAIN AN AERIAL VIEW OF YOUR LIFE

While I've focused a lot on the phenomenon of plasticity, I'm mindful that just because change is possible, it doesn't make it any easier. Plasticity, as you attempt to change behaviors, will sometimes feel like trying to bend a steel bar. It will take time, patience, perseverance, and a long-term "horizon" perspective. My goal is to suggest a perspective, perhaps unlike that which you've previously considered, that will enhance your resilience and success as you move forward.

Try to maintain an aerial view of your life and not get too bogged down on specifics. For example, while you might focus on exercising more and eating fewer calories as the path to weight loss, what you do in other domains of your life will have a critical impact on these goals as well. We know that people with more positive outlooks tend to be more successful with healthy behaviors. It would be tempting to say, "Sure, if I felt happy all the time, I'd be out walking too."

> We know that people with more positive outlooks tend to be more successful with healthy behaviors.

The truth is that people *are* capable of cultivating a positive disposition. Strengthening relationships, more effective conflict management, social engagement, prayer, meditation, and cultivating more meaning at home, work, and play may not in themselves burn calories. They do, however, create a context that will nurture and sustain your pursuit of more activity and nutritional change. This is the ticket you have to ride! The strategy of simply doing more exercise will not likely sustain itself in the long run. Do not look at your diet and your activity as isolated dimensions of your life. They're best viewed as critical parts of a larger, broader, mosaic for living. Filling your life with meaning, value and connection will serve to lubricate the gears of behavioral change.

> Do not look at your diet and your activity as isolated dimensions of your life. They're best viewed as critical parts of a larger, broader, mosaic for living. Filling your life with meaning, value and connection will serve to lubricate the gears of behavioral change.

THE PEP TALK

Expect that you may trip and fall. Expect peaks and valleys, progress and regress. Plasticity can lift you from tripping over your feet to becoming John Travolta in *Saturday Night Fever*. Okay, that might be hyperbole. The point is that the steps we take on life's dance floor are never beyond better rhythm and synchronicity.

We're designed for change, possibility, and opportunity. If your circumstances are better served by Vivaldi's *Four Seasons*, you don't want to find yourself stuck in a state of *Jumpin' Jack Flash*. You get the picture. Successful lifestyles and behavioral change must start with the awareness that your mind-body jukebox has more selections than you realize. You can also "burn" new recordings as well as "re-burn" old recordings that skip and stutter. Our mind-body jukebox has the tendency to pull out the same records repeatedly. Some have positive health consequences, such as playing the tune of attachment to a cherished friend, or not so positive, say, playing the tune of recurrent fear and social isolation. It's your jukebox! It's your quarter! Why play selection "*A-25*" if "*C-12*" is a better tune?

Imagine that the buttons pushed on your mind-body jukebox both consciously and subconsciously affect mood, thought, feeling, and behavior. Imagine that the buttons you choose to push radically influence blood pressure, blood lipids (like cholesterol), stress level, blood vessel or vascular health (increasing or decreasing risk for strokes, heart disease, kidney disease, etc.), cancer, inflammation, infection, response to medication, need for medication, vitality, mortality, and longevity. It's extraordinary that your brain—the mediator of thought, feeling, body, and behavior—can adapt its response 180 degrees from harm to health.

Are you ready for change? Remember that every other dimension of your life, including work and sleep, will also strongly influence your ultimate success.

RISK-TAKING

An important dimension of lifestyle change is the capacity for risk-taking. Behavioral change and decision-making are greatly influenced by an individ-

---

As you read on, keep these important principles planted in your mind.

1. Small positive lifestyle changes are doable.
2. Small positive lifestyle changes yield a big return on the investment (ROI) in enhancing health and wellness (see the Four-Week Addicted-to-Health Plan in Chapter 2).
3. Positive lifestyle change of any magnitude begets positive lifestyle change. The more you change . . . the more you change. The more you do, the more you do.

ual's perception of the risk involved and benefit achieved in any undertaking. Remember:

- Your perception of risk will be influenced by the emotional charge and fear value you attach to a particular circumstance. Prior experiences, your memory of them, and the emotional charge your amygdala attaches to them will drive this influence. An example of this might be the perception that exercise is "too risky" because someone you know had a heart attack while exercising. Or you may be fearful of a potential complication from a medication or procedure because a family member once experienced a serious complication to something similar.

- *We tend to fear that which threatens us more in the short-term than that which threatens us in the long-term, even when the actual long-term risks are more ominous.* For example, an individual may be much more worried about their next attack of gout (painful and harmless) than they are of their cholesterol of 350 (silent and deadly).

- The experience/anticipation of reward from a cascade of dopamine, endorphins, serotonin, oxytocin, and GABA (to name a few identified neurotransmitters involved with reward) may create a feeling so positive as to motivate any behavior that will likely reproduce that feeling. People will be willing to assume more risk to receive such a response. The "reward" from smoking, for example, is so powerful in its addictive drive, it overwhelms any knowledge of risk.

- Your prefrontal executive center becomes the arbiter in attaching value to perceived risks and rewards, ultimately defining the basis for your decisions.

RISK-TAKING AND MEDICAL DECISIONS

This underscores the importance of sharing your perceptions or thoughts, feelings, values, and preferences as they relate to medical decisions you may be confronting. All other things equal, individuals will interpret and respond to their circumstances in unique ways. This isn't hard to understand when you look at the individualized nature of experience, memory, perception, and interpretation that form the basis of perceived risk and perceived benefit. There are, however, some generalizations about human behavior as it relates to risk that are important to appreciate. They're important because the perceptions and the emotions that establish a risk-taking threshold may be incomplete, misguided, and counterintuitive.

When I was in medical school more than twenty years ago, the trend was to shift the emphasis of medical decision-making from the physician to one shared by the patient/family. We are still transitioning from paternalistic to partnership models of care, communication, and decision-making. And most people want to know more and to play more active roles in their care. That's wise. The catch is—this requires that you have more knowledge and skill as you contemplate the risks and benefits of a particular intervention. Because your analysis and ultimate decisions have implications for living longer and living better, the stakes are high.

Therefore, it's important to know that from a mind-emotion-behavior-body-health perspective, when it comes to risk-taking:

Emotions will trump logic most of the time.

The implication is that we tend to place our own "spin" on the information available to suit our bias (rationalization, the arch enemy of action and change). For example, an individual saying, "My father smoked and never exercised a day in his life and lived to be eighty." Some risks will *worry* us more than others even though *knowledge* of the actual risk is insignificant. George Gray and David Ropeik, of the Harvard Center for Risk Analysis, in their book *Risk* note the following:

- We fear risks over which we have little control more than those we can control. For example, some people fear flying more than they fear driving an automobile even though the latter is riskier than the former.
- We fear that which has attached an emotional, visceral charge more than we do that which does not. For example, many people fear guns more than they fear swimming pools, even though pools are a far greater source of death from drowning than guns are from shootings.
- We fear new risks more than old familiar ones. For example, some have an over-exaggerated fear of being struck by lightening and an under-exaggerated fear of dying from a cardiovascular catastrophe.
- We fear imposed risks more than risks we choose. An individual may fear a cardiac catheterization procedure more than they fear smoking—

the problem that led to the need for the catheterization in the first place.

- We tend to fear risks without clear benefits more than those with a clear reward. An individual may fear taking a medication for cholesterol-lowering because she feels fine now and is unable to "feel" the benefits that may take years to be realized more than she fears taking a strong anti-inflammatory medication for pain (despite side effects and the likelihood that the pain will resolve spontaneously) because of the short-term reward of pain relief.

- An individual's value assessment of risk-reward is often greater when a symptom exists (treating a sprained ankle) than when the risk is silent (allowing high blood pressure to go untreated). Motivation for treatment of the sprained ankle, despite its low health risk, may trump motivation for treatment of the high blood pressure, despite its substantial risk.

The take home message is that the worry and fear you attach to some of your behaviors may be small relative to the risk that the behaviors actually pose. Alternatively, the worry and fear you attach to some of your behaviors may be great, relative to their minimal risk (e.g., fear of exercise because of the back pain you're experiencing). Individuals with lifestyle syndrome, diabetes, high blood pressure, and high cholesterol may have five times a greater risk of dying prematurely compared to someone who doesn't have those problems! This risk can be reduced by as much as 90 percent with well-integrated interventions. The actual risk of mind-body techniques, exercise, and dietary change are negligibly small. The benefits are substantial! An important dimension to self-care is risk management.

An important dimension to self-care is risk management.

The tools you have to manage your risks are much safer than many of the drugs I would tend to prescribe. As you reassess the risk associated with your current lifestyle, focus on those thoughts, emotions, and behaviors where logic has been undermined by emotion and rationalization.

LIFESTYLE OR METABOLIC SYNDROME

Perhaps the greatest public health threat in the U.S. today is that posed by "lifestyle syndrome," referred to by physicians as metabolic syndrome. For

many reasons—fast food, fast calories, increased
stress, and more sedentary behavior—we've seen
an epidemic of obesity in our society. Recent
data suggests that almost 30 percent of Americans
are obese! We're not talking just overweight, but
substantially overweight. If you include being
over an ideal body weight to this mix, the num-

> Perhaps the greatest public
> health threat in the U.S.
> today is that posed by
> "lifestyle syndrome," re-
> ferred to by physicians as
> metabolic syndrome.

ber is over 60 percent! It's now estimated that poor diet and sedentary
lifestyle with the resultant weight gain will overtake tobacco as the leading
cause of death in the U.S. The economic impact in direct medical costs—
doctor visits, medications, hospital stays—in addition to such indirect costs
as lost wages due to illness, disability, and early death is well over 150 billion
dollars.

This is also a serious problem among children and adolescents. Approximately 16 to 18 percent of young people, ages eight to nineteen, are overweight. Health-related problems like diabetes, high blood pressure, insulin
resistance, and high blood fats are now recognized in kids this age. These are
no longer considered problems of just adults. (If this is something you and
your child/children can work on together, you're likely to attach greater
meaning to the behavioral change. Greater meaning equals greater motivation and reward.)

Clinicians now refer to BMI or body mass index as a measurement that
takes weight and height into consideration. An ideal BMI is less than or
equal to twenty-five. A BMI between twenty-five and thirty usually implies
being overweight, and a BMI greater than thirty would be considered obese.
I'm not making a moral judgment here about weight. This is just the way it
is. You can see where you are by examining the table below.

BMI is less accurate in individuals with larger than average muscle mass,
for example, weight lifters, body builders, and professional athletes. The features of lifestyle syndrome can be characterized as follows:

- A waist circumference greater than forty inches for a man, greater
  than thirty-five inches for a woman.
- A more widely accepted criterion is waist-to-hip ration. For example, a waist-to-hip ration greater than .9 in men and greater than .85
  in women is consistent with increased abdominal girth from fat.

BMI	19	20	21	22	23	24	25	26	27	28	29	30	31	32	33	34	35
Height (inches)	Body Weight (pounds)																
58	91	96	100	105	110	115	119	124	129	134	138	143	148	153	158	162	167
59	94	99	104	109	114	119	124	128	133	138	143	148	153	158	163	168	173
60	97	102	107	112	118	123	128	133	138	143	148	153	158	163	168	174	179
61	100	106	111	116	122	127	132	137	143	148	153	158	164	169	174	180	185
62	104	109	115	120	126	131	136	142	147	153	158	164	169	175	180	186	191
63	107	113	118	124	130	135	141	146	152	158	163	169	175	180	186	191	197
64	110	116	122	128	134	140	145	151	157	163	169	174	180	186	192	197	204
65	114	120	126	132	138	144	150	156	162	168	174	180	186	192	198	204	210
66	118	124	130	136	142	148	155	161	167	173	179	186	192	198	204	210	216
67	121	127	134	140	146	153	159	166	172	178	185	191	198	204	211	217	223
68	125	131	138	144	151	158	164	171	177	184	190	197	203	210	216	223	230
69	128	135	142	149	155	162	169	176	182	189	196	203	209	216	223	230	236
70	132	139	146	153	160	167	174	181	188	195	202	209	216	222	229	236	243
71	136	143	150	157	165	172	179	186	193	200	208	215	222	229	236	243	250
72	140	147	154	162	169	177	184	191	199	206	213	221	228	235	242	250	258
73	144	151	159	166	174	182	189	197	204	212	219	227	235	242	250	257	265
74	148	155	163	171	179	186	194	202	210	218	225	233	241	249	256	264	272
75	152	160	168	176	184	192	200	208	216	224	232	240	248	256	264	272	279
76	156	164	172	180	189	197	205	213	221	230	238	246	254	263	271	279	287

Interestingly, fat in this area is more likely to produce many of the nasty metabolic effects that increase diabetes, cardiovascular, and cancer risk than fat around the butt and hips.

- Abnormal blood lipids
  - High triglycerides (greater than 150)
  - Low HDL (good cholesterol) less than 40 in a man and 50 in a woman
- Insulin resistance (a "pre-diabetic" or diabetic risk factor)
- High blood pressure
- Significantly increased risk of cardiovascular complications like heart attack, stroke, and premature death.

These features are often silent (minimizing the perception of risk) until the proverbial you-know-what hits the fan. This raises the important point that *feeling well does not equal good health.* Lifestyle syndrome is an epidemic, and while life expectancy in America has almost doubled since the turn of the twentieth century, it's estimated that we may soon begin to see this trend reverse as a consequence of weight-related morbidity.

Scientists who study aging estimate that the maximum potential for life expectancy in humans is 120 years, or approximately six times the age of maturation, as seen in other animal species. The oldest person ever documented was a French woman named Jeanne Calment, who lived to be 122. Many of my patients are well into their nineties, and some have reached one hundred years old. And while a genetic predisposition to longevity exists, it's only one piece of a complex puzzle. I've never met an overweight ninety-five-year-old. As humans we have the potential to influence our aging and vitality in a most remarkable way. In truth, as the pace of biotechnology, genomics (study of genes), proteomics (study of proteins that control virtually every function in our bodies), and nanotechnology accelerates exponentially, no one really knows how long we are capable of living.

So, a not so funny thing happens on your way to gaining two to three pounds a year over the holidays for most of your adult life. As fat settles around your mid-section, a cascade of mostly silent mediators of disease begins to take over. We know that even modest reduction in weight, e.g., 5 percent or ten pounds in a 200-pound individual, can dramatically turn these bad mediators of disease and premature death in the opposite direction. Hence, the case for the power connected to small changes.

> We know that even modest reduction in weight, e.g., 5 percent or ten pounds in a 200-pound individual, can dramatically turn these bad mediators of disease and premature death in the opposite direction. Hence, the case for the power connected to small changes.

Though lifestyle syndrome is one of many examples of the often silent and insidious, yet reversible health threats to you, I emphasize it because of its prevalence and enormous public health implications. It also connects with the public health challenges of high blood pressure, diabetes, and high cholesterol. It also serves as a good example of tying together mind-body-behavior strategies for change and improvement. Remember, you're not a victim of your DNA nor are you powerless to change the potentially dangerous trajectory you are on.

Let's briefly return to the concept of allostatic load (see figure 8.1), specifically, the influence of allostatic load on your health, how it is expressed in your life, and how it can be effectively diminished.

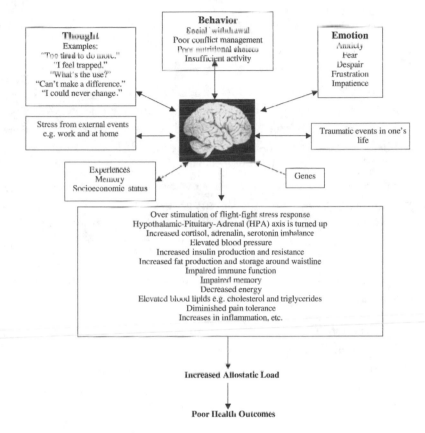

Figure 8.1   The Concept of Allostatic Load from a Behavioral Change Perspective

THE POWER OF PERCEPTION

Nothing influences behavior more than perception. Perceptions that limit the capacity for change lead to behaviors that perpetuate the status quo of poor eating habits and sedentary living. In turn, these behaviors serve to reinforce the perception that change is impossible. Charles Dwyer, PhD, of the Wharton Business School, suggests that perceptions are:

- Subjective
- Personal
- Arbitrary

- Idiosyncratic
- Fragile
- Infinitely malleable

Your complex biological imprints of perception, emotion, and behavior become the familiar sign posts that reinforce responses consistent with what the sign posts are telling you: "You've reached your limit. Change has never worked before." Instead the signposts should read: "Turn your canoe around. You're heading for a waterfall."

While familiarity can be a crucial asset like recognizing patterns that signal an imminent threat, familiarity doesn't always serve us well. We're all too familiar with the status quo of the sedentary state and the bliss of eating a bag of potato chips. When we become more aware of familiarity's habitual magnet sucking us back into the behavioral status quo we can begin to change. The challenge is exposing these habitual patterns as opportunities to change the following:

- Perception: Thinking differently or reframing circumstances.
- Emotion: Transforming doubt with confidence, fear with hope.
- Behavior: Actually doing something you didn't think you could do.
- Body: Seeing discomfort as a message to keep moving instead of withdrawing.

Many of the mind-emotion-brain-behavior-body biological imprints deeply imbedded inside you can be deconstructed and reconfigured. That's what plasticity is all about. Realizing and acting on this potential will enhance your brain's reward, meaning-maker, and attachment responses, eventually neutralizing the behavioral patterns that you assumed to be forever fixed. A subsequent reduction in stress will soon leave you feeling better and poised to do more. This biological transformation will result in a dramatic improvement in how you feel. Your dopamine and endorphins will say, "Yeah, Baby, yeah. I can do this. I feel great. I want more." I would suggest this to be your mojo, your source of power. Your goal is to access it and to make it work for you! Here are a few examples of how this construct works in different life scenarios.

TAKE MATTERS INTO YOUR OWN HANDS

Physicians often share the frustration of trying to influence behavioral changes in their patients. In fact, the medical evidence reveals the sobering reality that many physicians simply stop focusing on educating patients about behavioral change because it's too time consuming and often futile. The message here is that you must take matters into your own hands! While knowledge is empowering, it's not sufficient by itself to influence behavioral change. Your doctor can arm you with information, but he or she can't force you to exercise and to eat better.

What you'll find is that your initial success with fundamental behavioral change (i.e., a change of a deeply rooted habit as opposed to trying the newest fad) will be more likely to take hold if the behavior is rewarded. For example:

- **Creation of meaning:** "It will mean a lot to me if I can lose a few pounds and lower my blood pressure; my health and family mean too much to me to allow these risks to continue."

- **Creation of value satisfaction:** "I value reducing my risk of diabetes because I don't want to take insulin shots forever." "I want to be around for my grandchildren." "I value wearing clothes I look good in."

- **Reward:** Fulfilling a goal with positive meaning attached to it will turn on the reward system and subdue the stress response, enhancing mood, creating a state of inner satisfaction, and serving to further motivate the behavior. For example: "Wow, my weight is down five pounds, and my pants are beginning to feel loose. This feels great! I can't wait to do more tomorrow."

Mind-Emotion-Brain-Behavior-Body

Examples of the impact behavioral changes (exercise/dietary habits) have on thought, feeling, and health.

Old Behavior	**New Behavior**
Sedentary couch potato	Moderate activity, e.g., daily walking
Addicted to sugar-sweetened colas	Switch to sugar-free beverages

Old Thoughts/Perceptions	**New Thoughts/Perceptions**
Exercise:	
Status quo is acceptable	Status quo = time bomb
I look pretty good for my age	I could look even better
I'm too busy to find the time	3 hours per week is really not much
My back won't allow it	It will make my back feel better
Distracted	Focused

Food:	
Status quo is acceptable	Status quo = time bomb
I love this stuff	I'm heavier, my heartburn is worse
I can't stand diet soft drinks	This stuff really is not that bad
I miss the soft-drink habit	I can't believe I drank so much
How much difference could stopping make?	What a difference!

(−)   (+)

Old Emotions	**New Emotions**
Weary	Energized
Resigned	Confident
Overwhelmed	In control
Lacking motivation	Motivated
Anxious	Calm
Less resilient	More resilient
Craving	In control

Old Body	**New Body**
Fatter	Thinner
Larger waistline	Smaller waistline
Poor endurance	Better endurance
More heartburn	Heartburn gone
Poor sleep	Better sleep
Lifestyle syndrome risk	Reduced risk
Increased allostatic load	Reduced allostatic load

Mind-Emotion-Brain-Behavior-Body

Examples of work-related stress (you regularly interact with a colleague who pushes your buttons and increases your stress levels on a daily basis) and family-related stress (you are upset because your spouse works all the time, spending little time with the family; he/she seems grossly unaware of this imbalance).

Old Thought
Work:
This person is self-centered, controlling, and too comfortable with the status quo.

New Thought
I need to work with this person in order to achieve the desired outcome.

Family.
My husband cares more about work than his family.

My husband needs help with his awareness of how out of balance his life is.

Old Perception
Work:
Obstacle, antagonist, mediocrity serves

New Perception
Source of influence, collaborator, serves my values

Family:
Driven, insensitive, self-centered

Overwhelmed, burnt-out, vulnerable, at risk

Old Emotion
Anger, frustration, and impatience

New Emotion
Tolerance, empathy, acceptance, patience

(−)

(+)

Old Brain Biology
Fight-flight response
Increased CRH, cortisol, adrenaline
Limbic (amygdala) dopamine dominates

New Brain Biology
Decreased fight-flight response
Decreased cortisol and adrenaline
Surge of oxytocin and endorphins
Frontal lobe dopamine prevails

Old Behavior
Confrontation, avoidance, posturing

New Behavior
Tend and befriend, engagement, Collaboration

Body
Increased burden of allostatic load
Poor long-term health outcomes

Body
Decreased burden of allostatic load
Better performance and reduced health risk

Chapter 9

Nutrition: You Are What You Eat

"Let food be your medicine
and medicine be your food."

Hippocrates, 400 BC

Understanding the distance between where you are and where you would like to be—when viewed as an opportunity as opposed to an insurmountable obstacle—is a critical step in the creation of momentum for positive behavioral change. Your ultimate goal should not be confused with the short-term goals necessary to tip your mind-emotion-brain-behavior-body (ME-B^3) in the direction of positively reinforcing momentum. For example, your goal might be to lose twenty pounds or to run three miles; however, losing five pounds and walking one or two miles a day may serve as doable goals that will set the reward response into motion.

The 2005 Dietary Guidelines for Americans focuses on eating less, doing more, and making wiser choices. While knowledge *plus* action is required for change, the evidence is increasingly clear that being well informed not only improves health outcomes, but also enhances the perception of being in greater control. A sense of control is critical for controlling the magnitude and duration of your stress response and your resilience to challenge and change. People who age successfully will tend to feel more in control of their lives. They are also more likely to stay the course in response to a setback.

That said, information about dieting and nutrition is overwhelming and riddled with marketing that taps into our desires for a quick fix. These strategies are not usually an invitation to alter lifestyle in an enduring long-term manner. Losing weight is much easier than keeping it off. If you can't keep it off, you've accomplished nothing other than to reinforce your mindset that change is impossible.

As the power of mind-body-behavior goes, what will ultimately work best in the long run are behaviors that "light-up" areas in your brain that you will then biologically desire to reinforce. I know this is a bit abstract. The point is that you are capable of crafting thought and behavior in ways that will enhance your reward systems and your "meaning-making" neurobiological circuitry, which in turn gives you the motivation to move forward. Enhancing emotional neurobiological circuitry leaves less space for fear and risk-aversity (not always a bad trait) and more space for confidence, joy, contentment, and motivation. More begets more. You're indeed capable of cultivating dimensions in your life —relationships, social stimulation, larger networks of friends, family, and community—that have clear connection to the creation and maintenance of neurobiological responses that reduce stress and enhance the bliss of attachment. All of which massages the thoughts and behaviors that produced the positive responses in the first place.

> As the power of mind body-behavior goes, what will ultimately work best in the long run are behaviors that "light-up" areas in your brain that you will then biologically desire to reinforce.

Let's look at diet and nutrition in a practical way, one that will leave you more cognizant of how low some of the lifestyle- and behavioral-change fruit is actually hanging. One of the gaps in education that needs to be addressed is how best to translate the intuitive wisdom to eat less and to eat better into more effective strategies for success. The same can be said for activity, which I'll cover later. How much is enough? And how long should I be exercising?

I'll focus on measurable goals, distilling what I view as the "do not miss considerations" from what we know to be current best evidence. This is a moving target, and in some respects, it comes back to the basics of blocking and tackling, hitting and fielding, and the low-tech ABCs. Worthy points of emphasis include:

FRUITS AND VEGGIES

- Consume 4 1/2 cups of fruits and vegetables per day; or more specifically, 2 cups of fruit and 2 1/2 cups of vegetables per day. Approximately 1 cup of raw vegetables equals one serving, and 1/2 cup of cooked vegetables equals one serving. This would amount to *six to nine servings a day*. Sounds like a lot at first blush, though a worthy target to gradually work toward.

From a mind-body perspective, just reading the words "six to nine servings of fruits and vegetables per day" may conjure the image of a mountain of green, an insurmountable peak of produce, fiber, and botanical bore. Or the mention of fruits and vegetables may have conjured encoded memories of being a child, craving a Twinkie only to open your Batman lunch box and see neatly packed baggies of cut raw carrots, sweet pepper, and cucumbers. Perhaps your amygdala has "emotionally charged" your hippocampus, the library of every bad vegetable experience you've ever had, with feelings of disappointment, lack of pleasure, frustration, and palate-rejection. The remote memory of parental coercion to ingest as many vegetables as possible may now be highjacking your prefrontal lobe's capacity to say, "Wait a minute. Perhaps I only need to add two servings per day to achieve some benefit (indeed the case) without having to go the distance."

Or maybe you think, "I could never consume nine servings per day, so why try?" If that's your inclination, then track your veggie/fruit intake per day for a week and average it out. If you eat three servings per day, increase it to five. If you eat five, increase it to seven. Any degree of change will pay off, and the more you do, the more you do. Trust me. I grew up a meat-and-potato guy. Now I eat grilled portabella mushrooms. From filet mignon to portabella mushrooms? Until recent years, I wouldn't have thought it possible. Creating a meaningful goal you can fulfill will massage your reward response, shift your thinking from negative to posi-

> Any degree of change will pay off, and the more you do, the more you do.

tive, and make you more likely to repeat the good behavior. Soon you'll be off to the races!

Do-Not-Miss Fruit-and-Veggie Take Home Points (see the Four-Week Addicted-to-Health Plan in Chapter 2 for more information)

> Creating a meaningful goal you can fulfill will massage your reward response, shift your thinking from negative to positive, and make you more likely to repeat the good behavior.

- Excellent natural source of vitamins, minerals, and other phytonutrients (plant-based nutrients like antioxidants).
- If possible, organic is best to reduce exposure to pesticide residues.
- Cruciferous vegetables—broccoli, cabbage, cauliflower, kale, spinach, and asparagus—are excellent sources of B-vitamins and antioxidants.
- Berries have a lower glycemic load and are excellent sources of antioxidants, vitamins, and minerals.
- Beans, lentils and legumes are excellent sources of fiber and protein.
- Soy products—tofu, tempah, miso—are excellent sources of protein, isoflavones (nutrients with hormone-like effects).
- Create a variety of *colors* using a variety of vegetables, e.g., green leaf, tomatoes, yellow varieties, etc.
- Steaming will better maintain nutrients.
- Sweet potatoes are healthier than regular potatoes.
- Above-ground vegetables are healthier than root vegetables.

WHOLE GRAINS

Another area to emphasize is grains. Whole grains contain more protein, nutrients, and fiber. White, refined grains are persona non-grata. My friend and colleague Dr. Mark Liponis, coauthor of *Ultraprevention: The 6-week Plan That Will Make You Happy for Life*, refers to refined white grains as "the white menace." For the average recommended 2,000 calories per day allowance, the equivalent of three slices of whole-grain bread (three ounces of whole grain per day) is sufficient to meet these needs. This can come in the form of bread, cereals, and pasta.

The "white menace," for me, elicits memories of Wonder Bread, thick, smooth, and marvelous with peanut butter and marshmallow fluff. The white menace of cakes, cupcakes, and pastries sparks positive, delicious, and deeply imbedded amygdala-enhanced memories. This visceral response be-comes the architect of my mind's thought: "I can't eat the whole-wheat stuff all the time. What about sub rolls? All whole grain all of the time? No way. I can't fathom life without refined starches!" The subsequent behavior: sticking with what I know makes me comfortable, warm, cozy. It's also very tasty.

New thought: "Substitute white-refined for whole grains twice per week." Consequence: "If it doesn't say whole grain, I'm not buying it." To overcome the amygdala when it's working against you requires some prefrontal lobe as-sistance, for example, "I don't have to do this all at once. I never imagined such small change could have such an impact on my cholesterol, waistline, and blood glucose level. My mood and my energy level is saying 'thank you.' More whole grains please."

As you make changes to your diet, remember:

- Limit refined wheat-grain products.
- Aim for 30 grams of fiber per day in your diet.
- All-bran cereal is an excellent source of grain and has a lower glycemic load than most other cereals.
- Brown rice is healthier than white rice.
- Small changes reap big rewards. Fascinating system, isn't it?

WHAT ABOUT CALORIES?

The primary purpose of food is to provide energy or fuel to do what needs to be done to survive. Most of us eat more than what is required to achieve that objective. Consider portions and portion sizes. I'm always amazed at how small a recommended portion really is. Most ME-B^3 activity as it relates to serving size can best be described as "portion distortion." We all tend to overestimate portion size. For example:

- Three ounces of meat is the size of a bar of soap.
- Three ounces of fish is the size of a checkbook.
- One ounce of cheese is the size of a domino.

Some good strategies for reducing portion size include:

- Leave 25 percent of your meal behind. Wasteful but healthy.
- Eat more slowly. Shoot for twenty to thirty minutes minimum, par-ticularly when eating dinner.

- Use a smaller dinner plate and try to prevent foods from touching each other on the plate.
- Salads and fruits are good "low-cal fillers."
- One serving of cooked pasta is 1/2 cup. This is smaller than a baseball! The ME-B[3] vision of a serving of pasta is an overflowing plate shared in laughter with family, friends, and copious amounts of refined garlic-butter bread. Your palate's libido fully satisfied only after the plate is licked dry. That is one powerful imprint. "Are you now telling me that 1/2 cup is an official serving?" That simply does not exist in my ME-B[3] vocabulary. New thought: "Perhaps something in between with more salad, whole-grain bread, and more fruits and vegetables. Add some of that delicious, bubbly Italian carbonated bottled water for a bit of added gas-induced fullness and suddenly a half a cup may be tolerable." I can do that at least once per week or twice per month. The goal is to leverage a little plasticity to transform the lust for a full plate of pasta with the lust of a smaller waistline. Remember the ME-B[3] interplay:

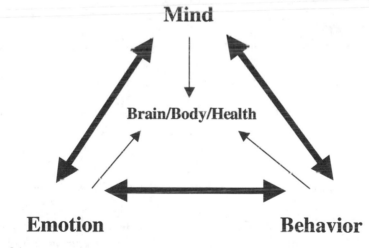

Figure 9.1

NUTRITION LABELS

Nutrition labels certainly give consumers important information. However, they can sometimes be very misleading. Consider a typical soft drink nutritional label (an oxymoron if ever there was one).

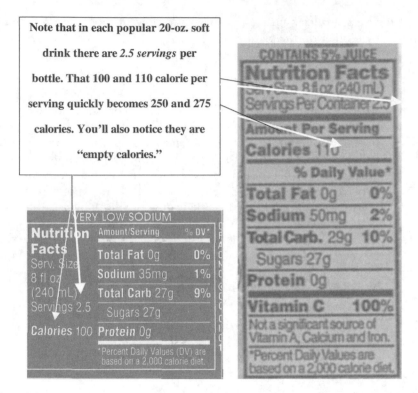

Figure 9.2

Note the nutritional information is based on "per serving." At first blush, when you glance at these labels, not too bad: only 100 calories in this delicious drink. Wait a minute. There are 2-1/2 servings in this bottle, translating into 250 quick calories. How bad can that be? After all, there's a picture of an athlete on the bottle (your subconscious brain activity is saying, "athlete, healthy, sweat, replenish, exuberance, and quench"). Many people don't equate the fact that burning 250 calories requires about one hour of moderate walking (3.5 mph). From a prefrontal lobe perspective, it just isn't worth it. When it comes to sugar-sweetened soft drinks, allow your prefrontal lobe to "put on the red light." Change one sugary drink per day to a bottle of water, and the consequences over the next three-four weeks will be:

- An adaptation of taste that renders re-exposure to the sweet "too sweet."

- You'll drink fewer sweetened drinks across the board.

- You'll lose some weight and assist with lower insulin and cholesterol levels.

- You'll have more energy. Please note: The "sugar-high or kick" after thirty to sixty minutes becomes an energy-draining metabolic sedative.

- Your prefrontal lobe-limbic dance for a better behavior will reward you like the dance you once had when that delicious soft drink swished your palate.

FATS

The theme is to shift from foods high in saturated fats and refined flours to fruits, vegetables, whole grains, lean meats, fish, and low-fat dairy (3 cups per day of low-fat milk or equivalent, like yogurt).

An excellent and proven diet to help you accomplish this is the "DASH" diet to stop hypertension (http://www.nhlbi.nih.gov/health/public/heart/hbp/dash/). Another excellent diet is the Dr. Dean Ornish diet (http://my.webmd.com/content/pages/8/3075_865).

Whichever diet you follow, total fat intake should be kept around 20 to 30 percent of calories (400 to 600 calories in a 2,000 calorie per day intake). Fats have nine calories for every gram. Polyunsaturated and monounsaturated sources such as fish, nuts, and vegetable oils are better for you. Limit saturated and trans fats. Basically, trans fat is made when manufacturers add hydrogen to vegetable oil—a process called hydrogenation. Hydrogenation increases the shelf life and flavor stability of foods. Trans fat can be found in vegetable shortenings, some margarines, crackers, cookies, snack foods, and other foods made with or fried in partially hydrogenated oils. Unlike other fats, the majority of trans fat is formed when food manufacturers turn liquid oils into solid fats, like shortening and hard margarine. A small amount of trans fat is found naturally, primarily in dairy products, some meat, and other animal-based foods.

Trans fat, like saturated fat and dietary cholesterol, raises the LDL cholesterol that increases your risk for heart disease. Americans consume on average four to five times as much saturated fat as trans fat in their diets. Although saturated fat is the main dietary culprit that raises LDL, trans fat and dietary cholesterol also contribute significantly.

Do-Not-Mist Take-Home Points on Chewing the Fat (see Four-Week
Addicted-to-Health Plan in Chapter 2 for more information and ideas)

- Minimize unhealthy fats—red meats, skinned chicken and turkey.
- Extra virgin olive oil is healthier than commercially processed oils like corn, safflower, sunflower, and mixed vegetables oils. The latter choices are high in omega-6 fatty acids, which enhance inflammation.
- Omega-3 fatty acids are healthy fats as they decrease inflammation in your body. Good sources include salmon, albacore tuna, walnuts, flaxseed, and avocados.
- Limit/avoid foods with trans fats and hydrogenated fats commonly found in processed foods.

THE CORPORATE DIET PLAN: BEWARE

A common pattern of eating involves fast food and empty calories that satisfy a hunger on the go. Our hectic lives leave little time for breakfast or planning healthier choices for daytime snacks. It's estimated that approximately 15 percent of U.S. adults don't eat breakfast. On the surface, this may seem advantageous, starting the day with fewer calories. However, the advice our mothers and teachers gave us about breakfast being the most important meal of the day has stood the test of time. It has also stood the test of science. Omitting breakfast will result in a low blood sugar, which becomes a potent stimulus for hunger and snacking later in the day. Hunger cravings lead to the overwhelming desire to eat refined, sugar-sweetened, carbohydrate snacks, providing immediate satisfaction. We all know that sometimes only a CARB will do.

Research suggests that the brain produces a protein messenger called neuropeptide Y that creates a satisfied pleasure and coping comfort. You may recall I touched on neuropeptide Y in the discussion of our bodies internal "anti-stress response." It's no coincidence we feel so good at the initial stage of carb consumption. This neuropeptide response, one example of many in the neurobiology of hunger, may promote binge eating or sustained grazing. This response is more pronounced if more than three hours have passed from your last food ingestion. This has implications for timing and choice of a snack. Try to avoid letting more than three or four hours pass without food and choose moderate amounts of non-refined carbohydrate alternatives like yogurt, nuts, and raw veggies.

Carbohydrate binging also results in a surge of insulin production and wider fluctuations of glucose and insulin. This is bad news with respect to the vicious cycle of empty calorie consumption over the course of the day. Boy, do I understand this and have tried excruciatingly hard to change the pattern. The problem is made worse by the easy availability of such choices in the workplace and at school. Sound recommendations include:

> Try to avoid letting more than three or four hours pass without food and choose moderate amounts of non-refined carbohydrate alternatives like yogurt, nuts, and raw veggies.

- Plan your eating choices over the course of the day. Try to avoid going more than three or four hours without eating something of low glycemic index (foods less likely to raise sugar, e.g., nuts, fresh vegetables, boiled egg, etc,. to avoid fluctuating glucose and insulin).

- Eat breakfast. Choose foods higher in protein like egg white omelets, unsweetened whole grains and low-fat dairy like yogurt (my personal favorite).

- Choose a mid-morning and mid-afternoon snack that will satisfy your hunger and have a lower glycemic index (less of an increase in your blood sugar after eating).

- At mealtime, consistently eat a balanced diet with salads, fruit, fish, and whole grains.

- Choose an evening snack as you would one earlier in the day for school or work. Temptation will follow you everywhere. Remember, any strategy for successful lifestyle and behavioral change is one you can live with every day.

People who travel a lot in their work are challenged to be mindful of the difference between foods prepared at home and foods prepared in restaurants or purchased from vending machines.

ALCOHOL: CAN I DRINK MYSELF TO HEALTH?

The short answer is yes, but of course in moderation. Moderation means two drinks per day maximum for men and one drink per day for women. Note that drinking fourteen beers on a Saturday night (two beers per day per week) is not the same as consuming one to two drinks each day. It appears that any source of alcohol—red wine, white wine, beer, or a Cosmopolitan—will provide the benefit. (The ethanol provides the benefits from a cardiovascular perspective.)

The beneficial effects of alcohol largely come from elevated HDL levels. HDL levels are the good cholesterol types that clear plaque-forming bad cholesterol, or LDL, which lead to atherosclerosis or narrowing. Alcohol stimulates the liver to produce "apo A1," a major constituent of HDL. Alcohol also seems to render our blood less sticky and, to a small extent, improves the sensitivity of our body to insulin.

Alcohol also has a down side as higher daily amounts can damage the liver, increase the risk of some cancers, and lead to inflammation of the stomach with bleeding. Small daily portions with or after dinner are not a bad idea if you're so inclined.

THE OMEGA-3 STORY

For many years, it's been recognized that diets high in omega-3 fatty acids reduce the risk of heart disease. These natural "healthy fats" have many potential health-promoting and disease-preventing benefits like reducing inflammation and inhibiting blood clotting. Current recommendations from the American Heart Association are to incorporate two portions (three ounces per portion) per week of fish that are higher in these fats. Examples include salmon (a choice I'm now conditioned to make subconsciously), trout, herring, sardines, and albacore tuna (be informed about mercury toxicity). Other good sources of omega-3 fats are tofu, soybeans, canola, walnuts, and flaxseed. Check the AHA website for more information: http://www.americanheart. org/presenter.jhtml?identifier=4632.

Restricting salt is a good idea; 2,000 mg per day or 1 level teaspoon of table salt should be the limit. In general, color is always a plus, for example, romaine instead of iceberg lettuce, or sweet potatoes instead of regular potatoes.

As we reframe our thoughts and perceptions to influence the mind-emotion-brain-behavior-body complex, I'm reminded of another example of the power of small changes. Remember, the old thought we discussed: "Over the last five years, I've only gained ten pounds or two pounds per year.

That's pretty typical. I'm a member of a large club." Well, substitute that old, damaging thought with this new one: "If I consume 100 to 200 calories per day less or burn 100 to 200 calories more each day, I could avoid the gain altogether."

Again, most people will underestimate intake (portion distortion). A target of reducing 300 to 500 calories per day will make a huge difference in your life and perhaps in the lives of your children! I did this by cutting out two sweet, delicious, carbonated, refreshing, stimulating, addicting cans of a well known cola brand. I went from "no way" to "no more" in about two to three weeks! Small change, big results.

SWEETS: WALKING THE LIMBIC HIGH WIRE

Until about three years ago, I was the poster boy for concentrated sweets. I would purposefully leave some of the entrée behind in order to make room for the sweet limbic reward to follow. Ahhhh . . . the bliss induced by a piece of cheesecake. My wife will still comment in amazement how rarely she sees me consuming concentrated sweets these days. The addiction to sweets is a good example of our reward system responding "sweetly" to a behavior that has significant implications for health promotion, disease prevention, and perhaps longevity.

Sweets are the reigning champs of the "discretionary calorie" category. Discretionary calories are the difference between the calories you ingest and the calories necessary to maintain your nutritional needs. The short-term neurobiological fallout of consuming sweets is a potent dopamine-endorphin-like response, not unlike that of a good workout or other sources of pleasure and satisfaction; in other words, eating sweets creates a biological response that promotes a desire to repeat itself. The suggestion is that a piece of cheesecake can elicit—in concert with thought, anticipation, expectation, and fulfilled promise—a response not unlike that of an opiate.

> The suggestion is that a piece of cheesecake can elicit—in concert with thought, anticipation, expectation, and fulfilled promise—a response not unlike that of an opiate.

While not as potent a stimulant of opiod-endorphins-dopamine and other reward pleasure neurotransmitters, there is clearly some overlap in these responses. When I speak of dessert, I speak of "loving" dessert. I don't like dessert. I *love* dessert. *It's love, not like.* I don't like chocolate and coffee. I love chocolate and coffee. I love them, desire them, feel great when I ingest them, and as I withdraw, I crave more of them. That's a pretty potent neurobiological footprint, wouldn't you say? I'm okay with the coffee, except at night (I'll address sleep in a moment). If you inhibit the effect of opiates in animals, the animals become less interested in eating. There's interest in exploring implications of this in the treatment of bulimia where binging on foods, often high in concentrated sweets, is common.

The dilemma here is that the ME-B^3 is working against us, not for us. In hunter-gatherer times, there may have been a survival edge in binge eating to store fat as a fuel source in times of unpredictable access to food. The average hunter-gatherer did not have a grocery store on every corner or a fast-food stop as they roamed the African savannah. Rewarding caloric intake as a fuel source becomes less of a survival advantage when foods (calories) abound! This is a biological footprint begging for plasticity, begging for the waves of prefrontal lobe mediated oversight to wash them away, enabling new footprints to be formed.

None of this will be easy. As you moderate your intake of concentrated sweets, you can anticipate a withdrawal response. Craving, needing, and wanting your amygdala-limbic system is a virtual disco inferno. It's very hard to override. Doing it gradually helps, for example, cutting out one concentrated sweet per day and substituting it with fruit, walnuts, or raisins.

If you go the free-fall route, as I did, expect full withdrawal. Expect to want to eat an entire Ben and Jerry's ice cream cake when no one is watching. Make sure close supportive friends are nearby. Make sure you're ready to take a walk to provide an alternative source of endorphin production (your brain will think your exercise is a Twinkie). A commitment to cut even a small amount will, to some extent, mitigate the mag-

> Make sure you're ready to take a walk to provide an alternative source of endorphin production (your brain will think your exercise is a Twinkie).

nitude of the craving. And if even a small degree of weight loss ensues, you'll begin to see a similar, though less potent, reward response in the form of better-fitting clothes, improved health profiles, and better moods and confidence levels.

Now there's some fuel for the prefrontal override that will soon begin to see one slice of cheesecake as the equivalent of a forty five-minute jog. Your prefrontal lobe can send a stronger message to your amygdala-limbic party animals conspiring behind the curtain to remind you how good it will taste and how good it will feel on your palate. Once your prefrontal lobe is high-jacked, you're doomed. I'll come back to this in the chapter on conflict management. Yes, the skills necessary to effectively manage conflict are not dissimilar to those necessary to avoid dessert. Gaining some control over this response is possible, especially with small, doable targets, for example, reducing one serving each day of either baked goods, processed meats, or unhealthy snacks. This is also a great way to reduce sugar and fat intake and to tell your amygdala-limbic co-conspirators to take a hike. "No ice cream sundae is going to reduce my chances of playing with my grandchildren!"

Remember, insulin in high-circulating concentration is the enemy.

Do-Not-Miss Take-Home Bullet Points: Sugar—How Sweet It Isn't

- Try to limit carbohydrates to no more than 30 to 40 percent of your total calories.
- If you are a diabetic, pre-diabetic or have metabolic syndrome, aim even lower, e.g., 20 to 30 percent.
- Limit foods with a high glycemic load, e.g., breads, pasta, sugar, desserts, pastries, white rice, potatoes, etc. (www.nutritiondata.com/glycemic-index.html)
- Eat more whole grains.

WHICH DIET IS BEST?

There are many diets out there. You know their names. You may be on one. If someone I haven't seen in a while comes up to me and says, "Mark you look good. Have you lost some weight? What kind of diet are you on?" I say, "I'm not on a specific diet. I'm just eating better." The many popular diets out there may work in the short term, say, for six months to a year. Beyond that, if you can't stick with it, it won't work.

Some people try calorie counting, which can easily become an obsession, and who wants that? By making more effective choices like far fewer refined starches and sweets and more fruits and veggies, walnuts, and Merlot (in moderation of course) with more salmon and low-fat dairy, you inherently reduce your caloric load without the perpetual burden of calorie-counting. An ideal pattern of eating is one that eventually allows you to live on autopilot.

The D.A.S.H. and Ornish recommendations mentioned previously in this chapter are less like diets and more "ways of living." I feel that's an important distinction. My diet is probably most closely aligned with those approaches. What will work best for you is that which eventually becomes a way of living. If you make this "way of living" approach work while you're in your thirties, we're talking about another fifty to sixty years of life. In your forties, perhaps you can expect an additional forty to fifty years. In your sixties? What about another thirty years! This design of ours, when the genes and the milieu are right, can definitely get us there. Healthy choices can help us live longer and, perhaps more importantly, improve the quality of those extended years.

Programs like Weight Watchers also work well and outdistance some of the popular diets for better compliance, providing both structure and clear choices. Meal replacement strategies like Slim Fast are also effective. Whatever path gets you there, terrific. The other point I would make is that reducing calories, particularly the nutritionally empty calories, when combined with regular activity, is a formidable dynamic duo. Do not hesitate to push your activity gradually toward a brisk heartbeat and stronger, deeper, and faster respirations. These are the physical hallmarks of burning fuel. The more oxygen moving through your lungs, the stronger your fire becomes.

The three characteristics of successful weight management that best predict success are:

- Eating breakfast
- Exercising regularly
- Weighing yourself daily

FOOD AND BRAIN HEALTH

An interesting connection undoubtedly exists between what we eat and the health of our brains. There is some suggestion in animal studies that moderate reductions in caloric intake slow age-related changes in the brain. Memory, learning, and coordination tasks remain sharper for longer periods of time.

Calorie restriction may alter the formation of destructive "free radicals," metabolic by-products that induce cell death. There is also evidence that some foods may be more "mentally healthy" like strawberries, blueberries, and spinach. These have greater "antioxidant" effects reducing cell damage from free radicals. Diets high in saturated fats may have the opposite effect. Eating less and eating better have major benefits to health preservation and vigorous aging, independent of reductions in weight.

Other mind-body integrative approaches to assist with weight reduction that are being funded by the National Institute of Health include:

- Qigong and acupressure (see Chapter 7: Mind-Body Medicine)
- Meditation-based treatment for binge-eating disorders
- A counseling and diet program at Wayne State University designed to help breast cancer survivors makes lifestyle changes to lose weight and reduce recurrences.

Chapter 10

Exercise: Motion Is the Lotion

"Sweeeeeeeeeeeeet surrender . . . is all that I have to give."

Sarah McLachlan, "Sweet Surrender"

In addition to walking and other energy-burning cardiovascular aerobic exercise, resistance and strength exercise using free weights or other equipment is very important. In as little as twenty to thirty minutes, two to three times a week, you'll see significant improvement in strength and stability. Ideally, this would be integrated with your aerobic routine.

The goal is to focus on specific muscle groups and find a weight that will allow you to do ten to twelve repetitions, with that last rep being just barely doable. As you strengthen, and as the ten to twelve reps become easier for you, increase the weight by 10 percent. There's some evidence that a single set of twelve good reps can build muscle as efficiently as three sets of the same exercise. The emphasis is that a modest effort yields marvelous results. Strengthening will enhance muscle tone, which essentially forms the scaffolding of our skeletal system. Resistance work may reduce your risk of falls, often due to balance instability, which comes from de-conditioning due to disuse of muscles.

> The emphasis is that a modest effort yields marvelous results.

Such strengthening is very important as falls become a major source of injury and death as people age.

As we age, we also tend to lose "lean body" or muscle mass. Contrary to popular myth, muscle does not turn into fat, it just gets smaller or atrophies. Fat stores, totally separate, just get larger. Enhancing muscle mass increases your energy expenditure as muscle uses more energy than fat. You'll therefore burn more calories even at rest! You'll also strengthen your bones and joints and enhance your body's sensitivity to insulin, a huge cardiovascular benefit.

Be patient. Believe in yourself. Three to four weeks of sustained change will tip you in the direction of greater control.

More control = better health.

Gaining more control over both the calorie input and the caloric expenditure in your life will do as much for your overall health as anything I am aware of.

Is there a behavior that can rival the opiate-endorphin "love-bliss" response of concentrated sweets and have a health impact 180 degrees in the opposite direction? The answer just happens to be "yes," and it comes in the form of movement. The current guidelines for activity are as follows:

- thirty minutes a day of moderate activity to reduce the risk of chronic disease
- sixty minutes a day of moderate-vigorous activity to prevent weight gain
- sixty to ninety minutes a day of moderate activity to sustain weight loss.

Walking thirty to forty minutes or 5,000 steps or two-and-a-half miles per day is considered moderately active. Walking sixty to ninety minutes a day, 10,000 steps, or five miles per day is considered active. Of course activity that expends more energy or calories like jogging, rowing, or biking can accomplish as much in less time.

Activity should be looked at as cumulative over the course of a full day. For example, if you walk briskly for fifteen minutes two to three times a day, you're reaching a target of thirty-five to forty-five minutes total. Wearing an

inexpensive pedometer can give you a more quantifiable, measurable monitor. Gradually working toward 10,000 steps a day is a good goal.

Cardiovascular and overall health benefits of aerobic exercise relate directly to the increased consumption of oxygen "burned" during the exercise.
Recommendations from the American College of Sports Medicine—whether
swimming, jogging, biking, or using a low impact aerobic device like a
treadmill—works best if you target achieving 60 to 90 percent maximal
heart rate or pulse. You can calculate your maximum heart rate by subtract-
ing your age from 220. So for example, if you're 50 years old, your maximum heart rate target for aerobic capacity or maximal burn is around 170.
Working toward a target of 100 to 150 (on the well-conditioned end) at
least gives you a ballpark to play in.

EXERCISE AND THE BRAIN

In recent years, research has begun to uncover the specific benefits of exercise
on brain function that go beyond enhanced mood and reduction in the risk
of stroke. For example, some research suggests that exercise positively affects
the hippocampus, the brain structure vital for memory and learning. When
I was in medical school (more than twenty years ago), it was widely believed
that you were born with a "fixed" complement of
brain matter that slowly faded into the sunset as
we aged; a decline in memory and learning was
seen as an inevitable and natural tendency. We
now know this is not at all the case. It appears
the brain is capable of generating new brain
cells.

> It appears the brain is
> capable of generating new
> brain cells.

Many mind-body approaches, in addition to exercise, are known to reduce cardiovascular risk. There is evidence that suggests a higher prevalence
of vascular disease in the brains of individuals with Alzheimer's disease. It's
possible that reducing cardiovascular risk may lower the risk of acquiring
Alzheimer's later in life. The Nurses' Health Study and the Honolulu-Asia
Aging Study results support the connection between vascular disease and
Alzheimer's. Untreated high blood pressure, diabetes, and high cholesterol
were independently linked to changes in the brain of individuals with
Alzheimer's disease.

Another study from Stockholm that followed individuals for decades found a substantial increase in the risk of Alzheimer's in people who had lifestyle syndrome (obesity, high blood sugar, high blood pressure, high cholesterol). Regular exercise with omega-3 fatty acid supplementation/diet appeared to have some additive protective effects.

Throughout life, particularly in response to cognitive stimulation and social interactions, the brain can be nurtured in health-promoting ways. Reducing the stress response is likely one of many critical pathways in this connection. Stress overload and activation of the HPA and cortisol response systems does, particularly in animal models, damage the hippocampus. Individuals with Alzheimer's disease are usually on autopsy found to have significant change and loss of architecture in their hippocampus. While just scratching the surface of an extremely vital and interesting story, it appears that there is much we can continue to do throughout our lives, to nurture our brains, the very mediators of the world we live in.

The science behind exercise, in addition to its effects on reducing anxiety and depression, points to cognitive improvements in the ability to process data. While it may not make you wiser, it does seem to enhance your brain's microprocessor. A 2005 study published in the *Journal of Exercise Physiology* compared results of school fitness testing with academic performance. Over 850,000 seventh and ninth graders were studied. The average math scores on standardized testing were substantially (20 percent) higher in the group of students who were able to meet all six of the fitness performance goals compared to those who were only able to meet half.

Cognitive capacity can improve quickly with exercise. I always bring a legal pad with me to the place where I exercise. Inevitably after a good workout some creative thoughts emerge.

Arthur Kramer, a University of Illinois psychology professor, studied senior citizens and found that aerobic exercise yielded a 20 percent improvement on cognitive testing. His study was published in the *Proceedings of the National Academy of Sciences*. Dr. Kramer has also compared fMRI scanning in seniors before and after six months of aerobic exercise. The scans demonstrated patterns in the brain, indistinguishable from that of twenty-year-olds. Another recent study published in the *Journal of the American Medical Association* examined more than 18,000 older women. Those who were more physically active had a 20 percent reduction in risk of cognitive impairment.

In another study, published in the journal *Lancet*, nearly 1,500 people sixty-five and older were monitored for more than thirty years. Researchers found that people who engaged in leisurely physical activity at least twice a week as they passed through "middle age" had a 60 percent lower risk of developing Alzheimer's disease compared with their sedentary counterparts.

> Researchers found that people who engaged in leisurely physical activity at least twice a week as they passed through "middle age" had a 60 percent lower risk of developing Alzheimer's disease compared with their sedentary counterparts.

The message is that what we do while we are well substantially lowers our risk of both physical and cognitive decline as we age. If you put a mouse on a treadmill each day, they will navigate a maze much more accurately than the mice that do nothing. At autopsy, the brains of mice that exercised showed far fewer changes of the type associated with Alzheimer's.

EXERCISING YOUR MIND

There has been considerable interest in mind-enhancing specific exercises like "memory training." As Dr. Gary Small of UCLA's Neuropsychiatric Institute notes, "The idea is use it or lose it; work out your brain cells so they can stay active and healthy." I have particular interest in this area of research as I am now a member of the memory challenged club.

Have you had an experience recently where you forgot the name of a person you just passed on the street or had difficulty matching a name to a face? Understanding how we process and store memory makes it easier to understand how practice in this area can actually work. For example, the first step is to focus on what you wish to remember, for example, the name of a person. You're now using your frontal lobe to "tune in" on the individual. The second step is to create a visual image in your mind of the face of the individual. This adds an additional visual context, enhancing the process of memory consolidation. The third step is to attach a context that has meaning and emotional significance (remember your amygdala-hippocampus working behind the scenes). This will add an additional "charge" to the memory, making it more likely to jump off the memory shelf when you need it. I'll give you an example.

I tried this recently at a school meeting for my son Alex. Alex has Down syndrome and was starting a new middle school. Several people there are involved in his education and development. On my son's first day, it was very busy, lots of hubbub, new faces and names. You know how those first days of school can be. We were also in a new locale and school system. The point is that my memory capacity was very challenged, if not overwhelmed. A woman who I would see a week later at a team meeting introduced herself to me in passing as "Betty, the Occupational Therapist," who would be working with Alex. As I looked her straight in the eye (focused), I took a snapshot of her in my son's classroom holding some notes she records while working with students. I attached the face of a dear aunt named Betty to her face. Now all of this occurred in a matter of seconds.

A week later we had our first team meeting. When she entered the room there was the momentary "name to face" challenge, then Betty the O.T. became the face of my aunt Betty. "Hi Betty," I said and smiled, proud that I spoke her name before she had a chance to reintroduce herself. "It's nice to see you again." By using a memory tool such as attaching a story or context to what you want to remember, you can easily scan the vast library of your hippocampus and pull the desired memory off the shelf.

Perhaps in a similar fashion, integrating activities like reading, puzzles, and word-games into your daily routines can fire up old brain cells that are stuck on the couch and generate new cells and synapses, once thought impossible. Research supports the intuitive notion that the brain and its health, like heart and kidney health, have many remediable, disease-preventing capacities. These capacities can be enhanced by purposeful thought, behavior, and positive emotional stimulation.

As we understand more about the biology of memory and learning, we will see dramatic potential for effective treatment in diseases like Alzheimer's. There's a lot of interest in brain transmitters like acetylcholine, glutamate, NMDA (N-methyl, D-aspartate), and GABA (gamma-amino butyric acid) that play important roles in memory. Current and future treatments of memory impairment are targeting these messenger systems in the brain.

EXERCISE AND MOOD

While much of the emphasis on exercise focuses on expending more calories, losing weight, and reducing cardiovascular risk, there is also a profoundly positive effect on mood and emotion. For example, physical activity can be integrated with such mind-body techniques as Yoga, Tai Chi, and Pilates.

Yoga, an ancient Indian practice, integrates breathing and meditation with stretching through the repetition of a series of poses. Tai Chi is a Chinese martial art done in slow motion to enhance flow of energy of Chi and restore balance of mind and body. Pilates is a muscle-lengthening program.

As mind-body benefits go, integrating these disciplines with walking, aerobic activity, resistive exercise, and diet puts you into a totally different health-promoting orbit. Benefits not only include the physical but also the emotional. Regular practice reduces stress, counter-acts depression, and enhances mood. The beauty here, in addition to feeling happier and more upbeat, is that positive emotions in and of themselves profoundly influence all aspects of physical, emotional, mental, and spiritual health.

Remember, when it comes to exercise, your memories of prior attempts to maintain a routine and the amygdala's emotional stamp of futility may send the message that it's not worth it. You may tell yourself, "The motivation just isn't there. I can't do it." Your brain can easily deceive you into thinking it's not a good idea. But, if you persevere even for as little as four weeks, these old footprints in the sand will have less of an impact as they are washed away and new footprints emerge.

Chapter 11

Mood, Emotion, and Health

It's long been thought that the emotional dimension of our lives was an abstract and "separate domain" of health that coexisted with the physical domain. Despite having an obvious effect on quality of life, until recently, there hasn't been any appreciation for the physiological states that serve as the underpinnings of our emotions and how intricately integrated they are with thought, behavior, and overall health.

As is true for many aspects of overall health, emotional health also has genetic, environmental, and cultural influences. We know, for example, that depression, bipolar disease, and alcohol addiction frequently run in families. We're learning, however, that many dimensions of our overall emotional health are intricately connected with physical and spiritual health in an acquired fashion, amenable to change and adaptation.

This is fundamentally shifting our paradigm for screening, diagnosis, and multidimensional treatment strategies. Take depression, for example. Historical perspective examined depression as a sad mood, the dark trait of an individual, separate from all that influenced physical health. Now we recognize depression and its many contributors as having the neurobiological characteristics of disrupted brain neurotransmitters like serotonin and norepinephrine. We now recognize depression as an independent risk factor for cardiovascular disease and complications. Studies demonstrate the risk of having a heart attack is twice that of an individual without depression.

We recognize that individuals with a history of heart disease who are also depressed (and trust me on this, many go unrecognized and therefore undiagnosed and treated) have a much worse prognosis and are more likely to suffer complications and experience premature death.

Traumatic stress in childhood such as physical, sexual, or emotional abuse was associated with as much as a 30 to 70 percent increased risk of having a heart attack later in life. We now recognize that traumatic events are relived continuously and manifested by physiological fight-flight adrenaline and cortisol, known to increase heart risk.

> **We now recognize that traumatic events are relived continuously and manifested by physiological fight-flight adrenaline and cortisol, known to increase heart risk.**

We also recognize that alterations in mood like depression and anxiety frequently coexist with chronic pain. While this relationship was always thought to be cause-effect, for example, chronic pain leading to altered mood and anxiety, we now understand it to be much more complicated. A new framework suggests that events, biological in nature, are causing both pain and depression. Consider that an altered biological state in your brain could affect both your degree of pleasure and joy, as well as how effective the circulation of blood is in your legs, heart, and brain. Imagine the disequilibrium of your mind's neurochemical symphony that results in the perception of pain in your arms and legs, when in fact no apparent physical reasons exist for the pain. Domains of physical, mental, emotional, and spiritual health appear to have unifying mechanisms integrated in cause and effect. This is an extraordinary shift in how we examine disease, health, and healing.

In the connection between mood/emotion and behavior, we see clear evidence of less effective self-care in people with chronic depression and anxiety. Healthy nutritional choices and activity tend to be marginalized under the weight of chronic emotional stress. Smoking is also more common. People who score high on measurements of hostility tended to consume, on average, 600 more calories per day than those who scored lower. Loneliness and isolation, not surprisingly, are associated with more self-destructive behavior. In this intriguing construct, depression and chronic emotional stress look more like a systemic, physiological process than they do separate, ambiguously connected and abstract states of feeling.

Johan Denollet, of Tilburg University In the Netherlands, developed a tool to measure an individual's tendency to have a "type D (distress)" personality. Negative emotional states—worry, irritability, gloom, and social inhibition—were features most pronounced with the type D personality. Increases in the risk of heart disease and high blood pressure were associated with high scores for this personality type. Lower quality of life scores and premature death were also more likely to be seen in the type D personality.

Together these mind-emotion-behavior interconnections of health and illness are going to fundamentally change our approach to health care. The notion of targeting treatments that can improve mood, anxiety, pain, thought, concentration, and memory *and* reduce cardiovascular risk is very exciting. The fact that enhancing emotional wellness can reduce cardiovascular risk is quite remarkable. Recommending lifestyle changes that foster relationships, social connection, mood and hostility management, relaxation response, mindfulness practice, etc., broadens the path to optimal health, particularly when integrated with aspirin, Beta Blockers, and cholesterol-lowering drugs. These multidimensional strategies are consistent with the integrated dimensions of illness, health promotion, and disease prevention that are shaping this new frontier of health care. In this dramatic shift in understanding, more emphasis is placed appropriately on self-care.

Some preliminary evidence has linked positive mood with strong social relationships. Individuals with a more "positive mindset," as measured by standard tools of inquiry, had lower levels of a marker of inflammation that circulates in the blood called interleukin-6 (IL-6). The lower the blood level of IL-6, the lower a person's "inflammatory burden." This we know is clearly important in reducing the risk of heart disease, stroke, and probably

> In this intriguing construct, depression and chronic emotional stress look more like a systemic, physiological process than they do separate, ambiguously connected and abstract states of feeling.

> The fact that enhancing emotional wellness can reduce cardiovascular risk is quite remarkable.

cancer. The inverse is also true. People who are more isolated, lonely, depressed, and anxious generally have higher circulating levels of IL-6. The same can be said about "CRP" or C-reactive protein, another important marker of inflammation.

Here's an example of how diametric thoughts can unleash totally opposite brain, emotion, behavior, and bodily reactions.

Mind	**vs.**	**Mind**
"My friends and family mean a lot to me."		"I feel alone. No one cares about my life."
↓		↓
Emotion		**Emotion**
"It feels great to connect with friends/family."		"I feel sad and lonely."
↓		↓
Brain		**Brain**
Positive enhancement of mood, pleasure, attachment, and pain-modulating neurotransmitters		Negative enhancement of mood, pleasure, etc.
↓		↓
Behavior		**Behavior**
Going out, "connecting"		Staying home, withdrawing
↓		↓
Body		**Body**
Decreased risk of age-related disease		Increased risk of age-related disease

LEARNING TO CHANGE

If you're sad, anxious, or cynical, can you just turn on a switch that will leave you with a rosy glow? Are you genetically imprisoned in sadness or a glass half-empty mentality? Are you a victim of events in your life that have left you traumatized? Many things contribute to how we feel, and I don't intend to suggest that health can be reduced to the patterns of peptides in your brain, which can be easily manipulated. My intent is to examine these interesting connections and to bring to your consciousness the innate potential for adaptation and change.

Until recently, and my medical training/background is pretty good, I would never have imagined that enhancing mood (by whatever method) could reduce heart disease risk as much as a cholesterol-lowering drug might.

When you consider this, you can better appreciate why caring and supportive relationships and social networks improve health outcome. We can see how prayer and meditation, gratitude and forgiveness improve many health outcomes. These actions seem to connect in a manner that enables malleability and change. Lonely people don't have to be lonely. Though some may choose to be, it's not a healthy choice. People who feel they have little to contribute can contribute a lot. People who don't feel loved are capable of feeling love. People without friends are capable of having friends. Anger is capable of coexisting with understanding. Sadness can coexist with forgiveness. Loss can coexist with hope. If you take a moment to consider how your behavior could alter the thought, feeling, brain, and behavior of another person, you can begin to see your potential to touch others. In that sense, we are all healers of self and of others.

Let me share a story that puts this in perspective. My mother, as I have mentioned, had a host of complicated emotional and physical health issues during her life. Depression, heart disease, diabetes, and kidney failure, to name a few, devastated her quality of life. At the tender young age of sixty-two, my family and I thought she might need to be put in a nursing home. For those of you who are caregivers, you can relate to the pain of such a decision. After a series of hospitalizations and with heroic and loving care from my father and sister, my mother returned home. She was a shadow of the person we once knew, and her future was very uncertain. She had no desire to leave her home or interact with others, and her self-esteem had all but been extinguished. We looked into the options for senior care "day-hab" and more socially stimulating settings in the community. She was resistant and convinced that this was a waste of time (*thought*). She felt embarrassed by her level of function and dependence. She was sad and lost. She was untrusting of her ability to function in an unfamiliar setting (*emotion*). This impacted her *behavioral choice* to stay at home, limiting contact with others. This understandable integration of thought, emotion, and behavior would likely add fuel to the fire that her many medical problems posed.

I remember thinking at the time (knowing too much and at the same time not knowing enough) that her prognosis for living longer and living

well was not promising. When confronting profound life change, the anticipation of "what's next" is often worse than the actual experience. Our worst
fears can easily become the assumptions of what the future will bring. My
mother was adamant about not attending the local day-habilitation program.
Finally, with a lot of loving prodding from family and friends, she decided to
go. It turned out to be one of the most joyful and satisfying dimensions to
her life over the next few years, prior to her death. Her thoughts of being "incomplete and unable to contribute" were transformed. In receiving, she was
able to give. And in giving she was better able to receive. The experience was
more positive than any of us had imagined. Her mood, functional capacity,
and quality of life improved to a level I had never expected. It was a dramatic
transformation made possible by one loving family's influence on an individual's connection with others. The therapeutic dividends inherent in these
interactions changed everything. It wasn't the aspirin, the Lipitor, or the
Prozac (though they were playing a role).

AN AGING POPULATION

This is a particularly good example because it represents a growing challenge
in our aging demographic. Many people out there are aging, alone, and mar-
ginally compensated from a health and safety standpoint. Families are more
dispersed, and often the stretched fabric of family support cannot easily "lift"
a loved one. Our nursing homes sometimes become the "default option" often leading to an inexorable decline in an individual's health and quality of
life. While skilled nursing facilities can be the best or sometimes the only option for moving forward, they've become a growth industry, largely because
our community systems of care are simply not designed to keep people in
their homes and neighborhoods.

These are diseases of medical progress and point to the inherent limitations our health care system has in serving you or a loved one. Families confront greater challenges to garner limited resources to keep a loved one at
home. Coalitions of community resources—family, friends, social services,
home care, faith communities—need to be leveraged more effectively. The
end result would be better care, less expense, and improved quality of life for
many individuals whose trajectory is otherwise a poor one.

NURTURING THE PSYCHE

While traits and states of sadness and indifference may not be easy to change, it helps to understand their health implications. Nurturing the psyche is critical to optimal health. Optimistic women, in a study done by Karen Mathews at the University of Pittsburgh, have less thickening of their arteries. Introducing "calm thoughts" like thinking about a dear friend lowers the change in blood pressure during a stressful task. Work deadlines, traffic jams, and marriages with too little mutual attention will understandably have the opposite effect. Most of us have a lot of psyche nurturing that needs to be placed higher on our agenda. And remember, activity is a marvelous psyche-soother that over time will make you a believer in behavioral and lifestyle change. The more you believe, the more the change. The more you change, the more you believe you can continue to change, another positively reinforcing cycle.

> The more you change, the more you believe you can continue to change, another positively reinforcing cycle.

Over the last several years, there's been growing interest in the area of positive emotions. Historically the emphasis has been on the understanding and treatment of negative emotions like despair and anxiety. Returning individuals to emotional states that enabled a safe and meaningful quality of life has always been the desired outcome. Positive emotions tended to receive less interest despite a clear connection between them and better health outcomes.

Martin Seligman, PhD, a professor at the University of Pennsylvania and author of *Learned Optimism* and *Authentic Happiness*, and many of his colleagues have brought much needed attention to this fascinating area. Seligman sees happiness as a function of a biological "set-point" (we each have our own), the circumstances of our lives (over which we have no control), and that which is within our voluntary control. While complex genetic determinants and deeply emotional experiences may influence this "set point of happiness," it is increasingly clear that many of the biological expressions of positive emotions are within the realm of self-control and self-care, particularly when integrated with professional therapy and, in some instances, medication.

Cognitive Behavioral Therapy (CBT), for example, has emerged as a critical process for understanding and treating individuals whose lives feel

out of control. CBT is effective in assisting individuals with a greater understanding of how they feel (emotions), why they feel the way they do
(thoughts), and how they respond (behaviors). The goal is to help individuals repaint the canvas of their lives to integrate feeling, thought, and behavior in a healthier way. I have been focusing on the biology that serves as the
underpinning of this relationship. People can and are capable of transforming fear and anxiety into greater control and equanimity. The neurobiology
that accompanies this change, much like the improvement one sees with exercise, takes time, perseverance, and strong faith in the potential for change
and a strong expectation for a better life.

THE RESILIENCE OF THE HUMAN SPIRIT

I recently experienced an unforgettable encounter that speaks to the extraordinary resilience of the human spirit. It demonstrates the potential we have
as humans to transcend the darkest places. I had been giving a talk on spirituality and health at a local Temple, a topic that I find resonates across a diverse
demographic. After the talk, several people approached me to share thoughts
and provide feedback. A tall, well-groomed man, who appeared to be in his late
forties, made his way over. "Dr. Pettus," he said with some familiarity, "I don't
know if you remember me, but you saved my life over ten years ago."

  I did remember. It had been a beautiful summer day in the Berkshire Hills
of Western Massachusetts. The "deep greens and blues" that James Taylor's time-
less lyrics speak to were in full life. The scene was a lovely area overlooking the
Stockbridge Bowl Lake nestled in the bucolic mountains—quintessential
Norman Rockwell country. On this particular day, as people slowed their cars
for a better view, some passersby noticed someone sitting still and leaning
against the door of an open convertible sports car. A gut feeling (intuition can
be telling if you think of your gut as an extension of your forebrain) tells the
passersby to pull over. On closer inspection, they find an unresponsive young
man with a "butterfly IV" in his arm, some syringes, and several vials of potent pharmaceuticals. He had no identification, but there was a note, heart
wrenching, desperate, and essentially saying goodbye. He was, I would soon
learn, married and had a beautiful young girl who was still a baby.

  I was paged to the emergency department where the staff was desperately
attempting to resuscitate him. He had a host of metabolic derangements upon

arrival, did not appear to have normal organ function, was on a breathing machine, in a coma, and appeared to have placed several potent pharmaceuticals directly into a large vein in his left arm. Dialysis might be his only shot.

He was in a precarious place, and as he was a "John Doe," I had no family to communicate with. I did what I had to do. At moments like this I do pray for individuals whose care I am entrusted with. No one can hear me, but inside I ask for strength and equanimity. I ask for love and hope to fill the souls of those whose lives are on thin ice, for those whose lives I sometimes enter in a random way. A dialysis-trained renal nurse joined me, quickly setting up an emergency dialysis treatment.

As I examined him more closely, listless and on artificial life support, I wondered what circumstances had left him with no perceivable choice other than to take his life? After the "butterfly IV" was removed from his arm, there was enough sun exposure to have burned the superficial layers of skin around the IV, creating a "butterfly IV tan line," on this day, a sad symbol of despair. As I continued the examination, I came upon a ring he was wearing. It was literally the only material object "attached" to him. I looked at it closely and recognized the logo of an outstanding university and thought his name might be engraved inside. The nurses were able to remove it and indeed his name was there. His family was subsequently notified.

After several hours, he began to improve, woke up, and was able to come off the ventilator. I remember thinking, "He never expected to wake up." Our hospital staff had been phenomenal, helping this young man—who would surely have more struggles in life—avoid catastrophe on this beautiful summer day. It was, in my view, a true second chance at a life that just twelve to twenty-four hours earlier had appeared not worth living.

Though his youthful athletic body bounced back from a pretty significant "hit," his thoughts, feelings, and spirit were no more "whole" after a long dialysis treatment than they were before. I was left wondering what his future would hold.

Now, almost thirteen years later, here he was standing before me, smiling, grateful, exuding life, and still apparently searching for meaning (as we all are). His baby girl was now an adolescent. Seeing him happy and assured left me deeply satisfied and feeling great hope. I watched my mother rally many times from the dark depths of depression with the help of family and friends. Her unrelenting faith opened within her a fountain of perpetual belief and meaning. Such resilience is a force available to each of us if we are willing to tap into it.

THE "NUN STUDY"

The "nun study" is an interesting look at personality traits and their long-term effects on health. For more than thirty years, information has been gathered from the School of Sisters of Notre Dame, in Namhuto, Minnesota, and elsewhere. Extensive family and medical history has been available for this group. The nuns had similar food to eat, available medical care, and a style of living much more consistent than most groups enrolled in clinical studies. Many of the nuns also kept hand-written autobiographies allowing researchers, in retrospect, to examine "emotional content." Those who scored higher for positive emotional content at a young age (twenties) were two-and-a-half times more likely to be alive in later life than sisters who had a more negative emotional content. Nuns who aged well had distinct personality traits like a sense of humor. They adapted better and demonstrated a better sense of resilience than some of their peers. Positive emotions perhaps had the effect of dampening the magnitude and duration of the stress response (figure 11.1).

THE WORKPLACE AND ALLOSTATIC LOAD

While work can enhance reward, meaning, and attachment-social responses in positive ways, it also serves as a considerable source of stress. While work-

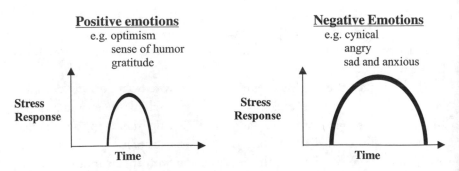

Figure 11.1   Hypothetical Effects of Emotional States on Stress Response

related stress is usually cyclical, the magnitude of the stress "peaks" and the frequency and duration of the cycles can dramatically influence health and wellness.

Deadlines, interpersonal conflict, budget constraints, and disagreeable colleagues can add tremendous stress to life. Memories from bad work expe riences and the emotional context these memories reside in, live on long after your workday ends. The fight-flight stress response so beautifully adapted for the African savannah is not as well adapted for twenty-first century corporate culture. As we all experience, the workplace affects our mood, energy, appetite, sleep, concentration, and in the end, our health. This, I find, is a generally shared experience. What sets us apart is our ME-B^3 response. Some, for example, eat more for the short-term dopamine/opiate reward; others furiously paddle a kayak against the wind.

The Whitehall studies of British civil service workers during the Margaret Thatcher administration point to the work-stress-health connection. At that time, there was considerable interest in the aggressive privatization of government functions. Those employees with the most authority and job security posted the "better" blood pressure, the least weight gain, and the lowest increase in cholesterol, and had greater amounts of restful sleep.

In addition, studies in Scandinavia have demonstrated a strong link between downsizing and illness, and Finnish researchers have shown that the risk of dying from a heart attack doubled after a major downsizing. This risk increased to five times normal after four years!

Swedish researchers after examining a large central health care database of workers (24,000), between 1991 and 1996, found that companies that merged/expanded with resultant expectation for increased productivity, change, and demand for adaptation, had workers who were 7 percent more likely to take sick leave of ninety days or more and 9 percent more likely to enter a hospital. Expansion of greater than 18 percent annual job growth was associated with increased worker stress and worse health outcomes.

White-collar workers, when tested in companies confronting such stressful transitions as reorganization, downsizing, and outsourcing, demonstrated:

- Increased BP
- Increased cholesterol
- Increased CRP, a marker of inflammation

In fact, recent data would suggest that most American workers are stressed out; 62 percent in a 2005 survey said their workload had increased over six months, and half say work leaves them "over tired and overwhelmed." This is not surprising given that 2005 data also shows that U.S. workers worked on average more than 1,800 hours per year; 350 hours more than German workers and slightly more than Japanese and East Asian workers.

Moreover, cell phones, wireless PDAs, and the ubiquitous Internet accessibility leave us virtually connected to work no matter how far away we may be or what time of day it is. However, it's interpersonal stress that leads the way in its insidious contribution to work-related stress and allostatic load. The stress-response induced from interpersonal tension or an overbearing boss will tend to pose a more significant health risk than a deadline, for instance.

The impact of work-related stress on an individual's health is hitting the radar screen of the employer, in part, because it has an enormous impact on the bottom line and success of the organization. It's calculated that work-related stress costs the U.S. $300 billion per year in health care and lost productivity due to:

- Increased absenteeism
- Increased work-related injuries
- Increased health care premiums—double-digit inflation for several years, down to 9.6 percent in 2005. *As an aside, spiraling health care costs have resulted in fewer employer-sponsored covered plans, down 70 to 60 percent at the time of this writing, and more financial responsibility on the worker to cover deductibles, from 10 percent to as much as 40 percent costs. This puts the biggest squeeze on low-income individuals whose wage increases are far below the increases they see in their health care premiums. It's an untenable situation. The increased allostatic load of being a member of a lower socioeconomic class is now accentuated. Eat or have health care coverage. Employers are likely to be further hurt by the impact health care costs has on their employees and on their bottom lines. This is a U.S. crisis!*
- Increased worker's compensation claims for injuries
- Increased presenteeism (being at work when you shouldn't because of illness, etc.), or just showing up with a work ethic best characterized as minimal "discretionary effort"

STRESS AND PERFORMANCE ENHANCEMENT

Stress *can* be beneficial in the enhancement of performance, though the "dose-response" has what I would refer to as a narrow "therapeutic-toxic" window. For example, before an athletic event, stress can be an edge, unless it becomes too great and too sustained, in which case the opposite occurs. You may be familiar with the Yerkes-Dodson Law. When too many demands are imposed on us, we become unable to perform.

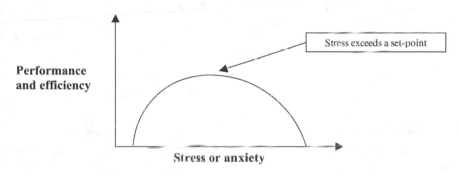

Figure 11.2   The Yerkes-Dodson Law

The Yerkes-Dodson Law is important not only from the standpoint of individual health, but also from the standpoint of employers. An employee on overload will not tell you he's over-stressed because of fear of retribution or fear of being viewed as a weak performer. It might look something like this:

- *Emotion and Memory* (thank you amygdala and limbic system) makes us remember prior experiences with a boss that led to feelings of shame, embarrassment, lack of confidence, etc., and thus we won't share pertinent information.
- *Thoughts* such as "My boss will think less of me" or "I'll never get that promotion" will "advise" you not to share information.
- *Behavior*, e.g., withdrawal and avoidance of co-workers and family, adds to stress.

The Workaholic

The rewards of work can be very positive, eliciting a dopamine-endorphin-opiate response that begs for more. More power, authority, prestige, pay, affirmation, and corporate-social bonding drive the configuration of the value pyramid. The biological imprint of work addiction is not all that different from exercise addiction. It can work for you or against you. The point is to know where you are on your performance-stress load curve. Also, think of your performance at work in the broader context of performance in other aspects of your life.

HOW TO COUNTERACT WORK STRESS

Consider this: research by Dr. Ronald Glaser and his wife Dr. Janice Kilcolt-Glaser demonstrates that the immune systems of highly stressed individuals—as assessed by markers like IL-6 (interleukin 6), where increased levels are associated with such illnesses as vascular disease and arthritis—is similar to that seen in ninety-year-olds. Prayer, in turn, lowers IL-6 levels, as does meditation. The take home message here is: **If you hate your job—start praying**.

The Mind Body Medical Institute (mbmi.org) is an excellent web site. It has a host of information on wellness, mind-body basics, and workplace health. Some basic steps (short of finding a new job, which is sometimes the most courageous option) to reduce some of that unhealthy stress include:

- Make time for breakfast each day (I hear you Mom!)
- Find time (only ten to twenty minutes per day) for meditation, listening to a relaxation tape, or practicing the relaxation response; I personally do the last one. The characteristics of the relaxation response that Dr. Herbert Benson at Harvard has been studying for the last thirty-five years is easy to do and can be effective in as little as five to ten minutes. It involves two basic steps:
    1. Repeat a phrase or word that has a strong belief attached to it. It may be a short prayer, a person's name, or a phrase. Repeat this with every breath.

2.   Dismiss external thoughts that try to enter your mind and return to full mindfulness of your breathing and word or phrase.

- Separate the "urgent and *un*important" from the "non-urgent and important" and channel your energy toward the latter. Urgent is in the eye of the beholder. Many demands on our time and energy are imposed by others who perceive a sense of urgency in their circumstances. You may not perceive the same sense of urgency. Learning to say "no, not now, perhaps another time" is an important step in the direction of placing your personal values above that of others.

- Try to avoid the national workplace pastime of talking negatively about other co-workers. It will not serve you well. The less you say about others, the more people will trust you because you say less about others. The more people trust you, the more they will share. The more they share, the deeper your relationships and understanding become. The deeper your relationships and understanding become, the more influence you will have in your workplace. Influence = control. The more control you have, the happier you will be! You get the picture.

- Get a good night's sleep. I highly recommend a bit of humor at bed time. Laughter right before you fall asleep is a superb "re-set" button for the day to come.

- Smile a lot. Smiles are disarming and deeply "coded" into our social fabric. Is it any coincidence that a child's first smile occurs in infancy? Will any behavior move Mom and Dad more profoundly? Seems like a pretty well ingrained survival skill. Hmmm, maybe I should use it more. No one has ever accused me of being a big baby for smiling.

- Laughter . . . there is no substitute.

- Develop better communication and conflict management skills.

- Try to integrate some activity into your working routine, e.g., taking a walk at break or at lunchtime.

- Cultivate relationships that leave you "feeling good." Minimize those (to the extent possible) that don't.

- Work on relationships you can't avoid that leave you feeling more stressed. This will take some time and can be very challenging. Contrast that, however, with the consuming trajectory you may be on.

- Do not take yourself or others too seriously; this is after all, just a job.

- Have pictures available to look at of those you love and fill your life with joy.

- See the Four-Week Addicted-to-Health Program in Chapter 2 for a synopsis of these strategies.

DON'T TAKE WORK STRESS HOME

If you find yourself beginning to think more about work when you're at home, big trouble. I was a master at this. As thoughts of work enter your consciousness, release them. Go for a walk, listen to some music, call a close friend (preferably one who is upbeat and a good listener), play with your kids, cuddle with someone you love (pets included), or get into a home project you have been putting off.

If possible, integrate some background music or use music at break time that's purposefully selected because it makes you feel good. Remember, this is all about self-care. Do not expect others to recognize and treat the unhealthy stress-burden that is pent up inside you. We all need more tools to foster resilience in our stressful lives.

It helps to periodically pause and take inventory of the tell tale signs that signal the excessive consumption that stress poses in one's life. It's cumulative, insidious, and remarkably hard to detect in those getting more mired down in it. You may notice:

- You're having trouble sleeping.
- You're feeling more impatient and irritable.
- You're deriving less pleasure from things you ordinarily love to do— read, exercise, or spend time with friends.
- Strained relationships with friends and family. This is exceedingly important as you now recognize the biological benefits of healthy relationships in terms of offsetting the stress response. Elicit feedback about the relationship as friends and family will likely notice change before you do and may not feel comfortable sharing feedback without an invitation.
- Losing appetite or, as is often the case, eating more and gaining weight. Remember, eating can elicit a short-term reward response that positively reinforces in the present and hurts like heck in the future.
- More frequent illness—headaches, colds, stomach symptoms, and excessive fatigue. You can now better appreciate the many forms of

the biological "fall out" of stress, including decreased immunity and increased inflammation.

Remember, you're not trapped. There are choices, some will serve you better than others. Keep a journal. Easier said than done, but it reveals a moment in time that creates opportunity for reflection and thoughtful adaptation. Transient and important thoughts and feelings are otherwise easily washed away in the high tide of stress. The other advantage of keeping a journal relates to how our memories work. Nobel Laureate Daniel Kahneman has extensively studied the disparity between our recall of events and what we were experiencing at the time of the event itself. He refers to this as "the experiencing self and the remembering self." His research shows that our memories of events are influenced by the emotional high and low points and by how the experience ends. A good ending to an encounter that may have been shaky is more likely to be recalled as a good encounter. A series of good encounters might be remembered as bad if the most recent one had a strongly negative emotion attached to it. A journal helps us recall the experience, in a way that our memory might recall differently.

BRAIN AND PAIN

More and more people are confronting physical pain in their lives. While we all can anticipate transient pain from a muscle strain, mild injury, or headache, there's a growing prevalence of chronic pain that poses a formidable burden of stress and diminished quality of life. It's estimated that fifty million Americans endure some type of persistent pain that can last for months to years. This includes back pain, headaches, arthritis, cancer pain, neuropathy, etc. While pain is a complex biopsychosocial phenomenon, there are some obvious contributors to the growing challenges of pain management.

- As an aging society, we can expect to live longer with whatever may be causing our pain—degenerative arthritis, osteoporosis, etc.
- A culture that suggests the solution to pain is an outside-to-inside approach, e.g., taking medication, having surgery, etc., as opposed to an inside-to-outside approach, e.g., physical therapy, more activity, social stimulation, meaning-making activities, and other mind-body strategies that enhance our natural opiates and modulate the per-

ception of pain. I certainly do not mean to imply that medications for pain aren't important. They are necessary for many to assure an acceptable level of comfort. However, ongoing mind-body integrative strategies, with the ultimate goal of minimizing medications that have side effects and potential toxicity, will likely serve you better in the long run.

- A dramatic increase in weight and sedentary lifestyles that enhances risk of injuries and interferes with adequate rehabilitation of pain.

- Growing prevalence of mental health problems like depression and anxiety syndromes that from a mind-emotion-brain-behavior-body perspective are linked with our bodies' pain modulation networks. It's now increasingly clear that change in mood and pain frequently coexist because they share similar biological processes.

- All of the above are, of course, pushed over the top by the unprecedented stress in our lives.

Another fascinating area of neuroscience and behavioral science research is beginning to uncover the biological underpinnings of our internal pain system and more novel multi-dimensional targets for pain management. Pain like fear, can protect us from potential harm as a stimulus to withdraw from the source of the pain. I want to feel pain if I'm holding a hot plate in my hand so as to avoid a burn (hot plates look the same as cold plates). Inflammation and the pain that accompanies a sprained ankle, for example, serve as a guide to limit activity, rest, and progress more cautiously.

However many other sources of chronic pain persist in the absence of an identifiable focus of injury or inflammation. We refer to this as nonnociceptive pain. This type of pain can persevere and be resistant to traditional treatments—medications, injections with analgesics, etc. It appears in those chronic pain syndromes that the brain's pain mechanisms fail to turn off or modulate appropriately, going into overdrive.

Research in pain management will lead to more effective analgesic interventions with fewer systemic side effects and addictive and abuse potential. Pain medications, at times extremely helpful and necessary, tend to produce more side effects as their potency increases. As a consequence, attempts to soothe pain in your lower back with more potent analgesics create sedation, fatigue, nausea, and constipation.

I want to briefly examine this issue from the perspective of ME-B³. As I have pointed out, our neurobiological design is capable of modulating pain by production of opiates, dopamine, and GABA, and overlaps intricately with our reward-motivation, attachment-bonding response, and higher levels of cognitive function. Again, at the risk of oversimplification, you can begin to appreciate the fine line between the downward spiral induced by ME-B³ interactions and the positively reinforcing cascade that can "lift" you from the downward slide (see figure 11.3).

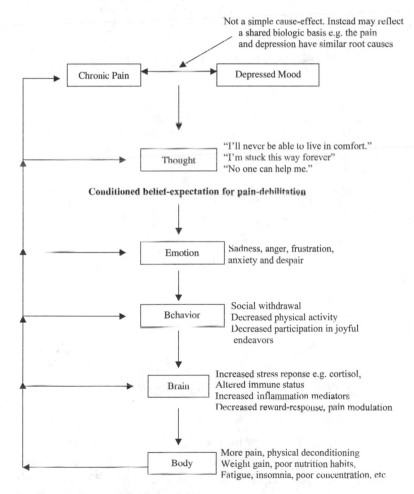

Figure 11.3   The Slippery Slide of Chronic Pain

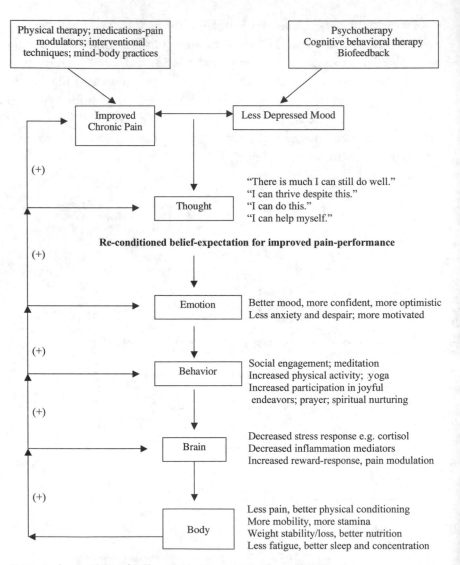

Figure 11.4   Possibilities for Changing the Negative Momentum of Chronic Pain

Consider chronic back pain for a moment. This is a common and challenging problem to treat. We've tended to point to a "logical" explanation for the pain, e.g., a bulging disc or a bone spur. And while these can be the basis for pain, we know that many individuals without any history of back problems will demonstrate bulging of the disc or a bone spur on a low back

MRI. More recent research suggests that the smoking gun may be more in the brain than in the low back. Functional MRI studies demonstrate widespread activation of pain sensation in the brains of individuals with chronic pain in response to a mild stimulus, e.g., a pinprick on the thumb. The response is less vigorous in individuals receiving the same stimulus without a history of chronic pain.

Research is demonstrating how our thoughts/perceptions can be modified to counter or override the experience of a painful stimulus. Recall the studies in Chapter 6 on the placebo effect. Cultivating thoughts of pain relief and an expectation of benefit totally altered the experience of a painful stimulus, an electric shock. This theme of thoughts, perceptions, and emotions acting through the "brain mediator" in a way that can accentuate or diminish pain modulation is a radically different way of examining a common and complex problem. Rehabilitation models that integrate ME-B$_3$ interactions may serve you much more effectively and safely than surgery. Exercise, the one activity we often avoid because it can aggravate pain initially (reinforcing the thought "I can't do this"), can improve muscle strength, flexibility, reduce disability, and improve pain by as much as 30 to 50 percent! With improvement in symptoms, exercise alters perceptions that reduce expectation for pain and enhance expectation for performance improvement. Without any alteration of low back anatomy, something is learned differently in the brain as activity, thought, and emotions become reconfigured. In some studies, six weeks of regular activity were sufficient to allow reduction in potent analgesics and the side effects they produce, a virtual win-win!

SMOKING . . . DODGING THE BULLETS

If you're a smoker and you can kick your butts in the butt, you're stepping on to the first-class section of the longevity train. There is nothing, and I mean nothing, that will have a more immediate effect on your health. When it comes to cardiovascular benefits, you'll begin to experience the benefits immediately. Each cigarette is best thought of as a bullet, capable of taking you out at any time and any place. Each puff carries that potential. The moment you stop, the bullets stop flying.

Effects on blood pressure, vascular constriction and dilatation, inflammation, blood clotting, and a host of other biological effects are immediately diminished when a person stops smoking. The risk of a heart attack or even death is reduced immediately when an individual quits smoking. The cumulative risks of vascular disease can be reversed considerably after five years of smoking cessation. The risk of cancer also becomes minimized after fifteen years of smoking cessation. Smoking is the ultimate threat!

> **The risk of a heart attack or even death is reduced immediately when an individual quits smoking.**

This is a hard habit to break as nicotine is powerfully addicting. That prefrontal "just say no" has a formidable competitor in the limbic "sweeeeet" reward response. With respect to quitting, I would emphasize these points:

- Find a way to quit cigarette smoking that will have a big-time immediate effect on your life. It will be hard, but it's doable. The current strategies that make success more likely include:
  - Clear understanding of the risks and benefits of quitting
  - Strong degree of motivation—health, family, friends
  - Readiness for change (often triggered by a meaningful event, e.g., a death or a birth of a child)
  - Pharmacological strategies, e.g., Bupropion (generic), nicotine patches
  - Partnering with a health care professional throughout the process
- See each puff as a shot heard in the distance, one of which may be intended for you.
- Cold turkey approaches are successful less than 5 percent of the time.
- Throw everything you can at the habit and remember, plasticity is on your side.

With the exception of the epidemic of obesity, nothing impacts public health in a more devastating way than smoking. Anyone who smokes will be quick to point out that knowledge of its many dangers is not enough to kick the habit. People can and do quit; however, even with aggressive multi-pronged approaches—education, counseling, nicotine replacement strategies (gum, patches, sprays), and craving-stabilizing drugs like Wellbutrin—the most successful nicotine cessation programs achieve a 25 to 35 percent success rate.

Recent neuroscience research has shed more light on the neurochemical effects of nicotine, why it's so addictive, and why it's so hard to quit. These insights will lead to more novel strategies to target the organ that produces pleasure in response to a habit that can be expected to shorten a person's life expectancy by at least ten years.

Researchers at the University of Michigan, using PET Scanning technology and a novel morphine like "tracer," have demonstrated brain responses for nicotine not unlike that seen with morphine and heroin. When individuals smoke, there's a surge of activity in the brain pleasure-reward-response circuitry. Dopamine and endorphins again are the key players. Dopamine and endorphin activity goes up in the anterior cingulate cortex region of the brain and goes down in the amygdala, thalamus, and nucleus accumbens. These neurotransmitter responses leave a person feeling more relaxed, calmer, more satisfied, and more in control. This, not unlike a "runners high," is a formidable state of reward, easily overwhelming any knowledge of risk. This after all, defines addictions and addictive behavior.

SLEEP: NOT TO BE TAKEN FOR GRANTED

It's amazing to me that despite the burgeoning biomedical research and the technical juggernaut of the twenty-first century, we keep coming back to the basics in regard to self-care in health promotion and disease prevention. The most effective interventions are under some degree of self-control— "low tech" interventions like eating better, being more active, seeking and fulfilling sources of value and meaning in your life, and oh yes, sleep. It's hard to fathom the impact that non-restorative sleep has on the health, safety, and the economic barometer of our social enterprise.

> The most effective interventions are under some degree of self-control— "low tech" interventions like eating better, being more active, seeking and fulfilling sources of value and meaning in your life, and oh yes, sleep.

Research tools are now making possible greater insights into the biological underpinnings of sleep, and the biologic/health fallout of chronic non-restorative sleep and insomnia. There must be some reason we require several hours of sleep per day. Allostatic load and the burden on health and wellness are clearly related to a lack of sleep. Neurotransmitters of interest are melatonin, acting as the brains "internal clock," hypocretin, and adenosine.

Current medications prescribed for sleep stimulate GABA (gamma amino butyric acid), inducing a state of drowsiness and sedation. Side effects like memory problems and a risk of potential oversedation and falls are significant downsides. I'd put a good night's sleep very high on the list of most important health-promoting activities with the potential to enhance concentration, improve mood and energy, and make more likely other health-promoting behaviors like increased activity. There are not many things that can help you cope with stress better than a good night's sleep.

Sleep is characterized by natural cycles of activity in the brain. Two basic states include REM (rapid eye movement) and non-REM, consisting of four stages. Each of non-REM sleep's stages can last five to fifteen minutes. Stages two and three repeat backwards before REM sleep is attained. Polysomnograms that measure brain waves during sleep show a 50 percent reduction in activity between wakefulness and stage one non-REM sleep. An individual aroused during the stage may not feel as if he or she has slept. Stage two is light sleep with periods of muscle relaxation and diminished heart rate and body temperature. Stage three and four are deeper levels of sleep with brain tracings showing slower, "delta waves."

During non-REM sleep, the body restores itself, regenerating tissues and strengthening immune function. As you get older, non-REM or restorative sleep drops off from two hours under the age of thirty to thirty minutes in people over sixty-five. REM sleep usually occurs ninety minutes after you fall asleep. REM sleep is cyclical with each recurring stage longer, the final one lasting an hour. Normally, heart and respiratory rate speed up and muscles may twitch during REM sleep. Dreaming, sometimes intense, occurs during REM sleep. Interestingly, there is heightened brain excitement on one hand and muscular immobility on the other. Have you ever suddenly become more conscious from deep sleep, aware you are awakening and unable to move? It's a frightening experience.

We tend to have less REM sleep as we age. It would appear that most adults need seven to eight hours of sleep each day. This increases for an individual who has been sleep deprived. Most people, and this has been my experience as I age, do not adapt well to getting less sleep than they need.

There are many reasons why people have difficulty getting a healthy dose of regular sleep. This is a topic far beyond the scope of this book. Sleep requires synchronized activity of the brain; and problems interfering with sleep have diverse biological fallout, much of which is related to an inability to optimally manage stress, and the manifestations of an increased allostatic load such as impaired memory, thought, depression, and decreased immune response. Increases in cardiovascular risk are now also recognized in people with impaired sleep. And if you have kids of adolescent age, as I do, there's a constant struggle to establish healthy sleep patterns. Why sleep when you can now watch *Trading Spaces* at 1 a.m. and Instant Message your friends until the last friend is no longer conscious? Optimal memory and learning requires good daily sleep, particularly "procedural memories," which help people learn skills like playing an instrument or perfecting a gymnastic move.

Some evidence shows that during sleep the brain may reprocess newly learned information. Sleep may be critical in getting newly processed information into memories that stick. When it comes to optimizing the learning experience, less TV and computers, and more ZZZZs please.

Some simple steps can lead to a good night's sleep:

- Try to avoid eating within two hours of bedtime

- Regular aerobic exercise is marvelous in promoting deeper sleep, though should be avoided two to three hours prior to bedtime.

- Try to go to bed at a regular hour each night. Your circadian rhythm (and the neurohormonal mechanisms that are involved with sleep) will be in better balance.

- Don't ignore the snore. It could be a manifestation of obstructive sleep apnea. This is a very common and often unrecognized health problem. You'll find lifestyle and behavior modification an essential part of this treatment.

- Minimize excessive light and noise. Your sleeping environment should be as quiet and peaceful as possible.

- Relaxation techniques at bedtime like progressive muscle relaxation or the relaxation response with focus on a calming word, phrase and slow rhythmic relaxed breathing can help calm, promoting better sleep.

- Caffeine should be avoided at least four to six hours before bedtime.

- If your pets tend to sleep on your bed, consider setting up a bed for them on the floor next to your bed.

- Nicotine is a stimulant and should be avoided, especially near bedtime.

- Alcohol, while it is sedating and can assist with falling asleep, tends to have more stimulating effects as it is metabolized during the night, particularly when ingested regularly in amounts exceeding one ounce (more than one drink).

- If you tend to work at home, try to complete your tasks at least one hour before retiring.

- Melatonin, a hormone secreted in the brain during the night that appears to help some people sleep, has been successful to varying degrees, particularly for jet lag. The dose amount and timing may influence success here. In my experience, people often require up to 3 to 10 mg, thirty minutes before bedtime to benefit. As an aside, Melatonin has potent antioxidant effects and may protect against many age-related diseases in lower doses than what are necessary to assist with sleep.

- The amino acid supplement L-Tryptophan has also been shown in some studies to assist with sleep. More information is needed.

Last, and by no means least, if you're sleeping with a partner, hold them close each night and tell them how much they mean to you. Also, spend a moment to reflect quietly on those things for which you feel grateful. This simple end of the day reflection will immediately begin to dissolve the stress of another day gone by and prepare you for the experiences that await. What better way could there be to end your day?

Chapter 12

Religion, Spiritual Practice, and Health Outcomes: Are We Designed to Believe?

"With all that science, can you tell me how light enters the soul?"

Henry David Thoreau

The connection between mind-body interactions and spirituality, science, and health is a fascinating one. It is here at the nexus of science and spirituality that ancient wisdom is made new, our motivation to seek answers is rejuvenated, and our context as human beings is broadened. In the dance of science and spirituality, our steps, interpretations, and expressions are both individual and shared. It is in this spotlight and on this part of the dance floor that I find myself spending more time and interest as a physician.

My interest is in part personal as I have valued religious and spiritual dimensions in my own life and was raised in a home that placed great value on faith. Many times, I've found my faith a buoyant comfort under duress. Another facet of interest is my work as a health care professional and consumer advocate. This work has brought me closer to people in more meaningful ways. It is within this nexus, in this spotlight, and on this area of the dance floor that I've felt more connected to others. Neither science nor spirituality alone could allow me to fully experience the depth and richness of this space.

I speak often about spirituality and health, and I always find this to be a topic people are interested in. There's an element of curiosity when a physician publicly addresses such issues. Perhaps this says something about how infrequently such an exchange occurs in a health care setting. My experience has been that people value this dialogue and are usually anxious to share. When I speak in public on themes of spirituality and health, I'm mindful of the need to define my language as words like "religion," "spirituality," and "faith" have many individual interpretations and are sometimes used interchangeably. In addressing health care professionals, I'm quick to point out the signpost on the road I am traveling that reads, "You are now leaving the Town of Facts and entering the Town of Faith."

It is in the Town of Faith where our certainty is based more on feeling than on fact. While issues of science and spirituality can ignite diverse and passionate perspectives, I feel there is sufficient space for these views to co-exist and inform. My primary interest is what our current understanding of the relationship between science and spirituality has to say about the biological underpinnings of religious and spiritual practice. It's fascinating to explore how these relationships awaken us to the powerful connections of mind, body, and spirit. They also add a critical dimension to the importance and significance of self-care.

I'm going to attempt to make the case for some thoughts I know will be provocative, perhaps contentious, and definitely based on varying degrees of good empiric evidence. I usually expect the ignition of passion in others, with meaningful and varied perspectives emerging. It is in this exhilarating nexus of science and spirituality that I find myself an intrepid explorer, wearing many hats.

As I noted, there's a danger in drilling too deep without first defining some terms. I view religion (from a Judeo-Christian perspective) as an organized set of teachings, doctrines, rituals, and practices that facilitate closeness to God. While religious experience is deeply personal and individual, there is usually a strong dimension of

> While religious experience is deeply personal and individual, there is usually a strong dimension of community that is experienced. Spirituality, on the other hand, is more a quest for understanding, meaning, and purpose that nurtures a deeper connection to our individual values.

community that is experienced. Spirituality, on the other hand, is more a quest for understanding, meaning, and purpose that nurtures a deeper connection to our individual values. It may or may not lead to the development of religious ritual and community. Faith, though often thought of in a religious context, implies strong belief and expectations of individual beliefs.

The biological underpinnings of faith and health that are shown to benefit individuals are not necessarily confined to religious practice or a spiritual experience of self-transcendence. Atheists who do not believe God exists and agnostics who are skeptical of the existence of God still may follow a framework of belief. For example, secular humanism is capable of eliciting similar health-promoting effects. The strength of your individual belief and the expectation of meaning derived from the belief, independent of the religious or spiritual underpinning, has inherent potential health value.

RESILIENCE IN THE FACE OF OUR OVERWHELMING WORLD

It's too easy these days to witness the many stories of human tragedy and suffering in our nation and in our world. Global communication has enabled the media to enter our lives 24/7 with details, usually of sad and emotionally negative events, happening around the world. The depth and magnitude of such human drama has never been more accessible. Watching, reading, and listening to the news can deflate the most buoyant of spirits. As I write this chapter, I am attuned to the horrible tragedies of Hurricanes Katrina and Rita that have devastated the Gulf Coast and Texas, and demoralized the collective spirit of our nation. I am witnessing with stunning sadness, the aftermath of the earthquake in Pakistan that has taken the lives of at least 40,000 people and has left millions homeless, lost, and broken.

And yet, like the unspeakable events of "9-11," from the rubble of grief and suffering emerges the resilience of the human spirit and an unprecedented collective consciousness of benevolence and courage. This benevolence has taken the form of heroic rescues, stories of survival, and people donating time and money to fellow humans in need. People desperate and broken sit atop piles of rubble that have buried their families and pray to survive another day.

William Levi, author of *The Bible or the Axe*, has experienced first hand the horrors of ethnic violence in southern Sudan. Millions of refugees wander without food, water, or medical care. Many of them are orphaned children who have lost their parents to violence. It's hard for most Americans to appreciate the magnitude of these horrors. When I asked William Levi what his greatest source of motivation was to survive another day, he responded, "Faith. Faith was the promise of a better day to come, drawing them forward one day at a time."

These compelling stories of hope, courage, faith, resilience, generosity, and compassion are powerful expressions of the universal human motivation to reach beyond the self. This universal tendency for self-transcendence and the human design that inspires it are the focus of this chapter.

SPIRITUALITY AND HEALTH CARE

Though the pendulum of medical education and health care is slowly moving in the direction of greater sensitivity and awareness of the role that spirituality and religion play in the lives of those we serve, the psychospiritual contexts of many people's lives and the spiritual wounds that accompany them often go unrecognized and unexplored in health care encounters. There are no X-Rays or blood tests that can pick up a spiritual wound. Health care professionals and patients are not often engaged in a manner that enables these issues to be sensitively and effectively addressed. As the Dalai Lama once said, "The practice of compassion allows us to see how much alike we really are."

> There are no X-Rays or blood tests that can pick up a spiritual wound.

While there are many reasons for this "disconnect," the nature of spiritual wounds sometimes makes them difficult to recognize and discuss. They rarely jump out and say, "Here I am. I need to be fixed." They tend to be more obvious when seen through the nonverbal look in the eyes of another than they are via the spoken word. The doors most begging to be open, in my experience, are often found in the quiet subtitles of our interpersonal interactions. And as I am sure you have experienced, health care professionals for many reasons are not often attuned to the nonverbal expressions that hint at greater meaning beneath the surface of our interactions. These critical dimensions to the health care experience are not in the same category as an objective, "tangible and measurable" concern like a broken bone, elevated blood pressure, high cholesterol, or a change on an electrocardiogram. So how does a spiritual wound manifest itself? Here are a few common expressions I have frequently encountered in experiencing spiritual wounds with others.

- Loss of meaning
- Loss of purpose
- Loss of hope
- Shame
- Guilt
- Isolation, loneliness, abandonment
- Suffering
- Reconciling unhealed wounds
- Diminished sense of self-value and worth

When I was in training more than twenty years ago, there was no formal instruction, discussion, or curriculum addressing spirituality. It was nowhere near the radar screen. Any discussion of religion or spirituality, in the context of health, disease, and patient care was best left to the individual and to pastoral care. And this exchange at best was left to chance. The only time prayer came up in medical school was prior to taking exams. The only time it came up as a resident was prior to another long night of call when we prayed for as much sleep as possible.

IMPORTANCE OF RELIGIOUS AND SPIRITUAL BELIEF AND PRACTICE IN THE U.S.

Many published surveys have examined American thought and practice relating to belief in God, religious commitment, and prayer. The data from these surveys mirrors the predominant Judeo-Christian religious practice in the U.S. However, there is a growing number of people in America who value and practice Islamic, Buddhist, and Hindu worldviews.

Most surveys consistently suggest that more than 90 percent of Americans "believe in God." Many (50 to 75 percent) view the Bible as the actual or inspired word of God. Many Americans (50 to 75 percent) say they pray regularly and, depending on the survey, 30 to 40 percent attend religious services at least once a week. This, in my view, has important significance regarding self-care.

In 2003, the Joint Commission for Accreditation Health Care Organization (JCAHCO), an independent organization that contracts services with

the government to assure safe and effective standards of care for Medicare recipients, published
data from almost two million individuals regarding preferences for medical care. This is a huge

> **Meeting spiritual and emo-
> tional needs was the most
> common priority noted.**

database! Meeting spiritual and emotional needs was the most common priority noted.

Most ancient worldviews see the process of healing and living fully as a natural confluence of the physical and the spiritual. While people have used prayer and spiritual practices for their own and other's concerns for thousands of years, only recently has more research been done in this area. In a study released in 2004 by the National Center for Health Statistics and the National Center for Complementary and Alternative Medicine (NCCAM), 62 percent of the 31,000 adults studied reported using a form of complementary and alternative medicine within the prior twelve months for treatment of an illness. Prayer was included as a form of complementary alternative medicine (CAM). As an aside, "integrative" is a much better term than complementary as the biological mechanisms that underlie spirituality, religion, and health are true integrations of mind, body, and spirit. Some of the findings include:

- 45 percent used prayer for health reasons
- 43 percent had prayed for their own health
- 25 percent had others pray for them
- 10 percent had participated in a prayer group for their health

The American experience of religious and spiritual belief and practice commonly, and in some instances, strongly influences:

- The context within which individuals examine and understand the experience of illness and healing
- Patterns of coping and self-care
- Medical decision-making, particularly regarding advanced directives and end-of-life care
- Dimensions and avenues of healing not routinely addressed in Western biomedical-oriented models of health care.

For many Americans, expressions of faith through prayer or worship are the first and most significant response to illness. As many as two out of three people say they would want their physician to address this dimension of their lives during illness, particularly more serious illness. Rarely, less than 10 percent of the time, do issues of religion, faith, or spirituality come up in the context of a health care encounter. There is a perva-

> For many Americans, expressions of faith through prayer or worship are the first and most significant response to illness.

sive disconnect between the role faith plays in health and healing and how effectively it is addressed by treating clinicians. Wounds, sometimes painfully obvious, are never acknowledged. Medical decision making, coping strategies, and sources of community support that might become an integral component of a multidimensional plan of therapy are never fully realized.

I have on occasion prayed with a patient or family at their request. I'm not suggesting that this is appropriate for all encounters. A visit for a cough is not the same as a visit to discuss whether or not to continue chronic hemodialysis. After a talk I gave in our community on this topic, a woman who had been in the audience approached. She said she had thought many times about asking her primary care provider about his views on faith and prayer but felt uncomfortable bringing up the topic. "Why do you feel uncomfortable?" I asked. "Oh, he's very busy, and I'm afraid I'll make him feel awkward," she replied.

Her hesitations are not atypical. Such conversations can understandably feel awkward at first because they're not perceived as appropriate. The perception is that they're too personal. This, I find amusing. Too personal? Have you had a colonoscopy, mammogram, or PAP smear recently? Are these standards of care less personal than a discussion of faith? I'd much rather talk about my views about God than to have a digital rectal exam to check my prostate. How about sharing a prayer instead of putting that illuminating scope up my rectum and through my colon?

The paradox is that most people would feel more comfortable waiting for their doctor to bring up the topic of spirituality because they don't want their doctor to feel uneasy and awkward. Most doctors I speak to (who find this topic important because doctors, after all, are people too) would feel more comfortable if the patient brought up the topic because they don't want their patients to feel uneasy by raising an issue that is perceived as inappropriate. As a result, it hardly ever comes up! It's ironic that a topic like this, so significant in its healing and self-care implications, can be perceived as taboo.

I remember being trained to talk to patients about sex and sexual preferences. These were mutually awkward and uneasy conversations to have. Then came along this virus called HIV. Now, under some circumstances, it would be considered substandard medical care not to have this discussion, given the implication for diagnosis and treatment. This is another good example of perception (awkward and inappropriate), emotion (shame, fear, and embarrassment), and behavior (avoidance) resulting in an outcome that falls way short of possibility. The health implications can be enormously significant.

I was appearing as a guest on a national television program to discuss this topic as part of a promotional tour for my book *The Savvy Patient*. I was sitting in "the green room" waiting to go on with another guest. He was a well-known gospel singer who several years earlier, while performing, became acutely short of breath. He quickly deteriorated into a critical state and ended up at the University of Michigan Medical Center. He required emergency surgery to save his life. What the surgeon found upon opening his chest was a huge collection of blood around his heart from a major blood vessel that had torn and was leaking. It seemed very unlikely he would survive this catastrophic event. The surgeon, while the fellow was under anesthesia, exited the operating room and asked the family if they wanted to come into the operating room to share their final wishes as his chances for survival seemed negligible. The family asked the surgeon to pray with them. Together they stood, hand in hand, around this young man confronting his mortality.

The surgeon, who did not consider himself religious, said (from a remote satellite television link as he shared his story) that he experienced an ineffable feeling of hope and optimism as he proceeded to do the best he could in response to the family's wishes. He described a deeply spiritual experience. The rest is history. Seven years later the singer's health was back, his strength was continuing to slowly improve, he had just recorded another gospel CD, and his purpose in life had never been experienced with greater inspiration and resolve. He had lived and experienced (as did his surgeon) a most remarkable story that could not have more aptly spoken to the points I had come to make.

Here's another example of how faith perspectives can influence the experience of illness and healing. Some years ago, I cared for E.C., a woman in her sixties. She had experienced severe depression for which she was being treated. She had kidney failure, requiring chronic dialysis to keep her alive.

She'd been on dialysis for years and was slowly failing. Her numerous medical problems took away her independence, and she was forced to be in a skilled nursing home facility. She was clearly suffering, and I struggled with her demise. Despite our best efforts, her quality of life continued to decline.

During a hospitalization she became quite tearful, took my hand, and said to me, "Dr. Pettus, I simply cannot go on any more. I have thought about quitting dialysis for some time. It's a decision that torments me." "Tell me more about how you feel," I replied, looking directly into her eyes that spoke of insurmountable grief and despair. She went on to say that she felt tormented because she did not feel God would agree with her decision to stop dialysis, a decision that would soon thereafter, end her life. Her faith and her relationship with God were too important to risk that. Her perception was that she would be eternally judged for making conscious choice to end her life, the most precious of God's gifts.

Now this is a deep spiritual wound if ever there was one. It is also an example of how a faith perspective can be a source of pain as well as comfort. When I explored this with her in more detail, I learned that she was a member of a local faith community. Many members of her congregation were in fact her closest and only friends. She had no family she was connected with. She had a close relationship with her pastor, but she hadn't shared these feelings with him. My partner and I arranged a meeting with her pastor, who along with other church members came often to talk with her. She was eventually able to reconcile her conflicts with the assurance that stopping dialysis would result in a "natural" death. She was able to see that dialysis itself that was not "natural." By stopping she would allow what was natural and from her faith perspective, acceptable to occur.

After more conversation and support, she made the decision not to undergo further dialysis. Her demeanor was calmer. She had an equanimity about her that I had not previously observed. She died soon thereafter with those she knew and trusted at her bedside, softly singing the hymns that had so often lifted her spirits and comforted her.

Not surprisingly, faith practices are an enormous source of comfort and satisfaction in the lives of many Americans. In a 2004 *Time* magazine poll, one thousand American adults were surveyed about sources of happiness in their lives. With respect to money, it's clear that once an individual can meet their basic needs, additional income does little to raise satisfaction with life.

The four top responses to behaviors most frequently chosen to improve mood:

- Talking to friends and family, 57 percent respondents
- Listening to music, 53 percent
- Praying and meditating, 45 percent
- Helping others in need, 42 percent

Martin Seligman, of the University of Pennsylvania, has extensively researched positive emotions. His work and that of others in the field has revealed that a person's depth of engagement with work, play, family, and faith were critical determinants of happiness. Using personal strengths to serve a larger purpose (we have examined this as "the meaning maker") is also strongly correlated with positive emotions. The biologic underpinnings of reward (the dopamine-opiate mediators of pleasure and satisfaction) and their neutralizing effects on the stress response are consistent with these findings. Religion, spirituality, and prayer, for example, are deeply engaging and meaningful human endeavors for many. Therefore, it's not surprising that people turn to faith when under stress and in need of comfort. The consequence is often one of just "feeling better."

THE MEDICAL EVIDENCE LINKING SPIRITUAL AND RELIGIOUS PRACTICE WITH HEALTH OUTCOMES

There's been a proliferation of published articles on this subject in the medical literature over the last ten years. Dr. Harold Koenig—co-director of the Center for Spirituality, Theology, and Health at Duke University—is a national leader in this field. He found, for example, that between 2000 and 2002, more than a thousand articles were published in this area as compared with just one hundred between 1980 and 1982.

Part of this growing interest stems from a shift in the American health care demographic. We're experiencing older age, more chronic disease, and more unique biopsychospiritual challenges of meaning and context that have intensified over the last generation. Issues of spirituality, religion, faith, and health perhaps have greater relevance as we confront these growing challenges of social health. We also have more interesting scientific tools like brain imaging and measurements of immune response that can now be applied in a more rigorous fashion to inform a biologic basis for these connections. While good research will raise good questions as much as it will provide good answers, there's never been a more interesting time to study the relationship between spirituality, religion and health outcomes.

I should make note of a few important themes that run like a loose thread through the fabric of this research.

- The overall quality of the research, applied methodology, and individuals studied vary considerably, making generalizations more speculative than certain.

- Many of the studies focus more on organized religion because there are some objective measurable elements like attendance at worship, prayer, use of devotionals, etc., that are somewhat easier to grasp than in the study of the more individual nuances of spiritual practice.

- The tools (usually surveys and questionnaires) used to assess religiosity and spirituality have varying degrees of validity and reproducibility. Also, different researchers define prayer, spirituality, and related concepts in different ways.

- Individuals studied are predominantly Caucasian Christians.

- Perhaps, people who go to church are healthier because you have to be well to get there in the first place (we refer to this as selection bias)

With that caveat emptor out of the way, I have studied this literature in detail, held it against my personal and professional experiences, and cannot escape the conclusion that there is an incredible connection here, valid, and enormously important. These connections have profound personal and public health implications. Here is a cross-section of what some of the studies examining the relationship between religion, prayer, spiritual practice, and health outcomes shows:

- Older adults attending worship regularly were half as likely to have elevated blood levels of interleukin 6 (IL-6). This is a marker of inflammation that can be measured in the blood. Other markers of inflammation were noted to be reduced as well. Lower is definitely better. You may recall that people with depression, chronic emotional stress, and hostility have significantly higher circulating levels of these inflammatory markers. Mindfulness meditation practice interestingly lowers IL-6 levels as prayer does.

- In individuals confronting chronic disease and advanced terminal illness, religious beliefs and a more personal relationship with God were more positively correlated with life satisfaction, contentment, and diminished pain and anxiety.

- The extent to which a patient's religious faith was a central motivating force in their lives, strongly predicted better outcomes in severe depression.

- Gratitude, forgiveness, God as personal support, and social religiosity were associated with reduced risk for depression, anxiety disorder, bulimia, and alcohol and drug abuse or dependence.

- In high school adolescents, worship attendance, prayer, and other measures of religiosity are linked to better decision making, lower rates of teen pregnancy, suicidal ideations, and other high risk behaviors. Higher academic and social competence was also noted.

- Women on chronic hemodialysis (certainly true of my mother) note better psychosocial adjustment and self-perceived quality of life satisfaction with religious and spiritual well-being.

- Attendance at religious service and the personal importance of an individual's relationship with God enhanced the likelihood of living longer. This was an independent factor after taking consideration of other health risks, e.g., smoking, high blood pressure, etc.

- Religious people, in addition to being less depressed and anxious than non-religious people, seem more resilient in response to setbacks.

- Prayer has been linked to reductions in cardiovascular risk.

- Religious and spiritual support has been effective when integrated with other therapies in assisting with symptom management in people with chronic and terminal disease.

Some current research sponsored by the National Institute of Health (NIH) is examining:

- Spirituality in the context of chronic illness. The connection between spirituality (as measured by standardized tools that examine meaning, peace, faith, religious coping, and religious activity) and health outcomes in individuals with HIV/AIDS

- Spirituality, immunity, and emotional well-being in individuals with cancer

- The interplay of spiritual practices with positive psychological states on resilience and health outcomes.

Many plausible reasons exist as to why a strong faith and religious or spiritual perspective could influence health outcomes. Healthier lifestyle habits, coping support, prayer (as a form of meditation and relaxation response), and more supportive social networks of caring friends are known to influence health. I'll elaborate more on the mind-emotion-brain-behavior-body (ME-B^3) mechanisms, which may play an important role in these effects.

I need to add that health benefits from "the faith factor" depend more on the individual intensity of a person's spiritual commitment than on their particular faith tradition. Of course, these spiritual-health connections would have come as no surprise to Jesus in the Christian tradition, Moses Maimonides from the Jewish tradition, or Avicenna from the Muslim tradition, to name a few noteworthy spiritual healing authorities of the last three thousand years. Hindu, Buddhist, and shaman traditions also see healing as a spiritual journey.

A "NON-SELF" PERSPECTIVE

A "non-self" perspective for examining life, particularly when ill, allows a transcendence of pain and suffering by offering a context of hope, meaning, and purpose. While these practices do not erase the problems that people confront, they often enable people to coexist in a more calm, meaningful, and satisfying way. This underscores the distinction between curing and healing, a distinction we struggle with in biomedical models of care. Curing implies the restoration of normal biological structures and functions, such as full recovery for pneumonia. Healing implies a broader peace, comfort, and capacity to coexist positively, even when a problem cannot be reversed—cancer, kidney failure. The evidence supporting mind-body integration is clear. Prayer and meditation can decrease levels of stress hormones that have many adverse health implications. Positive attributes embodied in world faith traditions, such as love, generosity, and forgiveness are also known to have positive effects on immune function, mediators of inflammation, mood, and cardiovascular health.

> Positive attributes embodied in world faith traditions, such as love, generosity, and forgiveness are also known to have positive effects on immune function, mediators of inflammation, mood, and cardiovascular health.

Stephanie Brown, a researcher at the Institute for Social Research at the University of

Michigan, and her colleagues have found that by helping others, people help themselves. The ancient wisdom that giving is better than receiving just may have been a prescription for good health, in addition to its inherent altruistic virtues. As Carolyn Schwartz, a social scientist asserts, "When you open your heart to other people to listen and care about them, it changes the way you look at the world and you're happier." The ME-B³ interactions we have examined, from a health and healing perspective, are designed to reinforce these ways of living. As it turns out, the Golden Rule is excellent advice for good health and it is inspired in all worldviews. For example:

- **Christianity**. Therefore all things whatsoever ye would that men should do to you, do ye even so to them: For this is the law of the prophets. *The King James Bible, New Testament*
- **Judaism**. That which you hold as detestable, do not do to your neighbor. That is the whole Law. *Talmud, Shabbat*
- **Islam**. None of you is a believer if he does not desire for his brother that which he desires for himself. *Sunnah*
- **Hinduism**. Such is the sum of duty: Do not do to others that which, to you, would do harm to yourself. *Mahabharata*
- **Buddhism**. Injure not others in the manner that would injure you. *Udana-Varga*
- **Confucianism**. (Here certainly is the golden maxim.) Do not do to others that which we do not want them to do to us. *Analects*
- **Taoism**. Regard your neighbor's gain as your gain, and your neighbor's loss as your own loss. *T'ai Shang Kan Ying P'ien*

I would be remiss not to touch on the potential negative impacts that faith perspectives can have on health and healing. All is not always positive in the interface of spirituality, religion, and health. Just as religion or faith perspectives can serve as an enormous source of comfort and positive biological repercussion, it can become a source of deep conflict and pain. There is nothing health promoting about holy wars. There are individuals whose faith perspectives are a deep source of conflict—feeling punished or abandoned by God, or not worthy of

> All is not always positive in the interface of spirituality, religion, and health. Just as religion or faith perspectives can serve as an enormous source of comfort and positive biological repercussion, it can become a source of deep conflict and pain.

good health. Some individuals may experience accentuated pain and resentment if they feel obliged to feel or think the way another person is suggesting they feel or think. Dr. Jimme Holland, a psychiatrist at Memorial Sloan-Kettering Cancer Center in New York City, refers to this as "tyranny of positive thinking." It's also possible that a more fundamentalist religion or spiritual mindset can lead to a dismissal of modern medical science. Horrible health outcomes are well described when an individual denies traditional health care on the basis that faith alone is all that's necessary. I'm a firm believer that for many individuals, prayer plus Prozac is better than either alone.

> I'm a firm believer that for many individuals, prayer plus Prozac is better than either alone.

SPIRITUALITY AND HEALTH: MIND-BODY CONNECTIONS, NEUROSCIENCE, AND THE FAITH FACTOR

When you examine the dimensions of faith, religion, and spirituality from a neuroscientific perspective, you can begin to see legitimized a physiological basis for the positive health outcomes reported in medical literature. This is truly a remarkable story. For example, consider the mind-emotion-brain-behavior body (ME-B^3) implications from what I have reviewed to his point:

- Attachment and bonding are central to the spiritual experience. Transcendence of "self" enables a greater connectedness to others. Community and social connections very much define the core of religious experience. An individual with a deeply personal relationship with a divine (non-self) presence is experiencing a deep connection with considerable meaning attached to it. An individual who is connected to others in a network of support and shared experiences is engaged in broader relationships. These support networks are an invaluable resource for surviving and surviving well, particularly as immediate family are typically more dispersed and less able to offer day-to-day support. As one of the most important contributors to aging well, we understand the effects that relationship, attachment, and social bonding have on regions in the brain that produce oxytocin, dopamine, and opiate/endorphins. This cascade of positive biology produces feelings of bliss, joy, and euphoria. The attachment reward response is also an effective mechanism for keeping the negative health effects of unrelenting stress in check. The cumulative consequences include fostering more positive emotions, eliciting health-promoting physiology, and reinforcing a level of motivation to pursue behaviors (like mindfulness meditation, or prayer) that positively reinforce this cycle.

- We know that creation of deep meaning and value satisfaction, in service of a greater purpose, enhances this same attachment-reward "meaning-maker response."

- Many faith practices promote healthier behaviors. For example, lower rates of smoking, alcohol consumption, and inactivity are often seen in active participants of faith-based communities. Personal relationships and marriage (health promoting) are also nurtured in this context.

- If the current understanding of the placebo effect suggests anything, it is that the depth of belief, conviction, and expectation can have profound health-promoting biological effects—enhanced mood, lower anxiety levels, and more effective pain management. Individuals cultivating the faith factor—strong belief, expectation of valued outcomes, and a meditative relaxation-prayer response—are creating an internal "spa-like" experience. Prefrontal lobe clarity of thought and focus are accompanied by reward enhancement, mitigation of the stress response, and reinforcement of health-promoting behaviors.

- The evidence is consistent with the neutralizing effects that positive belief systems, attachment in relationships, and creating and fulfillment of meaning have on the magnitude of the stress-induced fight-flight response.

- Many of the physiological effects of the faith factor that contribute to positive emotional states and behaviors, cultivate virtues like forgiveness, altruism, and generosity, which are known to be important contributors of health and resilience.

These themes are consistent with Martin Seligman's research on positive emotions linked to engagement, meaning, and lastly, pleasure. When a Buddhist monk enters a state of meditation, there is a dramatic increase in blood flow and activity in the left prefrontal cortex. This seems to be an important region in the brain as individuals experience positive emotional states. This is also the "executive center" that enables more effective interpretation and response to life events. As noted, the executive center is essential in keeping emotions like fear and anxiety in check. It's also a region that's important in our "reading of others," which in turn fosters empathy and forgiveness.

Interestingly when you study a baby's behavior in response to their mother leaving the room, two patterns of behavior emerge. Those who immediately cry have less activity in their prefrontal lobes than those who do not. While this may suggest we're born with a predisposition for emotional traits, there appears to be a high degree of plasticity, allowing the capacity to change in response to experience. Therefore, there's no reason to think that unhappy babies or babies who cry a lot grow up to be unhappy adults.

Additional evidence supports a connection between the left prefrontal area in the brain and the emotional center in the limbic system, such as the nucleus accumbens. Dopamine and endorphins or opiates appear as central neurotransmitters in this response. Brian Knutson, an assistant professor of psychology and neuroscience at Stanford, has been studying the link between motivators and decision making. Individuals who, for example, were highly motivated to receive a cash reward for successfully completing a task, showed increased activity, again in the nucleus accumbens. The implication is a connection between reason, emotion, reward, and behavior. I believe many people who attend worship experience these interactions.

When monks in meditative states or individuals praying note transcendent (non-self) experiences, brain activity increases in the left prefrontal cortex and is diminished in the parietal lobes, associated with spatial-time orientation. Individuals who induce this pattern of increased prefrontal lobe activity and parietal lobe suppression are filled with a deep sense of non-self and connectedness to others. This is a pattern of brain activity that may, at least in part, mediate an individual's "religious" or "spiritual" experience. Richard Davidson, a professor of psychology and psychiatry at the University of Wisconsin, has found individuals with positive emotional traits and increased left prefrontal lobe activity to have lower levels of cortisol, a stress hormone with many adverse health effects when elevated and sustained.

Positive thoughts, motivation, meaning, belief and expectation, prayer and meditation, and positive emotional states all seem intricately interconnected in their neurobiological footprints. And these interactions, as true of all mind-body interactions, are capable of being *induced*. "Spiritual experiences," such as the one shared between the heart surgeon and the gospel performer, are transforming experiences. Individuals have within themselves a transformation that has been *induced.* These induced changes affect thought, emotion, and behavior.

Psychologist Robert Emmons, of the University of California at Davis, has found a clear connection between exercise, other health-promoting behaviors (nutrition and compliance with treatment strategies), and expressions of gratitude and faith.

THE BIOLOGY OF FAITH: ARE WE DESIGNED TO BELIEVE?

The story of the universal, transcultural, and steadfast belief people share in a God or higher source is fascinating. The evidence (albeit of varying degrees of quality and scientific rigor) connecting personal and shared faith-based religion and spiritual practice with positive health actions is compelling and intuitive. Insights unveiled at the crossroads of behavioral health, neuroscience, neuroradiology, neurobehavioral health, neuroendocrinology, etc., though in their incipience, place the brain at the center of thinking, feeling, and doing. A biological and neurochemical dance of Astair-Rogers quality is revealed. At a higher level, a pattern of full mind, emotion, brain, behavior, and body-health integration is revealed.

Is the spiritual-health synergy simply a virtuoso of neurochemical homeostasis, swirling in three dimensions, enabling us to live longer and better? Is the calling of our connection to a divine source a reward-motivation response that places more emphasis on the design than it does on the divine? While I have theological, medical, personal, professional, and public health perspectives on the subject, more than anything, I'm most impressed that these interactions exist at all! I've also come to appreciate that the diversity of perspectives on these matters—while on some levels irreconcilable—can mutually coexist and inform. Transcending the diverse points of view regarding religion and spirituality is the desire to live longer and better. This, we can all agree, is a human priority.

Polemic passion about our origins, meaning, purpose, and destiny are easily ignited when reflecting on matters of science, religion, spirituality, and health. Conventional wisdom has always been to tread carefully when bringing up matters of religion and politics. The same can be said for matters of religion and science. Regardless of how our design of life came to be, it can be adapted in ways that enable great potential for a longer and more meaningful life. Such passion for insoluble debate should not come at the price of failing to recognize the health potential of what it is we are debating in the first place. Debating the origins of high blood pressure should not obscure the importance of diagnosing and treating it. Debating our origins should not obscure the fact that we are here and capable of hanging around longer than ever imagined. Reflections of our origins and our destiny should not obscure our being in the present, in the moment, and more aware of how we can play this instrument more beautifully. From a more pragmatic perspective: The evidence I have presented can, in no way, prove or disprove the existence of God, a higher source, The Big Bang, evolution, creation, etc. The only certain truth is that we exist.

> The evidence I have presented can, in no way, prove or disprove the existence of God, a higher source, The Big Bang, evolution, creation, etc. The only certain truth is that we exist.

When the amygdala-limbic fire of debate is ignited, we're more likely to see things in black and white, right or wrong, or as mutually exclusive. Anyone who enters this subject matter runs a high risk of pushing someone's amygdala button, having their own button pushed, and embarking on a white water rapid ride that leaves little opportunity to explore the subtleties of the landscape. But it's a mistake to let black-and-white thinking define what is really a rainbow of connections.

Jeffrey Kluger, a writer for *Time* magazine, did an interesting piece in the fall of 2004, asking the question, "Is God in Our Genes?" He noted that theologians in the third century BC, when Ecclesiastes was presumably composed, emphasized the universal human desire to discover the presence of God. And while more than two thousand years later, we seem inspired to continue to look for God; none of us is remotely capable of understanding what it is we are looking for.

Why do we believe? What purpose does faith serve other than perhaps a survival tool? Where does faith originate? Why do some seem more inclined to have it than others? Has the developmental complexity of our frontal lobes, the source of our higher reasoning, left us more cognizant of our vulnerability and need for comforting reassurance? Is faith a human construct, a lifeline we created in order to deal with the knowledge of a certain and eventual death? Is it the product of gene refinement selected over the generations because of its survival advantages, making the viability of the species more likely?

Faith appears to have a deeply embedded biological footprint. Strong belief, when associated with deep meaning and positive expectation, does seem to tip the allostatic load scale in the direction of health. There is some evidence that a chemical known as nitrous oxide may be stimulated in individuals experiencing these spiritual states. Nitric oxide has a relaxing effect on blood vessels, preventing the more harmful constrictive effects of norepinephrine and adrenalin.

Though many of the published studies linking spirituality, religion, and health employ imperfect scientific methods, this hardly discounts the mind-body implications. After all, if history teaches us anything, it is that the stories that emerge from the best science do not in the long run always turn out to be true stories. Take for example our understanding of ulcers. Generations of research associated ulcers with an overproduction of acid that overwhelms the protective barriers in the lining of the stomach. We now understand ulcers to be an infectious disease with an organism known as H. Pylori.

Absence of proof is not proof of absence. In any event, we reach further for understanding as we are "wired" to do. With that said, the science currently available is clear in linking many dimensions of religion and spiritual practices with a biological basis for living longer and aging well. And while we may not be any more certain why we are here, most of us would welcome being here as long as possible.

An evolutionary biologist would say perhaps that their theory is consistent with the emergence of faith and spirituality as naturally selected traits, important to best assure our ultimate survival. What we are seeing is the biological and neurochemical refinement of a primordial soup we have all emerged from. A bowl of alphabet soup will never be quite the same for me. This perspective would suggest religion and faith are superb survival tools that enable these human traits to persevere and with each passing generation, etch themselves more deeply into our existence.

A person of religious or spiritual faith might say that this is all consistent with a divine source, creating gifts that enable connections to self, others and to serve a higher purpose. What science is revealing is perfectly consistent with a higher power. After all, a higher source with benevolence and love as its "mission" would desire a design capable of doing what ours is capable of do-

> **What science is revealing is perfectly consistent with a higher power.**

ing, including evolving and adapting. If our purpose is to save the planet, we surely have some adapting to do. Thank God for making it possible.

A more reductionist perspective would point to a pure molecular or genetic basis for the ocean of biological and neurochemical events that essentially define who we are. Mind is body. Feeling is body. Religion and spiritual endeavors and ways of living are manifestations of genetic refinement over millions of years that reward survival-enhancing traits. And it would certainly appear these traits provide a survival advantage. As Michael Persinger, professor of behavioral neuroscience at Laurentian University in Ontario, would suggest, "God is an artifact of the brain."

Dean Hamer, chief of gene structure at the National Cancer Institute and author of *The God Gene: How Faith Is Hardwired into Our Genes*, has isolated a gene that when activated would lead to a feeling of transcendence. This biologically induced feeling suggests a molecular (genetic) influence on the experiences most of us would define as spiritual. Genes are clearly one of many factors that contribute to this experience. There is compelling evidence for molecular contributors (twin studies support this), however, the "nurture factor" appears to point to strong experiential and cultural contributions as well. Interestingly, Buddhist theory connects a spiritual gene origin with who a person was in a previous life. This gene from a previous life, when combined with the parents' genes, enables an inherent spiritual connection to past and future. Ironically, a pure reductionist perspective would support Buddhist theory. Isn't it great how this works?

Dean Hamer, whose research makes possible sophisticated and remarkable insights into our spiritual molecular roots, would note that his findings have no bearing on the proof or disproof of the existence of God. God or a divine higher source could surely coexist with these findings. After all, if I were God, I would want both nature and nurture working for me. As challenging as life is, we need all the help we can get to keep our complex lives in perspective! The distinction between religious and spiritual practice and belief should be reemphasized. While there may be some evidence for a genetic predisposition for spirituality or a feeling of self-transcendence, the rituals of organized religion and other faith groups appear to have a predominantly cultural and environmental influence.

I find I don't have any problem enabling different perspectives regarding our origin to coexist in my head. After all, one of my most important personal values to satisfy is to live long and well. And if I can't live long, I'll settle for living well. If tapping into my spirituality helps me do that—all the better. I believe we all have a capacity for spirituality regardless of our individual beliefs regarding our origins. The fact that mind-body-spirit dimensions can inspire hope and move us forward is more important than having solid answers about the past.

THE SOUL AND TRANSCENDENT MOMENTS

So where does the soul fit itself into this mind-body-biology construct? As Dr. Bruce Cohen, medical director of the MacLean Hospital in Boston, would say, the soul "is the house of the divine spark," separate from mind, body, and brain. "To the agnostic, the soul is in doubt. To the atheist, the soul is fiction. To the person of faith, the soul is a divine gift, permanent by it's very nature."

While issues of the soul should be left to individuals to contemplate freely, our spirituality—transcendent by its very nature—needs a home that the body cannot by itself confine. When a person smiles at me, something passes between us. When I hug my children or hold the hand of a patient, something passes between us. It may have both a mutually shared neurochemical basis *and* something that transcends our bodies, enabling the neurochemical response to occur.

My mother died in 1992. She was an incredible woman. Resilience defined her life as she confronted one health setback after another, one biopsychosocial quagmire after another. Her suffering, as I experienced it, enabled a deeper feeling of empathy for her and others as I got older. She was very funny, loving, and had a deep faith. I can close my eyes, sit quietly, and bring an image of her at a happy time in our lives into my brain. I can see her vividly. I can hear her voice. I can smell the scent of her perfume. I can feel her embrace and warm kiss on my cheek. I can experience the love she had for me in any place and at any time. I suspect if one were to slip me into a PET or fMRI scanner when I am more mindful of her, my brain would look identical to how it would look if she were actually sitting in the room, alive with me. From a neuroscientific perspective, she remains as alive inside me as if she were sitting next to me even though it has been fourteen years since her death. Her spirit, as it is translated in the design that resides inside me, is no less alive now than it was before she died. This is where our souls connect. It is the best case I can make for life after death.

APPLICATIONS FOR BETTER HEALTH

As careful as we might need to be in treading on the topic of spirituality and medicine, even greater care must be considered when giving advice. These are inherently personal areas with individually defined value, meaning, and preference. I need special awareness of this as a physician as my own biases should not, by virtue of being in a position of professional authority, violate the values, wishes, and preferences of another. That is a tenet of medical ethics that must be valued and practiced. It is not my intention, in any way, to push religion or prayer. It is my intention to suggest that by virtue of nature and nurture, we are spiritual beings. Or should I say:

**The design, as we better understand it,
is perfectly suited for spirituality.**

It's not my intention to suggest that saints live longer than sinners. Nope. I am suggesting, however, that many attributes of religious and spiritual perspective and practice have proven effect on many aspects of health and quality of life. Spirituality is not a disease or bad luck eliminator. It's about having the best garden for as long as possible. If I'm looking to sweeten my portfolio for a return on the investment (ROI) of energy expended, resulting in the best possible health and healing outcome, this is where I'm going to invest heavily. I would suggest that the ROI on the energy we invest in many other aspects of life is much less. I am beginning to track my energy investments more carefully. The ROI varies considerably. The beauty of this is that it works. It is designed to work. It doesn't have to be about religion, God, philosophy, science, reductionism, theology, creation, or evolution. It's about being alive and living well. It just is. There are no rules. I do feel that certain criteria should be met in defining the goals of your practice however you decide to practice it. Your practice should:

- Cultivate meaning
- Satisfy that which you most value

- Cultivate social, supportive networks of relationships
- Cultivate a stronger sense of non-self
- Give you greater awareness of the moment you are experiencing

While there are many more threads in this tapestry, those I have listed appear necessary for the fabric to develop. Here are some thoughts and questions to get you "lit" as you think about this more. Find a quiet spot where you will be undisturbed. Write down some thoughts in response to these questions:

- What gives your life meaning and purpose (think broadly—family, health, work, etc.)?

    1.
    2.
    3.
    4.
    5.

- What do you value or what are some of the most important things to you (be specific—a walk in the woods, listening to music, a particular friendship, etc.)?

    1.
    2.
    3.
    4.
    5.

- How well are your values being satisfied? Rate them on a scale of 1 through 5. One is poorly and 5 superbly.
- How do you go about satisfying that which gives you meaning (making time for yourself, writing letters to friends, mindfulness, meditation, etc.)?

    1.
    2.
    3.
    4.
    5.

- How can your thoughts, feelings, and behaviors change to bring you closer to satisfying that which you value (e.g., spend more undivided time with your spouse, read more, increase your activity, volunteer, etc.)?

    1.
    2.
    3.
    4.
    5.

- What could you do to more effectively connect with others (e.g., write more notes to friends, call a long lost friend or family member, do an activity with your kids, volunteer, etc.)?

    1.
    2.
    3.
    4.
    5.

- What are the most important relationships to you?

    1.
    2.
    3.
    4.
    5.

- How would you rate the quality of those relationships (use the 1 through 5 scale)?

- How can your thoughts, feelings, and behaviors change to bring you closer to relationships you desire (especially for those relationships you give a low score to)?

    1.
    2.
    3.
    4.
    5.

- What would you really love to do that you currently are not doing (e.g., taking a dance class, traveling more, writing poetry, healthier activity, etc.)?

  1.

  2.

  3.

  4.

  5.

- Cultivate the practice of mindfulness. It is ultimately about getting to know who you are. It is about uncluttering your mind and being in the moment. It is about observing yourself and your interaction with life. I highly recommend John Kabot-Zinn's *Wherever You Go, There You Are.*

- Practice the relaxation response. It is easy, wonderful and it works. Sit quietly, relax your muscles, and focus your attention to your breathing. As you exhale, softly repeat the word "calm" or a prayer, or whatever gives you meaning. Allow distracting and intrusive thoughts to pass through without resistance. Come back to your repetition of "calm" as you exhale each breath. Do this five to ten minutes twice each day.

- Check out some audiotapes, videos, DVDs, classes, etc., on yoga and meditation. These time-tested practices quickly become a way of living that will change your state of mind, body, spirit, and health.

- If you practice a particular faith tradition and feel disconnected, re-consider why you disconnected and if it's a value worth pursuing again.

- If prayer brings you comfort, do more of it.

- Find music that lifts your spirit (a goal here is to try to match the music with an emotionally positive memory) and dance while no one is watching.

- Tell your family and friends how much they mean to you.

- Volunteer your strengths to a cause that fulfills a greater good.

- Consider keeping a gratitude journal. At the end of each day, write a few experiences down for which you are grateful.

- Remember, from a health and survival perspective, it appears that the greatest service to self is service to others.

Chapter 13

Conflict Management:
Getting to Health

> "The gem cannot be polished without friction,
> nor man perfected without trials."
>
> Chinese Proverb

I have come to appreciate the sheer prevalence of conflict and the tremendous burden it poses on our relationships, stress load, health, and wellness. Conflict is the pervasive and inevitable consequence of a lot of people living with and depending upon a lot of other people. There are many thoughts and opinions out there, many diverse and varied lenses through which we observe and experience the world.

The sheer nature and volume of information shared per person per day is staggering. We are inundated with information, have more options than ever for communication, and have more complex stories to tell. The complexity of organizational structure and function has placed novel demands on the people who comprise it. In addition, organizational culture—whether work, marriage, church, parenting, or politics—is changing rapidly and requires more "fluid" adaptation to sustain harmony and effective growth.

Health care is a perfect example. Interpersonal dependence has never been greater. Many individuals contribute to the overall service experience in health care. There are now many more links in the chain, making it easier to kink. The multidimensional nature of the numerous interpersonal interactions involved in a routine health care encounter is stunning. Here's a typical example. An individual goes to their doctor because of a cough, fever, and shortness of breath. The doctor, concerned about the possibility of pneumonia, sends the person to the emergency department. Many personnel become involved in the evaluation and management—administration, insurers, physicians, nurses, phlebotomy (blood drawing) technicians, X-ray technicians, radiologists, pharmacists, medical students, residents, case managers, etc. It's not hard to understand how a breakdown in the process of care can commonly occur. And this is a very straight-forward scenario!

For physicians today, the skill mix that's required to navigate in an intensely interactive, interdependent, and pressure-packed context looks different than the skill mix required for the controlled autonomy that once defined the professional experience. The skill mix required for thoughtful analytical reasoning, in this case, making the diagnosis of pneumonia, looks very different than the skill mix required to facilitate the complex process of care—communication, empathy, and social awareness.

Many health care professionals and the individuals they serve are leaving more of their values unsatisfied each passing day. What we desire to experience looks and feels different from what we actually feel and experience. This is also true for consumers of health care. Our tendency to want to move from A to B, in a direct line, will be met with frustration as our interactions are usually not linear at all. It's not hard to understand why conflict is so pervasive in our lives. It's too pervasive to avoid and too important to ignore.

In this chapter we will review:

- The neurobehavioral mechanisms that drive behavior during conflict
- The important distinction between driving and being driven
- The relationship between poorly managed conflict and allostatic load
- Strategies for more effective navigation through life's conflict minefield.

Here's another paradox. While communication has never been easier, the ease with which communication breakdown occurs is stunning. Newer modes of communication like email inherently put a crimp on context. The receiver of the email is given more space to fill in the blanks. As more of our own stories are left for others to create, you can expect perceptual gaps to dot the interpersonal landscape with greater frequency. And they do. Perceptions drive much of our behavior. When they are accurate they serve us well. When they are not, they become your designated driver.

Effective conflict management is largely about influence. It's the ability to influence outcome by shaping perceptions in the minds of others. You need to be able to do this. That will require more effective storytelling on your part to close the perceptual gap. It will also require you to elicit a more complete story from the party with whom you are in conflict. In this transformation, you will be forced to become more vulnerable as you make possible a shift in your perceptions of another. This will not be easy. This will not feel good. It will not seem right. Do it anyway.

> Effective conflict management is largely about influence. It's the ability to influence outcome by shaping perceptions in the minds of others.

This may seem straightforward and intuitive, common sense really. However, as Mark Twain once said, "common sense is not common practice." It's much harder for individuals to embrace an alternative context (or "framework") within which to examine the context of the conflict. There is a vulnerability to doing this. It involves the uncomfortable retelling of a story whose words are familiar and certain to you. It will require rising above your fight-flight territories to higher, safer, more thoughtful ground. It will require walking by the candy store of quick, dirty, and targeted retribution.

Thank God for plasticity. Remember plasticity is the brain's capacity for change and adaptation. Alteration of thought and behavior will, in turn, alter your emotional balance. The mind-emotion-brain-behavior-body pattern you are accustomed to can be reconfigured to your advantage. Anyone can cultivate these skills. Plasticity is not the gift of a select few. My hair follicles stand on end when someone tells me that some are born to do it and others not. While some people have better knowledge and skill of conflict management, such skills can be developed at any stage in life. They're critical for our children to acquire, a major trump card if ever there

> While some people have better knowledge and skill of conflict management, such skills can be developed at any stage in life.

was one. Conflict, if not managed efficiently and effectively, will take a huge toll on your health, your quality of life, and your very desire to get up in the morning.

> Conflict, if not managed efficiently and effectively, will take a huge toll on your health, your quality of life, and your very desire to get up in the morning.

Conflict is a significant source of stress in our lives. As you examine stress as the biological burden of adapting to life's challenges, you can appreciate the health-undermining magnitude of conflict. Nothing will take the buoyancy out of your balloon more quickly than the perpetual stress of conflict. Conflict will ravenously consume the heartiest of souls. It is like fine beach sand. It can get into almost anything. It will reside in any nook or cranny it can find in your life. And it will tenaciously resist easy clean up.

I have become very interested in conflict theory and conflict resolution practice. My interest is, in part, to promote greater personal effectiveness, reduce the stress in my life, develop a marketable skill (creating meaning and value satisfaction), and to be a more effective problem-solver. I am an alumnus of The Harvard School of Public Health's Advanced Program in Conflict Resolution. I have learned a lot from the faculty of the Harvard Negotiation Project. Much of their work is integrated in this material, and a reading list of outstanding work in this critical area can be found in the Suggested Reading list at the end of the book.

There are no shortages of problems to work on in our lives. Effective problem solving, on which I will later elaborate, elicits a wonderful reward response (thank you dopamine and endorphins), brings you closer to others (thank you bonding-attachment oxytocin), and enhances mood (thank you serotonin). Effective conflict management will distinguish you as a "go to person." The more people go to you, the more stories you know. The more stories you know, the more relationships you build. The more relationships you build, the more trust capital you acquire. The more trust capital you have, the more likely you are to shape perceptions in others.

Learning to solve problems through conflict management is not unlike working toward better dietary and exercise habits. It's not always easy getting there, but once you've arrived, you're likely to want to stay. That's why many of the same faces end up on the most effective committees, working groups, and task forces.

Like most people, I don't like conflict, but I've come to see it as both inevitable and necessary to deal with. My health depends on it and so does yours. The very behavior of working with others to solve problems strengthens the synapses between my prefrontal cortex and my amygdala, with the icing on the cake an opiate reward with a sweet scoop of attachment-social connection. It feels good to tend to those you care about. Remember, the synapses that fire together, wire together.

> The very behavior of working with others to solve problems strengthens the synapses between my prefrontal cortex and my amygdala, with the icing on the cake an opiate reward with a sweet scoop of attachment-social connection.

There's just one small problem with effective conflict management. The intensity of the fight-flight response and the impact of physiological stress on memory processing, perception, and behavior will have a tendency to have an agenda of its own. All this theoretical stuff makes sense on paper. In the trenches, in real-time, in the heat of the moment, and in the midst of outrage and enrage, the most skilled of conductors may derail the train.

Because conflict will occur at home with those we love, at work with those we see each day, with friends, and with total strangers, we can anticipate the need to apply these skills with anyone, at any time, and in any place. Not every conflict needs a happy ending or even needs to be reconciled. It may be of such minor importance that the best strategy is to ignore it. A conflict may be consuming more time and energy than the effort is worth. For example, why expend excessive energy trying to get appropriate recognition by senior management when a better position may be available within your company or at another company. Having a good alternative (BATNA-best alternative to a negotiated agreement) might lessen your zeal to dive into a conflict, unless you can create the potential for an even better outcome than your planned alternative. Or you might be engaged in a conflict that is simply going nowhere as you spin your wheels. It's sometimes most efficient to agree to disagree and move on. Not every conflict is worth the effort of resolution. In other words, if the potential for value satisfaction exceeds the energy required to end the conflict, it may be worth pursuing. If the potential gain in value satisfaction is relatively low in relation to the effort required to end the conflict, then forget about it.

It's important to be mindful that while a particular conflict may not have a reconciliation that's worth the effort, there's a difference between resolving a conflict and preserving a relationship. For example, an inability to resolve a problem with a daily co-worker should not become the basis for an inabil-

ity to work together. It's also important not to be
too quick to write someone off due to the perception that it's not worth the effort. The process of
conflict management may create a mutual value
that is not currently recognized. In the complex
organizational context we live and work in, relationships are the most important source of capital. Relationship liquidity has no equal.

> In the complex organiza-
> tional context we live and
> work in, relationships are
> the most important source
> of capital. Relationship
> liquidity has no equal.

THE NEUROBEHAVIORAL MECHANISMS THAT DRIVE
BEHAVIOR DURING CONFLICT

When we perceive a threat, our cars of conflict start their engines and prepare to spin their wheels. The magnitude of danger attached to the threat will
directly impact your engine's RPM. Imagine a primal neurobiological response that a hunter-gatherer may have relied upon while walking through a
dark, thick jungle. Now imagine this is the same feeling you experience as
your CEO enters the boardroom. Any perception of threat will set a cascade
of responses into motion. And threats these days come in many forms. Have
any emails you sent left you desperate for an "unsend" button? Or have any
emails you received pushed your anger button? There is an inherent danger
in a system of communication that rewards efficiency of words within a limited context. Words, words, words coming and going in unprecedented volume at unprecedented speed. As a result, you quickly respond with a story or
perception that integrates motivation, intention, expectation, and assumption in response to the data before you.

As a quick "check" of your story's validity, a memory may be needed.
Below the radar screen, in response to the perception you have created (the
mind-thought contribution), you scan the vast library of prior experiences
that might relate to your current circumstances. Off your hippocampus shelf
of memories pops Volume 2: Episode 3 from a prior committee meeting. Yes,
you remember. Volume 2, Episode 3 occurred three months ago with the
same person who sent you the email that pushed your button big time. This
memory popped off the shelf in part because the person involved was the
same, and perhaps more importantly because your amygdala pumped it with
the emotional charge of anger, distrust, and hurt. Bingo! The perception you

have now mentally assembled about the current situation is consistent with what you recall about this individual—he is rude and unprofessional. So now you're not only certain of your perceptions, you're getting more and more riled as you think about it.

The amygdala essentially facilitates reconsolidation of the thought-emotion-memory interplay. This makes it more challenging for your prefrontal cortex to intervene by considering additional ways for the behavioral data to be assembled into a story that may look very different. The accuracy of our intuition is critical in influencing the outcome of conflict. Misreading another's intentions can be a disaster. Leaving the intentions of others to cursory inspection or chance falls into the category of root causes when you try to sort out what went wrong. As our external sources of data quickly enable a story to emerge, our internal processes of intuition affirmation run wild. Sensing the emotional significance of your "threat," your amygdala and hippocampus will spin the roulette wheel looking for past experiences that support the worse case scenario.

It's a funny thing about memory. It appears there's a tendency to believe what fits best with our version of "the facts." Just how accurately are our perceptions of the present informed by memories? Take for example the war in Iraq. I should preface this by noting that it's not my intention to make a political statement here. The primary motivation, as described, for invading Iraq was to uncover and destroy weapons of mass destruction or WMD. As time passed, it was increasingly clear based on available evidence that WMD did not exist. The media everywhere reported the gross miscalculations of inaccurate intelligence. It became a focal point of contention between John Kerry and George Bush Jr. in the 2004 Presidential election. Despite the unequivocal evidence against WMD in Iraq, people who felt the war was justified continued to believe the motivation to go to war to uncover WMD was legitimate. In this example, memory parts ways with reason. On the other hand, if you question citizens who did not support the war to begin with and who did not believe the WMD theory, when the facts were revealed (no WMDs), there was universal acceptance. We are, therefore, more willing to rely on misinformation if it's consistent with the "mental model" we've crafted for ourselves.

The certainty we attach to our original story can prove a formidable obstacle to accepting a perception that looks different. And as we all know, the information we base our stories on is sometimes more fiction than fact. I'm sure you've experienced this as many times as I have. As you call upon your recollection of memories, those that will most affirm your perceptions are retrieved. You find yourself thinking, "At first I wondered . . . now I'm certain." The jump from wonder to certainty does not require new fresh data. The data on my hard drive will do just fine, thank you. Of course this momentum can build quickly in a positive or negative direction depending on your original story. So there is good news and bad news. The good news is that our perceptions serve as a guide to our behavior. The bad news, in the words of Charles Dwyer, PhD, from the Wharton Business School, is that perceptions are:

- Personal
- Subjective
- Fragile
- Arbitrary
- Infinitely malleable

This is frightening when one considers how powerful perceptions are in shaping our interpretations and response to experience and our interactions with others.

In addition to perceptual gaps, values play a crucial role in the genesis and reconciliation of conflict. For example, you may—as you peel away the layers of the onion of anger—discover that at the core of a conflict, a value has been violated or has not been satisfied. You may share similar values to someone you're in conflict with and have different criteria for how the values are best satisfied. I've seen conflicts like this plodding forward without either party having a clear sense of what the other person values and what would have to happen to satisfy those values. For example, an individual chairing a committee may be upset with a committee member who is consistently five minutes late for meetings. Here's a brief analysis:

Chair person	Committee member
Perception:	
Tardiness is a real problem.	It's only five minutes.
Tardiness implies lack of respect.	I always come to the meetings and never get a pat on the back. No respect.

Values (ranked in order of importance):

1. Respect for colleagues' time	1. Seeing clients prior to meeting
2. Avoidance of meeting disruption	2. Respect for colleagues' time
3. Seeing clients prior to meeting	3. Avoidance of meeting disruption

Criteria for value satisfaction (ranked in order of importance):

1. Prompt timeliness	1. Showing up
2. Scheduling clients around meetings	2. Scheduling meetings around clients
3. Reviewing agenda beforehand	3. Bringing agenda with me

In this example, you can see conflicts of "prioritization" and "criteria for value satisfaction." The committee member who values many of the same things as the chairperson feels they are fulfilling their criteria for value satisfaction with their current behavior. This will be unacceptable to the chair given his or her different criteria for satisfaction of the same values. On the surface, it looks like a conflict over five minutes, but it's really a struggle involving perceptions and unexplored value systems.

My wife and I both value a clean home. Our criteria for clean vary somewhat. As a consequence, my threshold for vacuuming is a bit higher than hers. If she is, hypothetically speaking of course, upset with me because I don't mind a dirty floor, I'm likely to think, "C'mon, the floor's not that dirty." Her perception: "He doesn't care about having a clean house or he would vacuum." My perception: "She is fastidious about cleanliness. This looks fine." Any effective process of conflict management has to examine mutual perceptions, values, and criteria for value satisfaction.

Managing conflict when reexamined from a neurobehavioral perspective requires an awareness of the rapid response unleashed when a threat is perceived. When the relationship is too important to leave to chance, look to create value for you and your constituents. Remember that effective conflict management is not about getting even, it's about getting what you want. As you navigate these tricky waters remember that your prefrontal cortex needs to consciously and carefully distill an amygdala alert for fight and flight. Your biggest threat is an amygdala highjack.

EMPATHY: THE CURRENCY OF CONFLICT RESOLUTION

An important dimension to any interpersonal encounter, particularly in the management of conflict, is the ability to read faces. Most communication is nonverbal. Some of the most important messages ever communicated to me as physician have been nonverbal. For example:

- The look on a daughter's face when her parent, lying ill in a hospital bed, says, "Everything is fine. I'm ready to go home."
- The look in a person's eyes when they say they feel okay and what you see is fear, despair, and deep pride.
- The look of shame and guilt on your child's face when they say, "I don't know how it happened."
- The look on the face of an individual who is lost though not asking for assistance.
- The look on the face of an individual who says, "Please open the door" when the spoken message is "Leave me alone; do not enter."
- The look of anger and disgust that takes on the passive-aggressive interpretation of "Fine, fine, everything is just fine!"

You get the picture. And getting the picture is really what it's all about. People who are skilled negotiators and conflict managers are very attuned to what others are thinking and feeling. Equally essential, they are attuned to their own feelings and are skilled in the competencies of self-awareness (reading one's gut, knowing strengths and weaknesses, confidence and limitations, etc.) and emotional management (self-control, adaptability, initiative, achievement, and optimism).

> People who are skilled negotiators and conflict managers are very attuned to what others are thinking and feeling.

The opportunities for filling in your perceptual gaps rely on awareness of the subtitles. The paradox here is that an important nonverbal message begging for interpretation may push your "A (amygdala) Button." The net effect is an override of the flashing neon signal that is saying, "Pause here and fill in the blanks." For example, the look of anger and impatience on the face of someone you're negotiating with might prompt you to step back and reframe. Perhaps they don't understand my position and interests. Perhaps they are not in a position to make the decision and worry their supervisor will be upset with the options. Perhaps they are expecting something I have overlooked.

The faces we read, particularly in the heat of conflict, can influence behavior and interaction in powerful ways. Your amygdala-limbic backseat driver may be pushing you toward self-defense and ego satisfaction. Your prefrontal cortex, if attuned, should be prompting you to be more curious and information seeking. Here we have two opposing forces sparring behind the scenes inside your head with very different consequences for conflict recon ciliation and better health.

In research using PET and fMRI brain imaging, the amygdala is especially active during the viewing of fearful faces. Reading faces may be an additional strategy the amygdala uses in surveying the landscape for any signs of threat. We can all remember as children looking to the faces of our parents in an attempt to get a reading on the danger that might be present. Not having a full library of danger memories, we rely on those we do have to serve as our fear barometers. As I was writing this chapter, I recalled a memory from when I was nine. I was living with my grandparents in rural northeastern Alabama. It was a hot summer evening and as was typical that time of year, some pretty fierce thunderstorms were moving through. On this late afternoon, a storm came through with substantial winds and large hail, the likes of which I had never experienced. The look on my grandparents' faces would serve as my arbiter of imminent danger. They calmly brought me down to their basement, showing little overt worry, their faces calm and reassuring. Within moments, a twister would move through, taking the roof off my grandparents' garage and destroying the schoolhouse next to us. Having not read fear on their faces, I felt little fear inside, despite what in retrospect, would turn out to be an unforgettable experience.

It's important to appreciate that the amygdala's ability to read deeply into a facial expression, particularly in the midst of conflict and high-stress, is somewhat crude. Its goal is rapid triage or risk stratification (danger vs. no danger). Many intermediary shades of gray will be lost in this cloud of black vs. white. You might, for example, be presenting a report to a difficult colleague. Your amygdala associates this person with negative emotions and quickly places a "caution sign" on the present circumstances. The person you are presenting to may have a perfectly neutral, non-threatening look on their face. This neutral look, under the influence of "The Big A," may have your prefrontal perceptions concluding, "She did not show much response at all. I bet she hated my presentation . . . in fact . . . I know she did. I was a failure." What the colleague may have been thinking is "Pretty good stuff." Affirmation and positive reinforcement would have worked well here to limit the confusion.

In another study, the amygdala "lit up" when healthy people viewed un-trustworthy faces. Researchers have shown that patients with damage to their amygdala judge faces to be more trustworthy and approachable than people with other types of brain damage. For example, an autistic individual will have trouble reading emotion in faces even when the emotion expressed is quite obvious. Conversely, people with severe social phobias see emotions that are not apparent to others. In one instance, the amygdala lays low in the face of threat, and in the other, the amygdala is hypervigilant when no threat is apparent.

As we consciously try to suspend the temptation to get even or to "right a wrong," we have to leap from the trajectory of satisfying self-interests to a trajectory of enlarging interests to include others. This enlightenment, as irony would have it, makes possible greater satisfaction of self-interests. This is a major leap and is critical in the breakthrough of irreconcilable conflict. It requires overriding two powerful and primal response systems. The first is our ubiquitous fight-flight stress response. The second is the short-acting, sweet-tasting, intoxicating, dopamine-endorphin surge that provides the sat-isfaction for lashing back with sarcasm, anger, hostility, or total avoidance. Effective conflict management requires distinguishing these primal responses acting as allies from those acting as obstacles. For example, there's a big dif-ference between a biological ally that heightens your awareness of a genuine threat and a biological obstacle that leaves you fearful of getting your lunch eaten when in fact a better meal is possible.

An epiphany that makes possible transformation of zero-sum deadlock can be found in the expression of empathy. Placing yourself in the shoes of another is the currency of understanding, the genesis of a new frame that will change what you see on the canvas. It can also powerfully transform how oth-ers see you. Empathy, once induced, is biologically expressed in a manner that is mutually reinforcing. Empathy, when genuinely expressed, makes more likely the reciprocity of empathy from another.

In recent years, there have been exciting developments in the neuro-science of empathy with the discovery of "mirror neurons." It had previously been recognized that before an individual performs a task like opening a jar, the brain circuitry necessary to coordinate the steps involved in the task would "turn on" before the task was actually performed. This activity is gen-erated in the frontal lobe "motor cortex." Interestingly, mirror neurons not only allow an individual to prepare for performing the task, but also are activated in response to observing someone else perform the same task.

It appears that mirror neurons may be integral to understanding the intentions of others, an "empathy center" if you will. Studies have shown that mirror neurons seem able to recognize context, attaching the capacity of an individual to experience what another individual is experiencing. In essence, mirror neurons become the bridge that connects our minds and emotions with others.

As Marco Iacobini and his colleagues at UCLA report, "People seem to have specific neurons that code the 'why' of some actions, predicting the behaviors of others." This discovery sheds insight on a neurobehavioral basis for understanding social interactions.

As we acquire and encode a repertoire of experiences, intentions, and emotional contexts, we become better able to re-create the experiences of others within ourselves. The more detail our mirror neurons capture, the more likely we are to feel what others are experiencing and to ascertain intent. If you capture the mirror image of anger on the face of someone you're in conflict with, you're likely to interpret an intent that is most consistent with the feeling of anger—intentions of retribution.

I've been an active medical educator for more than twenty years, and it continues to be a great joy and challenge to participate in the education of medical students and residents. A frequent question raised is whether traits like empathy, altruism, and humility can be taught. There's a school of thought that some of my colleagues would aspire to that says, "You either have it or you don't. You can't take a person without good bedside manner and teach them bedside manner."

As an educator, that hasn't been my experience at all. And if anything, *It's All in Your Head* is an attempt to provide evidence that the capacity for change is within us all and more likely to be influenced by nurture than by nature. For example, some health care professionals have had personal experiences as patients or caregivers that allow us to relate better to those we are interacting with in a health care setting. I had the painful irony of seeing both my parents develop kidney failure (my area of specialty), require dialysis, and suffer the setbacks of many unforgiving complications. Seeing other individuals experiencing this in their lives naturally elicited an understanding and a host of feelings that made it easier for me to connect empathetically.

The brain's empathy room, in my view, always has its light on. What separates us is our ability to enter the room (awareness) and apply skills that would render us better able to relate on an interpersonal level. Ironically, many health care professionals have been acculturated to stay at arm's length, leery of the slippery slide of getting too personal. Many health care professionals are empathetic *and* uncomfortable with its expression. Much more of a nurture issue.

Some people are transformed by virtue of a noteworthy event in their lives. It happens all the time, though it may come late in the game. I've cared for people who felt transformed in their final days and weeks of life, expressing feelings and thoughts that had been suppressed.

The research appears to suggest that when we observe another, our brains become awakened in patterns that mimic what the other is experiencing, allowing us to share the experience. Unfortunately, during a conflict we tend to focus on our differences, when it would be much better to focus on shared interests: the desire for a better outcome, the desire to provide for our families, the desire to limit physical and emotional consumption, and the desire for such basic fundamental human values as respect, dignity, integrity, and honest. All these are often lost in the heat of battle. Our shared experiences as humans far outweigh our differences. That is what makes empathy possible in the first place.

SEPARATE WHEN YOU ARE BEING DRIVEN
FROM WHEN YOU ARE DRIVING

You're driving your car to a familiar destination. It may be a few or perhaps many miles away. In what seems like a flash, you've arrived at your destination. Your conscious recollection of the details of the route you traveled is limited. "Did I stop at the light? Did I pass the convenience store?" The route you traveled, so familiar and so routine, has been imbedded in your brain. This imbedded "brain stamp" has integrated sight, memory, and motor skills, all necessary to safely get you to where you want to go. So precise is this circuitry etched, you can successfully carry out the task, a complex task at that, on a subconscious level. It's scary to suddenly become aware of having reached a destination without any recollection of the steps that got you there.

This common scenario serves as a good metaphor for how "your car" can be driven at a subconscious level. This is the Achilles heel of conflict management. Much of what may be driving your behavior—perceptions feelings, and memories—is doing so without your conscious oversight. Your ability as the driver to harness all the available information, distill it carefully, and respond thoughtfully is easily undermined as your stress response moves forward with or without you. Alternative and possible *breakthrough* perceptions, understanding, enlightened interests, additional options, and their consequences may never be fully realized.

If you feel out of control when confronting conflict, you're being driven. If the choice you are about to make increases the chance of a worse outcome, then you are being driven. Your amygdala is preparing you for imminent danger by invigorating flight-fight. Is it possible to know when you're at risk of being taken over by a surge of volcanic limbic lava? The short answer is that it is not at all easy, which is why most of us struggle when dealing with conflict. There are a few physical manifestations you or others may notice that say, "I'm entering fight-flight." Because of the stimulation of your adrenaline system, you may note.

- Racing heart
- Dry throat
- Rapid respiration
- Tightened muscles
- Increased perspiration
- Flushing of your face
- Difficulty concentrating and recalling
- An uncomfortable feeling in your gut leading to malaise or nausea

Other not so subtle manifestations of fight-flight on thought and emotion include:

- The overwhelming urge to lash back
- The urge to defend to the end
- Thinking of what you will say next while the other person is talking to you, instead of listening
- Having the gas gauge in your emotional tank higher than in your thinking tank
- Being absolutely certain without all the facts

- Seeing everything in black or white, no shades of gray
- Being unable to think of the better options that exist
- Spending more time looking back than looking forward
- Engaging in more blame-placing than problem-solving
- Being certain there is only one obvious answer

When fight-flight makes its move, the challenge is largely one of emotional management. The breakthrough epiphany is the awareness that your amygdala-limbic surge is looking to take over the wheel of your car. Sure, it might feel good at first: roof down, high-speed, wind blowing back your hair, navigating the tight curves, until uh oh . . . you're heading for a large patch of black ice.

THE RELATIONSHIP BETWEEN CONFLICT, THE BURDEN OF STRESS, AND ALLOSTATIC LOAD

When you consider the health-undermining biological fallout from conflict, you are truly given reason to pause. While some interpersonal conflicts like a nasty divorce are legion in their epic emotional, physical, mental, and spiritual consumption, many conflicts leave their effects in more insidious, transient, and cumulative ways. Repeated stimulation of your fight-flight response unleashes a cascade that can be viewed as a total body stress test (Figure 1). A life saving switch that was intended to be turned on and off quickly is too easily left in the "on" position as the stress in your life sweeps you away.

How your mood and energy are affected when confronting conflict is self-evident. Chronic sources of conflict, often seen in struggling relationships at home and at work, can be particularly debilitating. Chronic stress from conflict affects performance, concentration, enhances risk of illness, depression, anxiety, and increases the risk of substance abuse. Relationships, the very lifeline of resilience, become more tenuous and are more easily undermined. The stress load from conflict also tends to last longer as emotions that are attached run deep, are very personal, and provoke self-conscious feelings of guilt, shame, and humiliation. Bruises in this domain take much longer to heal, and they do so at the expense of greater cardiovascular burden. A primal system design that enables us to adapt to imminent threat becomes mal-

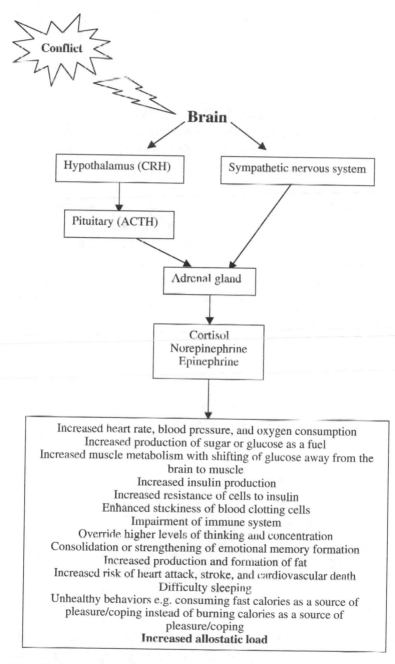

Figure 13.1 The Stress Response in Conflict

adaptive when your amygdala's button is repeatedly pushed and sometimes stuck in the "on-position."

BRINGING IT HOME: HOW TO MANAGE CONFLICT

When it comes to managing conflict in our lives, there is good news and bad news. The good news is we have a sophisticated tool called a brain that's capable of integrating thought, feeling, and behavior in the creation of value satisfaction. The bad news is we have a brain that places the priority of threat and danger over that of creative reasoning.

Much has been written on conflict resolution (see the suggested reading list), and many fine works have influenced my knowledge and practice of it. In the following section, I will integrate into the mind-brain-behavior-body ME-B^3 construct some important principles developed by people like Daniel Goleman and his pioneering work on emotional intelligence, Roger Fisher and Bruce Patten from The Harvard Negotiation Project, and Kerry Patterson and co-authors of *Crucial Conversations*.

Here is a summary of ME-B^3 contributions to conflict management.

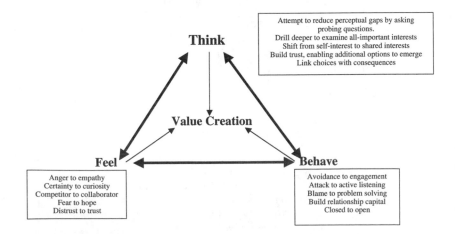

Preparation

Whenever you can anticipate the occurrence of conflict, preparation is key. If you can anticipate encounters that may predictably push your button, prepare for them. Anticipate an amygdala discharge that could elicit a behavior that may or may not serve you reliably. You will feel certain of your story and your perceptions will be locked in. Ask yourself, "Am I in a fight-flight mode?"

Ask yourself, "Am I in a fight-flight mode?"

It's also important to examine on an individual basis the price/earnings (P/E) ratio of conflict resolution. Is the price worth the earning potential? It probably is if:

1.   Your values can be better served by influencing behavioral change in the party you are conflicted with
2.   Your relationship with the party you are conflicted with is too important for disengagement
3.   You can build intellectual and relationship capital to serve you better in the future.

If the P/E ratio is not favorable and has no reasonable chance of being modified, ignore the conflict. Move on. Stay healthy. And enjoy the show.

Typical Obstacles and Their Antidotes in Conflict Resolution

Let's bring some of these principles of conflict resolution home by reviewing the obstacles we commonly confront and how we can stay in greater control of the interpersonal car we drive.

Obstacle	Antidote
Goal	
Getting even	Getting what you want
Win at all costs	Satisfy values and strengthen relationship
I get more, they get less	We both get a lot more
Brain	
Amygdala-Limbic Highjack	Prefrontal cortex mediation
	Prefrontal-limbic impulse control
	Reward/attachment
Expression	
Perceptual gaps	Assume they exist
Value differences	Empathy
	• Ask explicit questions
	• Relearn their story
	• Retell your story
	• Explore interests in more detail
	• Put only objective data on the table
Emotional attachment	**Retreat**
• Blame	Relaxation response
• Villain-victim	Awareness of being driven
• React	Get an objective reality check
	• Manage emotions

Memory distortion	Assume a bias exists
Looking back	Forward thinking
Linear thinking	Examine multiple dimensions
Only one best option	Best of many options
Subjective	Link choice with consequence
One sum	Objective and legitimate standards
	Create value

Go for the Plasticity

You may be convinced that this stuff is too warm and fuzzy, or of little value. Try it—you may experience plasticity in action. Remold the plastic that tells you to follow the script that has become habitual and commit to trying another context. The goal here is to purposefully create another story and make possible clarification of existing perceptual gaps. Think of it as Monday morning at the Improv; it's doable and interesting. This is the brain exercise equivalent of taking your prefrontal lobe for a jog. The process of asking questions of the person you're in conflict with will help you to create a new path. For example, ask your fellow conflictee:

- How do you see things right now?
- How do you think I see them?
- What is most important to you about _____?
- What is the information you have that forms the basis of how you see things?
- What do you think will happen if _____?
- What do you hope to see happen moving forward?
- What additional information might you have that I am lacking?

Coping Strategies

Inevitably your amygdala will have conspired with your hippocampus to charge your story with "ignited passion," reinforcing your perceptions of fear and threat. See it. Close your eyes for a moment and feel it. Then hook up the prefrontal hose to the hydrant to cool it. If you are in fight-flight mode as is often the case in conflict, prepare to bring in some reinforcements to manage your emo-

> If you are in fight-flight mode as is often the case in conflict, prepare to bring in some reinforcements to manage your emotions.

tions. Here are some strategies to keep your hands on the wheel as you race forward:

- Retreat
- Silence is safe when the fire is burning
- Listen, with your eyes and with your ears (often a lost opportunity)
- Relaxation response (make it portable, comfortable, and accessible)
- Seek objective, trusted third opinions
- Recognize and resist the allure of the retribution reward. Imagine it's the equivalent of eating a pound of chocolate. It tastes good going down and hurts you in the long run.
- Instead of lashing back, express your frustration in the form of burned calories. My personal approach now is, "I'll show you . . . I'm going to get healthier."

Problem-Solving Mode

Once your prefrontal cortex (mediator) and amygdala (conflict) are in better balance, reach for the reward (dopamine and endorphin opiates) by entering the problem-solving mode.

Be purposeful in your objective to create value satisfaction and meaning. Judgment hinders the imagination. Creative options are unlikely to emerge if your amygdala is not in check. Getting it in check is a prerequisite to this step. Sustaining it requires an awareness of what position your "on/off switch" is in.

Pause, retreat, and check your compass. Reduce any resistance to creative thinking. Place options in the open. What are the consequences of the options before you? How do they compare with where you're at and where you would like to be? Are there objective standards or benchmarks available to test your data and options against? This change in momentum is what Leonard Marcus, a negotiator at Harvard, would refer to as a shift from self-interest to enlarged and enlightened interests. It is in this enlightenment that value creation emerges. You'll notice that a great deal of effort may be necessary before the dopamine kicks in. If you feel frustrated in your attempt to move the momentum forward, remember:

- You are the all important agent of self.
- You may be the more sophisticated and skilled of the conflict managers involved. Help your constituents help themselves. Remember,

you can't influence behavioral change without an understanding of another person's perceptions and values. You have the challenge of helping another you are conflicted with. Perhaps you can help them serve their values better, and in the process, find yourself in a better place.

- Make a quick list of the likely consequences of the trajectory you are on.
- How does it look when compared to the outcome you would find most acceptable?

Chapter 14

Social Connection: Born to Bond

How highly an individual perceives their quality of life appears to be a significant predictor of improved health outcomes. While many factors contribute to this, social satisfaction consistently rises to the top of the pyramid. The standardized instruments used to assess social satisfaction emphasize the quality of a person's relationship both to self and others. Individuals who score high on these surveys rate cultivation of relationships with family and friends as a priority value. The bottom line—support and connection to others fills a perpetual need for sustaining life satisfaction and for living well.

YOUR BRAIN AND SOCIAL CONNECTION

Let's briefly review how your brain's design encourages a connection to others. If there's one neurobiological system that brings together thought, feeling, behavior, and survival advantages, it's that which rewards social connection. As I've pointed out, social connection and social satisfaction have proven value when it comes to stress reduction, health promotion, and disease prevention. When it comes to health, there is no substitute!

> If there's one neurobiological system that brings together thought, feeling, behavior, and survival advantages, it's that which rewards social connection.

Recall that when mammals are compared to other living creatures, they consistently display these distinguishing social behaviors:

- Nursing and maternal care
- Communication for maintaining maternal-offspring control or "the separation cry"
- Cuddling and play

It would appear that we mammals are wired to commit to a family-like social structure. This has intuitive survival advantage as the ability to adapt to change may be better leveraged over a socially connected group.

Consider what happens inside you when you embrace someone you adore:

- Medial cortex of the frontal lobe increases serotonin responsiveness enhancing mood, feelings of joy, and positive emotions
- Endorphins are enhanced, modifying pain, improving comfort, and generating a satisfying state of bliss and contentment
- Your limbic system networking with your prefrontal cortex enhances a dopamine-oxytocin "dance" of love, attachment, and positive emotions
- Your hypothalamic-pituitary-adrenal axis (HPA), always poised to react to threat, is rendered more relaxed, resulting in decreased cortisol production. This reduces the "stress response," enhancing immune function, lowering blood pressure, inflammation, risk of diabetes, etc.
- Your locus coeruleus decreases its production of norepinephrine or adrenalin, reducing heart rate, blood pressure, anxiety, and oxygen demand.

. . . and all of this from hugging or cuddling with someone you care about.

These intricate networks, when cultivated (like providing more water and sunlight to this part of your brain's secret garden), reward cooperative social relationships and inhibit selfish impulses. The virtues of non-self perspectives are what define altruism. Altruism, extending kindness and compassion to others not because you have to but because you can, is a virtue identified in highly resilient children, adolescents, and adults.

Resilient individuals usually have cultivated important supportive social networks and attachments. Outstanding leadership and noteworthy acts of courage are often seen in individuals who value altruism: They *think*, "serving others is meaningful to me," they *behave* in ways that satisfy this value, and as a consequence, they *feel* better. All of this positively reinforces and motivates ongoing consistent behaviors. This is how the design appears to work. In other words, the more acts of non-self one engages in, the more acts of non-self one engages in. And in the end, the rewards to "self" are incredible—greater joy, happiness, contentment, meaning, better health, and longer life as your allostatic load is reduced. All of this and more, and it don't cost a penny? Where do I sign up?

Conversely, individuals who are more isolated, disconnected, and socially disenfranchised score much lower on quality-of-life satisfaction surveys; experience more mental illness, substance abuse, addiction, and cardiovascular disease; and are more likely to be of lower socioeconomic status.

If you compare performance capacity as it relates to healthy behaviors—good nutritional habits, regular activity, non-smoking, having coping strategies—a significant difference emerges between the socially attached and the socially disengaged. One simple explanation for these differences is that there are healthy people (the "lucky ones") and unhealthy people (the "unlucky ones"). People who are healthy will naturally be more upbeat and energized and have a desire to connect with others. "I'd walk, too, if I was in good health." "I'd volunteer with Habitat for Humanity if I felt better." "I would have more social activity if my health was better." Anyone whose health is poor confronts a risk of isolation as a consequence of losing independence, autonomy, and being infirm. Tempting though it might be to reduce the connection of health and social satisfaction to self-perpetuating cause and effect, it's far more complicated than that.

The point of this book is that there is no trajectory in our lives that we are not capable of changing, regardless of when we become aware of the potential to change. While some people possess personality characteristics that may make it easier to connect with others, it's a perceptual myth that you either have it or you don't. People who are unable to effectively connect with others need their social pilot light lit and the right relationships and social context to fuel it.

> While some people possess personality characteristics that may make it easier to connect with others, it's a perceptual myth that you either have it or you don't.

It's again worth re-examining the mutual contribution of nature and nurture to social satisfaction and attachment. On the nature side, we're born to bond. The very survival of hunter-gatherer groups was contingent on leveraging knowledge, skill, and responsibility to confront an uncertain and unpredictable reality. Our current reality by the way, is no less uncertain or unpredictable.

It takes longer for our children to grow to the point of being able to survive independently (as a parent of two adolescents I'm still not sure how long that is). The profoundly powerful attachment a mother has to her baby has a deeply rooted basis in brain structure and function, thanks to the blissful bond engendered as oxytocin, dopamine, and endorphins dance the dance of love. Nature's legacy to us is the gift to connect with others, and our design handsomely rewards thoughts, behaviors, and emotions that cultivate connection. This has clear survival advantages, connecting us to our "offspring" at a time of total dependence and enhancing the quality and quantity of our lives by connecting us to communities of support. The bottom line: The more you connect, the more you connect.

> The bottom line: The more you connect, the more you connect.

Which brings me to the nurture contribution. Here again is where we begin to identify countless possibilities for greater quality-of-life influence. A recurrent challenge emerges. How can someone transcend what may be perceived as insurmountable obstacles—health problems, impoverished living conditions, abuse, and feelings of loneliness, fear, shame, abandonment, isolation, and despair? There surely are no easy answers for major health setbacks or the perpetual stress of lower socioeconomic status.

Many individuals struggling to cultivate networks of support simply need more help. As noted, many factors influence social satisfaction and pose formidable obstacles. These obstacles vary considerably in their degree of difficulty. Examples include:

- Physical, developmental, or intellectual disability
- Behavioral health problems—depression, bipolar disease, anxiety syndrome
- Personality characteristics—shy, angry, hostile
- Self-conscious emotional states—shame, guilt, humiliation, embarrassment
- Low income

- Low educational level
- Insufficient knowledge, skill, or resources—literacy, language, ability to drive, use a computer, etc.
- Unhealthy behaviors—smoking, poor nutrition, substance abuse and addiction, sedentary lifestyle.

Individuals who confront such obstacles in their lives often feel over-whelmed. Existing systems of support—federal, state and local—may be con-fusing. Self-conscious emotions like shame, embarrassment, and deep pride make reaching out more difficult as our vulnerability becomes more trans-parent. Close (geographically speaking) networks of family have become spread thin as siblings disperse for jobs and education. More parents work multiple jobs to make ends meet resulting in precious little additional free time and energy. We're treating diseases of medical progress that are chronic and often progressive in nature. People are living longer and often at the ex-pense of compromised independence, performance capacity, and ability to navigate safely. I'd make the case that social disengagement is a significant public health issue and, in many instances, a remediable contribution to poor health outcomes and quality of life. I'll look at some of the evidence sup-porting this contention.

Shift Your Perceptions

Don't look at the ability to cultivate social relationships as a personality trait that you either have or don't have. Think of it as something that can be worked on and de-veloped, much like getting more exercise or eating better. You may need help in this dimension. That's okay. We all do. There's a big difference between being a social crea-ture who needs help cultivating his or her relationship garden and having no potential whatsoever to connect with others. I submit that the latter category is a percep-tual myth. Even connecting with a pet enables more posi-tive health outcomes.

We all have a tendency to view our individual chal-lenges in life as unique and unusual when in fact we're re-ally members of a very large club.

SOCIAL SATISFACTION, ME-B³, AND HEALTH OUTCOMES: THE EVIDENCE

For more than thirty years there has been a growing body of evidence in the field of psychoneuroimmunology (PNI) connecting psychosocial stress with illness and alteration in immune function. For example, researchers at Carnegie Mellon University and Ohio State University have shown that people who report strong social supports have more "robust" immune responses.

Conversely, studies have also demonstrated that social disengagement affects aspects of immune function and inflammation. Redford Williams, MD, Professor of Psychiatry and Behavioral Sciences at Duke University, has long studied the relationship between hostility and poor cardiovascular health. As a result, he's recognized the need and potential for training individuals to develop and apply more effective social skills through his "Life Skills" programs and workshops.

Dr. Williams' work, and that of others in this field, has provided growing evidence that points to an association between social isolation and hostility and increases in adrenaline driven or "sympathetic activity." The stress response may be turned on to a greater extent when individuals are isolated, depressed, and anxious. And as seen in other states characterized by an unchecked fight-flight stress response, increased cardiovascular risks and shorter life expectancy are reported.

An international study involving more than fifty countries demonstrated much worse health outcomes when individuals rated their degree of social satisfaction (at home, work, and community) to be poor. High-risk behaviors like smoking and poor diet were more prevalent. There were also pervasive differences in endocrine and immune function when marital conflict was present and associated with hostile behavior.

In 2003, the second part of the Whitehall study (cited in Chapter 11) that examined work-related stress and its relationship to health was published. The higher a person's social position and perception of control in the workplace, the lower the markers of inflammation like interleukin 6 (IL-6), C-reactive protein (CRP), and fibrinogen compared to those who perceived minimal control and status. Remember that less inflammation is desirable! Mild depression was also found to a greater extent in workers lower in the chain of power and control. Lower social status and locus of control were also associated with an inability of blood vessels to expand appropriately and also with greater immune/inflammatory expression.

A greater waist-to-hip ratio (more abdominal fat storage), evidence of pre-diabetes, and high triglycerides were all more prevalent in lower-status workers. You may recall that these are features of the "metabolic syndrome," which carries a four to five times risk of significant vascular disease. In all, more than 160 prospective studies have demonstrated a link between degree of perceived social support and status with coronary artery disease risk.

A large survey from Sweden, a country with a national database that is capable of tracking the health of all its citizens, looked at how often dementia (like Alzheimer's) was diagnosed in people over the age of seventy-five. Broader networks of friends and support were associated, as an independent factor, with a significantly lower risk of acquiring dementia.

In individuals with end-stage kidney disease, a journey characterized by enormous and unrelenting health challenges, self-rated quality of life was clearly connected to how highly they rated their support network and spiritual beliefs. We begin to see these connections emerge as one of the many potential healing benefits of religion and spiritual practice, as those involved with a spiritual or religious community tend to form more social networks and attachments.

I've been very active in advocacy for individuals with developmental disabilities. I can think of no dimension of life that contributes more to perceived satisfaction and quality of life as that of full social integration. I've witnessed profound transformation of the human experience made possible by more thoughtful social integration at school, home, work, and community. The smile on the faces of many adults confined to a lifetime of institutional settings, now living, working, and playing in our communities, says it all.

Robert Sapolsky, PhD, a biologist at Stanford University, has been studying primates for more than thirty years. Like people, primates live in large groups and place great value on social hierarchy. He's observed that primates who cultivate their social skills—sitting with other primates, grooming other primates, etc.—have the greatest likelihood of success and dominance. No attribute predicted the "success" of the primate more significantly than effective social skills. If baboons have an unstable social network, are fed a typical American diet (30 percent fat) and exhibit aggressive, dominant, and hostile behaviors, they end up like the CEO who nobody likes, everyone avoids, and who has a heart attack at age fifty. When aggressive, non-social baboons are taken to the cardiac catheterization laboratory (to look at the blood vessels in their hearts), they have twice the atherosclerosis or narrowing that their more social, less hostile fellows have. They also have higher cortisol and other markers of inflammation that we know to be a consequence of a fight-flight response that is in the "on" position to excess.

From research done by Redford Williams at Duke and others, we know that individuals who tend to get angry at the little things had accentuated fight-flight responses compared to those less easily provoked. Does this sound like anyone you know? Social competence and effective supportive networks are associated with reductions in anger and hostility and render a more "controlled" response to imposed stressful events.

Evidence from studies in animals and humans link neurotransmitters like oxytocin, dopamine, and endorphins to feelings of romance, attraction to others, and bonding. Trust, a *feeling* that defines meaningful relationships (and a seemingly scarce commodity these days), shares the same neurobiological pathways and is a critical dimension to motivation, reward, and behaviors that reinforce connection with others.

There are some interesting gender differences relating to the utilization of bonding and attachment as an antidote to the stress-response. At the risk of gender stereotyping, some of these generalizations may resonate with your own experiences. In *The Tending Instinct*, Shelly Taylor, PhD, a social neuroscientist at UCLA, and Laura Cousin Klein, PhD, at Penn State University, have researched the importance of friendships as a protective response to the stressors of life. Their research shows that women prefer to "tend and befriend" as opposed to fight and defend, in response to conflict and crisis. In married couples, men rely more on their wives than women do on their husbands when confronting stressful circumstances, in part, because women have cultivated stronger networks of emotional sharing and support outside the marriage.

At the risk of oversimplification, it seems the combination of oxytocin and dopamine and their distribution in the brains of women compared to men, in addition to estrogen, provides a powerful tool for empathy and social awareness (a "social thermostat" if you will) that values connection with others. I suspect any woman who has given birth to a child and breastfed experiences the profound power of attachment and bonding that men can only contemplate. Somehow the male bonding experience of a weekend fishing expedition is not quite in the same league as the female bonding experience of shared childbirth and breastfeeding.

Women also tend to discuss their feelings while men tend to prefer to give advice. My wife prefers a good love story. I like an action-packed thriller. Sound familiar? In a health study from Harvard Medical School, women with more friends and social ties reported fewer physical ailments and more joyful lives. There was also more resilience after losing a spouse (one of life's greatest stressors) when women rated their social satisfaction high prior to losing their spouses.

In an Australian longitudinal study of aging that followed 1,500 people over the age of seventy for ten years, a strong network of friends was linked to a 22 percent reduction in mortality, greater resilience, better mood, coping, and self-esteem.

From HIV/AIDS, cancer, heart disease, and a host of other chronic medical problems, support groups have been shown to be important for coping, symptom management, and quality of life. Previous studies have also demonstrated possible survival advantages in married individuals confronting melanoma or bladder or prostrate cancer when compared to those who are single and suffering the same illness. Some studies have demonstrated reduction in the inflammatory marker IL 6 in women with ovarian cancer receiving effective social support. In HIV/AIDS, group therapy can reduce "viral load" and enhance important markers of immune function.

A person who suffers from social isolation and depression is twice as likely to die over a period of five to ten years than someone who is not isolated or depressed. Add to that the stress of a more demanding job and less control, as is often seen in lower socioeconomic status, and the death rate is four times higher.

> A person who suffers from social isolation and depression is twice as likely to die over a period of five to ten years than someone who is not isolated or depressed.

STRATEGIES FOR CULTIVATING SOCIAL CONNECTION

While it makes perfect sense that being immersed in a supportive network of friends and family can foster resilience, improve quality of life, and make more likely better health outcomes, the obstacles to full cultivation of this innate tendency to bond are not easily overcome. Here are some action steps to help you increase your social connections or, perhaps more importantly, to help someone you care about who is at risk of social isolation.

- Make a list of three enjoyable social activities in your life that mean a lot to you. If you don't have three, think about possibilities that might connect you socially to your areas of interest. The options are practically endless, but here are some ideas to get you started:
  - Join a recreation league—bowling or coaching a youth league
  - Take a class—yoga, meditation, aerobics, or arts and crafts
  - Volunteer at a soup kitchen, hospice, hospital, or any number of local nonprofit groups such as Habitat for Humanity
  - Participate in a book club or sewing group
  - Become active in your children's school
  - Join a faith community or participate in a local mission project
- If you confront a chronic health ailment, figure out if your community has resources that support you and your needs. The fellowship and sharing of information provides many benefits. Groups commonly organize themselves around such health issues as cancer, chronic pain, fibromyalgia, and diabetes, to name a few. In addition, cardiac rehabilitation programs (usually available at hospitals) offer superb physical, social, and emotional support. Contact your doctor, hospital, or Department of Social Service to find a support group that meets your needs.
- As suggested in the next chapter on forgiveness, consider an important relationship in your life that has become "undone." Write a letter or call the individual as a courageous (and health-promoting) extension of your desire to "forgive and let live." You will enable healing to unleash itself and serve your long lost friend or relative by accepting the challenge and the vulnerability of reaching out.

There is no shortage of great causes and opportunities out there to share your time and talent, which as you've seen, reward health and quality of life in countless ways. Remember, the paradox—that which you feel would be great, but have little time for, will (after moving forward) reward you with more energy and more opportunity. You may also be rewarded with more time for living.

IF YOU OR SOMEONE YOU CARE ABOUT
NEEDS HELP CONNECTING TO OTHERS

This is a very common scenario. Many individuals, who would otherwise thrive in the presence of others, are limited by circumstances beyond their immediate control. It's easy to label someone as a loner or anti-social when in fact they may be confronting depression, social anxiety, or alcoholism. You may have a loved one who insists on "staying in," socially isolated and afraid to venture out because of a disability, care-giving responsibility, depression, fear, or anxiety. It's common for individuals who have a health issue to feel incomplete in the presence of others. There may be self-conscious emotions of shame or embarrassment to deal with. These are formidable obstacles.

If you are at a distance from a loved one, you may not appreciate the depth of these social challenges. People, particularly as they age, don't want to be a burden on family or friends. They may assume that their circumstances are just part of the aging process. I can't tell you how often patients have told me, "I had my good years and memories. I don't need much and don't want to be a burden on anyone." Acceptance of social isolation as an inevitable stage of aging, particularly for those who have lost a spouse of many years, becomes the mindset that makes reaching out for assistance more difficult. Often I have assisted individuals who are reluctant to reach out for fear they will be perceived as vulnerable and have their independence and autonomy taken away. The paradox here is that the courage to reach out is often what is necessary to remain independent and self-sufficient.

Earlier, I gave the example of my mother's reluctance to participate in our local community social day habilitation program after sustaining a series of major health setbacks. Her walking was unsteady. Her speech at times was slurred. Her independence was compromised. Her depression and anxiety made it impossible for her to feel the fire still very much burning inside her. Her depressed mood obscured her ability to appreciate her potential to share and connect with others. We literally had to force her to participate as a "trial." One month later, she was smiling, sharing, singing, connecting, giving, receiving, anticipating, and awakened to the precious moments of her life. People who confront chronic illness and disability often have a tendency to forget how important their lives are to others.

PERHAPS YOU FIND IT CHALLENGING TO MAKE
AND KEEP SOCIAL CONTACTS

Some considerations:

- Again, first consider whether you may have a treatable medical problem. For example, many people with social anxiety, depression, or bipolar disease just assume that's "the way they are," unaware that a remedy exists. If you're uncomfortable discussing this with a health care professional, talk to someone you trust—a friend or pastor. They may be able to assist you as these are challenging paths to walk alone.

- Pets. When it comes to loving, nonjudgmental, and steadfast companionship, pets rule! I must say I have a bias as a longtime dog lover. I've cared for many patients whose pets were the most important living souls in their lives. I'd often hear comments like, "My pet knows when something isn't right with me." "My pet is so comforting to me." "My pet welcomes me like she hasn't seen me in years." "I feel good when I'm holding my pet." Many hospitals and clinics use trained dogs for therapeutic pet visitation. Patients, families, and medical personnel are all drawn to the presence of a pet. Many studies demonstrate improvements in mood, immune function, and quality of life in pet owners compared to non-pet owners. Some dogs have been able to sense seizures in their owners before they actually occur. They are very attuned to changes in our moods and emotional states. I'm certain that my parent's dog did as much for their moods as their medication ever did. Pets are a buffer to isolation and loneliness. They're an important source of meaning and purpose for their owners. They do not attach conditions to the love and loyalty they express. In a perfect world, there'd be no abandoned pets and no lonely people who would benefit from owning one.

- The National Institute for Mental Health (NMH) offers some good advice on making and keeping friends. It's important to remember that while we may be born to bond, the social skills that allow us to connect are not always intuitive and within our grasp. The NMH noted attributes that better enable individuals to thrive in a relationship. They include:
  - Independence and self-sufficiency
  - Caring and upbeat demeanor
  - Talking about others in a positive way

- Honesty
- Reliability
- Ability to balance talking with listening
- Empathy
- Cleanliness
- Being nonjudgmental
- Social awareness of the need for personal space

- Make a list of your close friends and take inventory of what is positive about the relationship and what leaves opportunity for improvement. How would your friends characterize you? In your self-assessment inventory of likes/dislikes, where is there room for improvement? Think of a time when you created a change in your life that made your life better. Examples might include ending a relationship that was more toxic than therapeutic, joining a health club or reading group, being less the center of attention and more an active observer.

- Make a list of circumstances in your life that make relationships difficult—illness, stress, excessive work hours, distance, fear, money, transportation, etc. Now make a list of some options for resolving some of these challenges—cutting back on work or other obligations, exploring public transportation or carpooling, seeking more comprehensive medical care for a potentially treatable problem, etc. Make a list of action steps and follow through.

It's hard to imagine a better antidote to the biologic stress in our lives than cultivating networks of supportive relationships. As I advise our new medical residents who are entering a challenging culture of interpersonal development and professional growth, "The best way to survive and survive well is to make as many friends as you can."

Chapter 15

Forgive and Let Live: A Change of Heart that Will Change Your Health

"There is no revenge so complete as forgiveness."

Josh Billings

From a health and healing perspective, forgiveness serves you well. It's efficient. It's sophisticated. And it takes a big bite out of allostatic burden. The evidence is compelling that cultivating a mindset of forgiveness, particularly toward a transgression that may be insidiously wearing you down, significantly enhances emotional and physical well-being by unleashing a diverse and significant host of positive health effects. Despite its healing powers, however, forgiveness—from a neurobiological perspective—is hard to apply.

The good news is that forgiveness is a skill that can be developed. Don't give your DNA too much credit here. It's not a matter of having

> The evidence is compelling that cultivating a mindset of forgiveness, particularly toward a transgression that may be insidiously wearing you down, significantly enhances emotional and physical well-being by unleashing a diverse and significant host of positive health effects.

a "forgiving heart" or not. You're not predestined for forgiveness or unforgiveness. You're predestined to adapt to what serves you best. Cultivating your capacity for forgiveness is about reducing the burden of stress in your life and aging gracefully and well. The neurobiological imprints of forgiveness *can* be developed toward this end. This is very important. You, too, can create a cascade of positive biological fallout by reconfiguring ME-B^3 as it relates to the practice of forgiveness—biological effects that in turn become addictive and reinforcing.

> The good news is that forgiveness is a skill that can be developed.

> Cultivating your capacity for forgiveness is about reducing the burden of stress in your life and aging gracefully and well.

The second point is that forgiveness, though inspired by many world-views of religion and spirituality, can thrive outside such a context. A practice of secular humanism can also foster forgiveness with implications for greater control, mitigation of the stress response, and development of attachment and reward. In addition to promoting health, forgiveness has the added benefit—whether coming from a secular, spiritual, or religious perspective—of fostering social connection, compassion, and understanding.

WHAT FORGIVENESS IS NOT

The potential health benefits from forgiveness are often not realized because individuals may not be clear on what exactly matters in the process and what the goals, from a health perspective, really are. It helps to understand this by considering what forgiveness is not. *Forgiveness is NOT:*

- Condoning an act or behavior that hurt you deeply
- Compromising your moral and ethical principles. Forgiveness enables your ethical and moral principles to stand uncompromised and to coexist with a response that better serves your well-being
- An attempt to simply forget and move forward as if nothing ever happened
- An act that should be contingent on an apology from the person/ persons who hurt you
- An obligation to reconcile a conflict with someone who treated you badly

- A substitute for justice. Pope John Paul II had the nobility to visit Mehmet Ali Agca in Rome's Rebibia prison after he had tried to assassinate him. He was there to offer forgiveness. This was hardly a substitute for justice.
- Pretending everything is okay
- Something you can be forced to do.

These are but a few common misperceptions about forgiveness that create an enormous wedge between the adverse health effects of an unforgiving mind-set and the potential to apply an entirely different framework that makes forgiveness possible. This is an *epiphany* as you contemplate the possibilities inherent in the transformation of a deeply rooted grudge to an attitude that allows anger to coexist with health-promoting thoughts, emotions, and behaviors. People often struggle to realize this difference because they perceive forgiveness as an unnecessary and unfair gift to the perpetrator instead of a gift to one's self. Forgiveness is a gift to you, not to your transgressor.

> Forgiveness is a gift to you, not to your transgressor.

Any experience you have that creates the possibility for forgiveness implies wrongdoing by another. The depth and extent of the wound varies depending on the nature of the transgression. Something you value greatly may have been violated. As your initial experience of an offense is stored away in your memory, an emotional charge is tagged to it, reflecting the shock, hurt, anger, shame, or humiliation that you may have felt at that time.

Recall the interactions between the amygdala and the hippocampus in the initial encoding of this event. You will likely repeatedly replay this event in your mind because transgressions that carry the greatest health burden are those we're most likely to relive over and over again. Each time the event or events are replayed, the memory becomes reconsolidated or strengthened, reflecting the story of hurt you have experienced. The nature of the original formation of memory and of the process of reconsolidating (reliving-strengthening) of the memory will accentuate your thoughts/perceptions (your "hurt story"), the emotions attached to your memory (anger, distrust, and betrayal), and the fight-flight stress response adapted to protect you and to maintain a level of high-alert and hypervigilance for future transgressions (see figure 1).

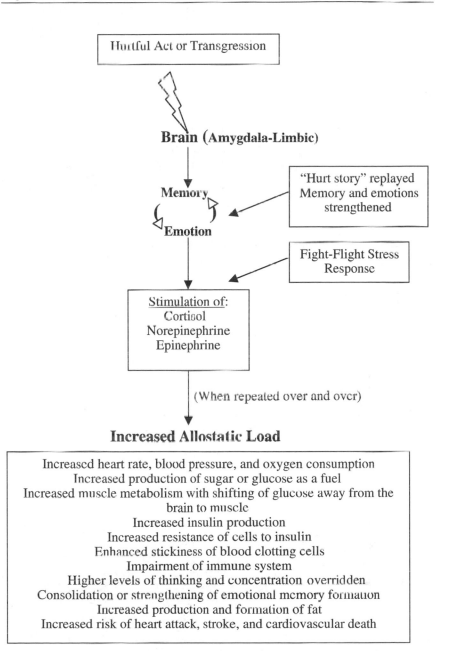

Figure 15.1   The Stress Response in a State of Unforgiveness

Hearing the transgressor's name, voice, or any subsequent contact will push the button that replays this physiological cascade. This is another powerful paradox, the forgiveness paradox. It goes something like this. The health burden, or allostatic load, created by the amygdala-limbic, emotional/memory response becomes both the

> Hearing the transgressor's name, voice, or any subsequent contact will push the button that replays this physiological cascade.

reason to consider forgiveness as well as the obstacle to forgiveness. For example, an expression of forgiveness necessitates overriding this powerful amygdala-limbic, memory-stress response that was adapted to protect from possible danger or threat in the first place. It requires (as is true in conflict management and interpersonal skill development) that your executive center or prefrontal cortex subdue this primal response to fight-flight that is telling you to dig in to the bitter end.

This primal defense system, though adapted to protect you, if repeatedly turned on or kept on becomes maladaptive and can hurt you even more. The result is a huge double whammy. You are hurt by someone else and your natural response to the hurt, in the long run, may add even further damage. This accentuation of the initial hurt may be masked by how sweet revenge feels or how insistent your amygdala is in prompting you to remain steadfast in holding a grudge.

> You are hurt by someone else and your natural response to the hurt, in the long run, may add even further damage.

REVENGE

Revenge is the natural desire brought to life by fight-flight. Righting a wrong and getting even are what the bright flashing neon sign on the landscape of fight-flight beckons us to do. Revenge is sweet. It's interesting that sweet is used to describe revenge. Something about it tastes great, like a mountain of ice cream and chocolate sauce. The biological reward induced by revenge (dopamine/opiate response) will surely satisfy the value of getting even, just as cocaine satisfies the user. The bliss, reward, and motivation leave little consideration for the domino of downside effects as noted in figure 15.1.

As I pointed out in the chapter on conflict management, it's hard to resist the sweet nectar of revenge as its origins in the amygdala-limbic system easily take over the controls from our prefrontal executive center. Revenge is to forgiveness and conflict management what the poppy field was to Dorothy and her intrepid friends as they earnestly ran on the yellow brick road to Oz. Too much time in the poppy field and you're not likely to reach the Emerald City (unless your prefrontal cortex can make it snow on your limbic system).

From a health or biological burden perspective, a hurtful initial event comes back to hurt you repeatedly each time you relive the transgression. This is a conceptualization of how different the trajectories of unforgiveness and forgiveness can look from a mind-body perspective (figure 15.2).

> From a health or biological burden perspective, a hurtful initial event comes back to hurt you repeatedly each time you relive the transgression.

THE SCIENCE OF FORGIVENESS

British studies examining individuals using fMRI have taken a closer look at patterns of brain response in test subjects responding to scenarios involving various interpersonal transgressions. Subjects were asked to respond to social scenarios where the intentions of the subjects in the scenarios could be inferred (an exercise in social reasoning). Scenarios that the test subjects judged as worthy of forgiveness revealed increased activity in the left medial and basal portion of the prefrontal cortex. This is consistent with research suggesting these regions may be important in allowing us to "read others" (empathy) and for forgiveness to unfold. It is our executive center that is again critical in reconfiguring thought/perception and the ability to subdue the impulses for revenge and for holding a grudge.

Forgiveness requires an override (*Thank You Plasticity*) of your defense systems by your prefrontal lobe. This is a familiar theme that biologically defines the challenge to transformation. It's the frontal lobe's capacity to separate a hurtful story of transgression that replays and strengthens itself to a story of understanding and empathy that allows a story of hurt to coexist with a greater health-promoting response. Sure, your anger will feel justified. Your principles are important. Your betrayal may require a court. Justice may need to be served. Shifting from a state of unforgiveness to forgiveness should not be equated with reconciliation of the relationship or obviating the need for justice. The anger may feel justified and that's okay.

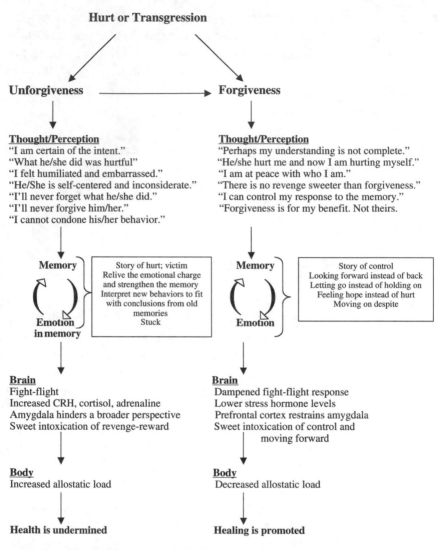

Figure 15.2 The Health Implications of Transforming a Mindset of Unforgiveness to One of Forgiveness.

It's not necessary or realistic to think that feelings of betrayal have to dissipate before forgiveness can emerge. I know what you're thinking. It's not easy to "let go" after someone has hurt you. Remember, forgiveness is not about forgetting. It is an awakening of choice, an option that places the point

of control on you. Let's briefly explore some recent research that makes the following points:

- Forgiveness can be learned and developed.
- Forgiveness can alter the health burden
  trajectory of unforgiveness through its
  biological effects, consistent with a reduction in allostatic load or burden.
- There are no acts, no matter how egre-
  gious and heinous, beyond the capacity for human forgiveness (Pope
  Paul II would have attested to that).

> Shifting from a state of unforgiveness to forgiveness should not be equated with reconciliation of the relationship or obviating the need for justice. The anger may feel justified and that's okay.

Some of the most exciting research in this area has come from Frederick
Luskin, PhD, clinical science researcher and director of the Stanford Forgiveness Project. He is also the author of *Forgive for Good: A Proven Prescription
for Health and Happiness*. Luskin has shown that structured training in strategies for applying forgiveness has clear and immediate benefit on physical and
emotional stress. His initial work involved Stanford students who underwent
forgiveness training. An important step in this learning process was simply
clarifying what forgiveness is and what it is not, with an emphasis on health
promotion. Strategies or steps for cultivating forgiveness were then emphasized and taught. When this process was applied to older adults with unresolved interpersonal hurt, several measurable outcomes emerged that were
significant relative to those who never received forgiveness training. After
eighteen weeks, the follow-up results included:

- Decreased levels of hurt and anger using self-assessment, standardized tools
- Decreased self-assessment of stress load
- Decreased symptoms of dizziness, pain, gastrointestinal distress, and
  muscular tension.

In an impressive display of the capacity and power of forgiveness, Luskin
studied adults from Northern Ireland, from both Catholic and Protestant
communities, who had lost immediate family members in the violence there.
As expected, many of these people insisted beforehand they could never forgive the perpetrators for their transgressions against their loved ones. The individuals received a one-week forgiveness-training program that Luskin de-

veloped at Stanford; assessments were performed before and immediately after the training with additional six-month follow-up data available. Participants in the training demonstrated:

- A 40 percent decrease in symptoms of depression
- Decreased stress, anxiety, and hurt
- A 20 percent decrease in anger
- Improved appetite, sleep patterns, energy, and general well-being
- Changes in blood pressure, most pronounced in individuals whose anger had diminished.
- *Remember, the motivation for forgiveness is to heal the forgiver, not the "forgivee."*

Studies examining individuals harboring unforgiveness, who were asked to replay their story of transgression, demonstrated the following signs of a "turned-on" stress response:

- Increased heart rates and blood pressure
- Increased brow muscle tone
- Increased cortisol levels

Other recently published studies of note linking forgiveness with health outcomes include the following:

- A Duke University study examined forgiveness in individuals with chronic pain. Standardized measures were used to measure forgiveness, and the dimensions of forgiveness varied greatly in the people they studied. Higher forgiveness scores were associated with lower levels of pain, anger, and psychological distress.
- A University of Wisconsin study examined the effects of forgiveness interventions on anger in individuals hospitalized with substance dependence. Decreases in anger, depression, and anxiety were noted in individuals receiving the intervention compared to those receiving standard therapy. Better self-esteem and resilience were also noted with forgiveness interventions. Importantly, these beneficial effects persisted at a four-month follow-up.
- A University of Tennessee study looked at cardiovascular responses when forgiveness is applied to interpersonal conflict. Over one-

hundred college students who had experienced interpersonal betrayal by a parent or friend/partner were studied. Lower levels of blood pressure, heart rate, decreased muscle tension, and skin conduction (a measure of adrenaline induced sweat production) were seen in individuals whose levels of forgiveness and empathy were higher at baseline. The magnitude of rise in these cardiovascular correlates when re-living the events of betrayal was also lower in these individuals. The "forgivers" also lowered their stress response to baseline more rapidly. When the "unforgivers," those who nursed grudges, were compared to "forgivers," the following differences emerged: unforgiving thoughts prompted more negative emotions, eyebrow muscle tension, skin conduction, heart rate, and blood pressure; forgiving thoughts prompted greater perceived control and comparatively lower physiological stress responses.

FORGIVENESS AND END-OF-LIFE CARE

It's been well documented and certainly my experience as a physician that forgiveness is an enormously important dimension to healing in end-of-life care. The types of health problems we now see tend to be more chronic and progressive by nature. End-of-life care, often thought of as cancer care, now commonly includes individuals with advanced heart, kidney, and lung diseases, and Alzheimer's. Individuals who confront their mortality will naturally begin to re-think their life priorities, replaying many prior memories, moments, and reexamining that which is of greatest value and meaning. Forgiveness is often essential to clarify and to reconcile this process.

People who are unable to forgive themselves or others are more prone to experience symptoms of depression and social isolation. They lose their capacity to appreciate what their lives mean to others: what a difference their lives have made. Forgiveness, in addition to its stress-response mitigating effects, enhances interpersonal functioning and social support. Together, forgiveness and its cascade of healthy outcomes have a more enduring effect on blissful levels of dopamine/opiate/oxytocin than does sweet revenge.

People I have cared for sometimes punish themselves with guilt and the perception that their illness is an act of punishment for some wrongdoing. "If my actions are responsible for all the events in my life, I must have done something to deserve this." This perception can prove an enormous obstacle to unleashing the healing potential within you. This perception will also diminish your tendency to reach out to others for help and sometimes delay seeking timely medical attention. Adequate self-care erodes, threatening the very foundation of who you are.

HOW TO DEVELOP AND APPLY FORGIVENESS

How can one develop and apply forgiveness more effectively in our lives? Consider starting with a shift in perception:

STEP #1

Old Perception	**New Perception**
I could never forgive this act or forget what he/she did.	Forgiveness is a learnable skill that starts by separating a hurtful event, over which I had little control, from the hurtful response to the event, over which I have full control.
He/she hurt me badly.	I am now hurting myself.

STEP #2

Take inventory of the events in your life where unforgiveness prevails. Any instance where you hold a grudge can be included. Add a value score one through five; five meaning the transgression is big as compared to a one or two for a minor grudge.

STEP #3

When you drill more deeply into a particular experience of unforgiveness, allow yourself to become more mindful of what rooms in your brain are "lit" as you relive the events. It might be easier to practice with an experience you attach a lower score to and work your way up. For example:

The Mind Room: Perceptions/Thoughts (a.k.a. your hurt story)
- "This person is bad, mean, and cruel."
- "I will not compromise my principles."
- " Forgiving him/her would condone the act."
- "I will look soft to my colleagues if I forgive them."

- "I'll get you my little pretty and your dog Toto too."
- "I've never been so humiliated."

The Emotion Room (feeling central)		The Brain Room (mission control)
Anger	Anxious	Fight-flight vs. Self-control
Hurt	Fearful	Looking back vs. Looking forward
Distrust	Betrayal	Hurting them vs. Helping self
Humiliation	Vengeance	

The Body Room	The Behavior Room
Less energy	Withdrawal
Intermittent bursts of increased HR/BP	Social isolation
Altered sleep	Less motivated to exercise, eat well
Worsening physical pain	Avoidance
Trouble concentrating	Ineffective interpersonal management

As you become more mindful of how your rooms are lit, write down some examples of your thoughts, your hurt story, and the feelings that define the experience for you. Develop an alternative story that allows hurt to co-exist with a response that has a different constellation of rooms lit in your brain's home. For example:

Mind
- "I am angry and hurt, *and* I cannot continue to allow this transgression to affect my health this way."
- "The less this person's behavior affects me, the less control they have over how I feel."
- "Which of my values has been violated? I'll take action to better satisfy them."
- "I accept what happened and I must move forward."

Emotion	Brain
Less anger	Diminished fight-flight
Less fear	Reward/motivation

More confidence	Diminished cortisol
More control	Prefrontal cortex trumps amygdala
Less hostility	

Body	**Behavior**
More energy	Meditation/Relaxation Response
Improved sleep	Enhanced social networks
Lower cardiovascular risk	Healthier eating and exercise
Fewer physical symptoms	Improved interpersonal management

By focusing on that which you can control, you disable the transgressor's control over you. In addition to reframing your perception and linking the choices you have for your response to their consequences, you allow yourself to choose more consciously. Other strategies that employ mind-body techniques that can assist with detachment from prior transgressions are "transcendence" practices. These practices cultivate greater awareness of the distinction between an event that has occurred and your interpretation and response to that event. Excellent avenues for mindfulness practice include:

- Meditation
- Yoga
- Tai Chi
- Prayer
- Therapy
- Friends/networks of support

In summary, the current study of forgiveness demonstrates profound capacity for healing change. This is another great example of *plasticity* in action. Apparent health benefits include a reduction in the stress state of *unforgiveness*. The physiological consequences of unforgiveness such as cardiovascular disease risk, immune suppression, and possibly impaired memory and cognition can be offset significantly by understanding what forgiveness is and how you can learn to more effectively apply it in your life.

As Confucius once said,

"If you devote your life to seeking revenge, first dig two graves."

Chapter 16

Raising Adolescent Kids:
The Storm Before the Calm

"Youth are heated by nature, as drunken men by wine."

—Aristotle

I have two children ages thirteen and sixteen. I can be totally objective and unbiased when I say they're pretty terrific. They're sweet souls whose bodies, minds, emotions, behaviors, and brains are in a state of rapid-fire change. As a parent, I'm now navigating the perfect storm of adolescent behavioral management (somewhat of an oxymoron). So are my children. In researching the neurobehavioral breakthroughs of recent years, I couldn't help but contemplate the implication for parents raising adolescent children.

If you have already raised children through adolescence, kudos! You may find yourself reading this chapter, looking back on your experiences, and thinking, "Yes. That explains a lot of what I experienced!" If you have children that haven't yet reached adolescence, now might not be a bad time to start a support group.

While I'm a proud and loving parent who desires to have full control over my children's destiny, I've reached the sobering conclusion that the true CEO is the brain that sits in my teenagers' heads. Instead of repeated and

frustrating attempts to understand their behaviors, I have chosen to understand better their CEO.

I am not their CEO. And you, despite your most loving intentions, are
not your adolescent kid's CEO either. That's not to dismiss the significance
we make in the lives of our kids who are riding this emotional roller coaster.
We've all been there ourselves. Remarkable isn't it? Somewhere between experiencing this stage and aging to the point of parenting adolescent children,
we've crossed the great generational gap. Just as we want to use our knowledge to exert more influence, we see our teenager's brain trumped by capricious and insatiable drives for independence, social stability, and reward-
satisfaction. And that's okay. The behavior that we universally observe in our
adolescents is necessary en route to developing a better compass for navigating the uncertain and capricious waters to come.

My objectives in this chapter are:

- To briefly examine current understanding regarding the neurobiological underpinnings of puberty and adolescent behavior.
- To review the nature of behavioral risk-taking that reflects the rapidly evolving biology of puberty as it races ahead of the CEO's ability to provide more rational oversight.
- To contemplate the parental implications made possible by examining adolescence from a mind-emotion-brain-behavior-body (ME-B^3)
  perspective.

Historically it was thought that we were born with a full complement of
brain cells. The accepted premise was that these cells, neurons, and synapses
solidified themselves into a "fixed" pattern of structure and function by early
childhood, gradually dwindling in number and function as we age. More
recent research in brain development has revealed a much more dynamic
process than once thought. Consistent with the
themes I've examined thus far, this dynamic
process continues actively to adapt and change
during adolescence and early adulthood. The
implication is that of the dramatic potential for
plasticity and adaptation in a brain that was
once thought to be in its completed state.

The developing brain at this developmental
stage of life may be more plastic than at any

> The developing brain at
> this developmental stage of
> life may be more plastic
> than at any other stage,
> molding and configuring
> more significantly in re-
> sponse to a growing reper-
> toire of experiences and to
> the environment.

other stage, molding and configuring more significantly in response to a growing repertoire of experiences and to the environment. This, from a parental perspective, points to "ripeness" in the potential for influence (influence = power), despite not having complete control of your child's CEO. This makes us more like the chairman of the Board of Trustees who provides fiduciary oversight of the CEO. You get the picture.

Dr. Jay Giedd and Dr. Judith Rapaport, at the National Institute of Mental Health (NIMH) in Bethesda, MD, with colleagues from McGill University in Montreal, studied the brains of kids using fMRI imaging at two-year intervals. What they found was very interesting. While much of the brain is fully developed by age six, there remain areas that continue to change significantly well into late adolescence (adolescence as arbitrarily defined by ages ten through twenty). In babies, there's actually an overgrowth of neurons (brain cells) and synapses (spaces between cells where transmitters communicate to many other neurons), followed by a reduction of some of these cells and synapses that are not in regular use by the age of three. It would appear early on, that we begin to unload that which doesn't serve us.

What was also seen, and of some surprise, was that a similar overgrowth of cells and synapses occurred again just before puberty (age eleven for girls and age twelve for boys). This proliferation occurred in the prefrontal cortex, that area in the brain behind our forehead. It's as if the brain's garden is suddenly fertilized, watered, and in receipt of abundant sunshine. Then during adolescence, the frontal lobes demonstrate a "pruning process," in which—as in early childhood—there is a systematic trimming back of the branches and leaves that are not selected for use (note the word "selected").

As the garden is pruned back in adolescence, the neurons are wrapped in a protective coating called myelin or white matter. This has the effect of strengthening the connection between the signals passing from one neuron to the next. It's kind of like going from a telephone modem to broadband cable modem or DSL. Another interesting observation involves the cerebellum, located in the back of the brain, just above the top of your neck. This region has always been thought to regulate motor or muscle function, coordination, and balance. In adolescence, the cerebellum—in addition to the prefrontal cortex—shows some evidence of change. It "lights up" when kids are asked to perform mental tasks. It may be that the cerebellum functions as a co-processor, assisting frontal lobe activity in its cognitive capacity.

Please note that this stage of growth and refinement is occurring primarily in the prefrontal cortex. And recall that the prefrontal cortex is the CEO's office, controlling, planning, reasoning, thinking abstractly, surveying, and managing emotional and behavioral impulses. Interestingly, teens with schizophrenic behavior—characterized by disordered thought and impairment of impulse control and reasoning—have been found to have significant loss of gray matter in the prefrontal lobes. Other regions of the brain proliferate and prune as well, though these regions seem to complete this task at a younger age. For example, areas of the brain responsible for language and spatial orientation (temporal and parietal lobes respectively) show few changes beyond the age of twelve.

CRITICAL OBSERVATION #1: THE PREFRONTAL CORTEX OF AN ADOLESCENT IS NOT QUITE READY FOR PRIME TIME

Our challenge as parents is to recognize this as a time of both great vulnerability as well as great opportunity. A better understanding of the biological underpinnings of adolescence may help explain how your sweet, affectionate, and empathetic Sunday school role model has been transformed, seemingly overnight, into a sullen, labile, indifferent, withdrawn, unpredictable, and ghastly caricature from a Tim Robert's movie. But there are also important parental and public health implications in understanding the effects of the neurobiological process on adolescent behavior.

> Our challenge as parents is to recognize this as a time of both great vulnerability as well as great opportunity.

Though most adolescents do just fine during this volatile and capricious developmental stage, there are consistent themes in adolescent behavior patterns that are universally expressed in all cultures:

An increase in time spent with peers and a decrease in time spent with family
I no longer take this personally. My kids once considered me a walking Mardi Gras; now they desire to spend less time with my wife and me. A strong drive to venture away from the nest is a necessary right of passage to assure survival without parental dependence. From a developmental success perspective, he or she with the most solid network of social connections and placement on the hierarchy of social status will be at an advantage. As I've discussed in pre-

vious chapters, these social networks continue to serve us well throughout life both mentally and physically. There is a clear health advantage to deep and meaningful social connection. My teens perhaps are just jockeying for a better position as adulthood approaches. Anyway, I simply can't compete with cell phones, the Internet, and the ubiquitous Instant Message systems.

Your teen's capacity for empathetic expression may be conspicuously lacking.
In the chapter on conflict management, I introduced the recent discovery of "mirror neurons," which are concentrated in the frontal lobes and able to create patterns of brain activity that allow us to "feel" the experiences of others. Intuitive skills like reading the faces of others—expressions that signal fear, fatigue, worry, and weariness—are not fully refined in the adolescent. You may have noticed that your teen's awareness of and response to what may be an obvious need and empathy-inviting opportunity—helping with chores, assisting a sibling, problem solving a family issue—are underwhelming, to say the most. When you may feel most in need of empathetic support, your terrific teen may simply not "read the landscape." Instead of saying, "Mom you look tired," you hear, "Can I have the keys, I'm in a hurry?"

> You may have noticed that your teen's awareness of and response to what may be an obvious need and empathy-inviting opportunity—helping with chores, assisting a sibling, problem solving a family issue—are underwhelming, to say the most.

This is not to say that empathy is totally lacking in adolescents. I'm sure some of you are thinking, "Not my kid, he/she is sensitive." Sensitivity and empathy are different in nature. The catharsis of self—so strong in adolescence as the drive for independence strengthens—will limit abstract interpretation of the circumstances they confront. The anterior cingulate gyrus, deep in the prefrontal cortex, and the limbic structures, both important in the expression of empathy, have not yet completely networked. As a consequence, an adolescent may be very sensitive (not wanting to hurt another) and yet need help recognizing the opportunity to extend that sensitivity (reading the angst on another's face). This is another example of a developmental process that can be both a source of hurt and opportunity—an opportunity in that plasticity can help to sculpt a teen's awareness of others' perspectives, thoughts, and feelings. More on this later in the chapter.

Increased risk-taking and exploration

There is a sobering paradox in the life of an adolescent. On one hand, they boast the healthiest burst of bone development, muscle mass, energy, stamina, learning capacity, speed, reaction time, and immune function than at any other time in life. They are also at a 200 to 300 percent increased risk for mortality compared to kids less than the age of ten. And not surprisingly, the common causes of serious injury and mortality in teens are the result of high-risk behaviors:

- Accidents
- Recklessness
- Alcohol and substance abuse
- Suicide
- Depression
- High-risk sexual activity
- Homicide
- Eating disorders

Substance abuse, for example, has been on a rising trend in the U.S. Estimates suggest that approximately 50 percent of high school seniors consume alcohol at least once per month. By the time teens reach eighth grade, nearly 50 percent have had at least one drink and 20 percent have been "drunk"! It is estimated that 17 percent smoke cigarettes, the quintessential bane of health promotion efforts. Use of heroin and methamphetamines is increasing at an alarming rate. Of equal concern is that teens perceive less risk associated with these behaviors in recent years (from 20 percent in 1999 to 40 percent in 2004 perceive less risk).

We've all been there, and most of us—but not all—have been spared our lives and have avoided significant disability. There's a fine line between taking risks as a biologically driven desire to learn and experience and foolishly risking life and limb. A complete and wise frontal lobe would sure come in handy when such risky decisions are contemplated. As Ronald Dahl, MD, from the University of Pittsburgh once noted, "Adolescents make a lot of decisions that the average nine-year-old would look at and say, that was a dumb thing to do."

> Adolescents make a lot of decisions that the average nine-year-old would look at and say, that was a dumb thing to do.

CRITICAL OBSERVATION #2: AS THE ONSET AGE OF PUBERTY DECREASES, THE DURATION OF ADOLESCENCE INCREASES

If you study what happens during puberty, you can begin to separate hormonal-induced behavioral drive from those that are more a manifestation of a brain that needs more time and experience. In other words, some behaviors are a direct manifestation of puberty itself (the nature aspect) and others reflect the shortcomings of an executive center that needs more time and mentoring (the nurturing aspect).

You may have noticed that puberty is occurring at a younger age. In the U.S., for example, the average age of menarche has decreased from fifteen to sixteen in 1800 to twelve and a half today. Also, by the age of ten, breast and pubic hair development was seen in two-thirds of Euro-Americans and in 95 percent of African American girls.

As it is, the maturing process of the brain continues into the late teens and early twenties. With the onset of adolescence now occurring much earlier, the span of time that teens remain vulnerable to risk-taking behavior is increasing. Or you might say that the puberty-driven penchant to engage in risky sexual behavior, for example, is getting further ahead of the prefrontal cortex's ability to rein it in.

Puberty is defined by changes in male and female reproductive hormones. The hypothalamus in the center of the brain sets this cascade in motion, releasing a hormone called GnRH or gonadotropin releasing hormone. This stimulates the pituitary gland to produce FSH (follicle stimulating hormone) and LH (luteinizing hormone). These hormones stimulate estrogen release by the ovaries in women and testosterone release by the testes in men. Breast and testicular development begin. The adrenal glands (the same organs involved with fight-flight in their production of cortisol and adrenalin) are stimulated to enhance more androgen production. This contributes to pubic and axillary (armpit) hair growth. It is in this perfect storm of reproductive development that romantic desire, risky behavior, and reward-seeking are taken to new levels, threatening to overwhelm the executive center's capacity to effectively manage. Bring back any memories?

As if that wasn't enough, the pituitary gland also produces a surge of growth hormone resulting in dramatic changes in stature, muscle mass, bone development, voice, etc. These dramatic physical changes when combined with changes in sexual development may themselves elicit an "external" response from others, affecting thought and emotion. Thoughts like, "Wow, people find me attractive," or emotions like, "I thought we were just friends, now I'm confused by the mixed messages I'm receiving." Remember the profound capacity for thought and feeling to affect behavior. You can appreciate why I refer to this as "The Perfect Storm" of behavioral navigation. It can also be "The Perfect Storm" of parenting.

CRITICAL OBSERVATION #3: ON THE ADOLESCENT RACETRACK OF LIFE, THE ENGINES HAVE STARTED BUT THE DRIVER HASN'T COMPLETED TRAINING

Adolescents experience an increase in conflicts with authority.
I know this comes as a shock to you. I know I never conflicted with my parents (ah, the beauty of memory distortion). Now I try to see the behavior from a human developmental perspective. This allows me to transform an experience I could easily take personally to one that's attributed to a specie-necessary survival skill.

There's clearly a necessity for adolescents to "push themselves away" to grow and learn outside the predictable and boring confines of the nest. Adolescents (not unlike adults) also need to establish self-interest-based ego-satisfaction as they jockey for a higher place on the mythical ladder of popularity. (Though ultimately, it will be important to learn the difference between popularity, which so sweetens the feedback of our reward response, and relationships that support on a deeper and more health-promoting level. In other words, the difference between being liked and being sustained.)

Conflict is an inevitable byproduct of this need to establish an individual position of approval, acceptance, affirmation, and affection. The perception is that there's a lot of competition out there—so many teens, transiently and peripatetically, willing to assume risk to satisfy sensation—seeking and reward-craving drives. The "ignited passions," as described by Robert Dahl, MD, are lit by puberty and accompany a whirlwind of activity in the amygdala-limbic areas, resulting in emotional impulses that can quickly take over the race car, particularly when the track gets challenging. An amygdala-limbic highjack of a still vulnerable prefrontal cortex can set the brush of conflict in motion, quickly consuming the landscape in its path. Ignited passions

proliferate at a time when planning, logic, reasoning ability, inhibitory control, and problem-
solving skills have not fully developed. While
your driver's race car is poised to speed into the
emotional-motivational-reward wind tunnel,
your race-car driver is mostly untrained and
without a map. Expect collision to look like
conflict.

Ignited passions proliferate
at a time when planning,
logic, reasoning ability, inhibitory control, and problem-solving skills have not
fully developed.

As an aside, male teens and female teens demonstrate behavioral patterns
in response to conflict that sometimes look different. While young men will
tend to engage fight-flight, settling the conflict in a vacant lot, young women
understand that the best way to seek revenge is to undermine the social stability of the adversary. For young women, it's social. For most guys, it's force
or alpha-like behavioral domination.

Another paradox here is that most adolescents by age fifteen can sit
down, take a computer generated test, and generate adult capacity for abstract thought, reasoning, and decision-making. However, when "test" conditions are reproduced in "the wild," the multidimensional and spontaneous
world out there, these competencies break down. When my teens appear dysfunctional in their emotional and interpersonal skill capacity, I see less rebel-
lion and more a need to offer guidance. After all, they're victims of cognitive
delay, unable to effectively manage the emotional catapult of puberty.
Unfortunately we cannot use this excuse as adults.

CHANGES IN SLEEP PATTERN

The neurobehavioral basis for the alteration of sleep-wake patterns in our
teens is still not well understood. What is well described and what I have experienced is perfectly consistent:

- Teens go to sleep later
- Teens wake up later

In a perfect world, where the learning capacity of teens was maximally
exploited, school would start at 10 a.m. and finish at 6 p.m. No adolescent
on earth will experience maximum learning capacity at 7 a.m.

BEHAVIORAL PATTERNS IN ACTION

Let's look at a common scenario that highlights some of these behavioral patterns and the underlying biology that fuels them. You're fifteen-years-old. While at a social gathering at a friend's house, you're introduced to a sixteen-year-old, a junior at the local high school you attend. There's an immediate spark of attraction. Some innocent touching on the arm and shoulders turns into a series of innocent kisses. Soon you have to be picked up by your father as the party draws to an end. As you sit in the back seat on the way home, you feel on top of the world. Your feelings are a whirlwind of surprise, bliss, ecstasy, romance, satisfaction, and anticipation. You are in love. You are certain of it. Despite exchanging less than five-hundred words and knowing very little about the stranger you just met, you contemplate that this could be the one you spend the rest of your life with. The consumption of thought about this stranger intensifies. You can hardly bear the thought of having to wait another thirty-six hours before the next contact. All you can think about is your next connection. This relationship, in its infancy, has almost instantaneously risen to the top of the motivational pyramid. Eating, family, and sleep have become secondary. No one can convince you that this is not as serious as you think. Seeking reward and attachment leave little room for an alternative interpretation.

Your parents sense something is up. They're seeing less of you. You're spending more time multitasking—talking and text messaging on your cell phone, sending Instant Messages on the computer—as a flood of communication with friends pours in and discussion with parents tickles to a drip. You say less at the dinner table and leave more food on your plate. Your parents gingerly probe for an avenue of insight, a glade of light into your consciousness. You offer little. "They would never understand what you're experiencing anyway." Your academic studies and piano lessons are less of a priority right now. You would relinquish them in a heartbeat to share another romantic encounter with this new friend.

Sound familiar? Love at first sight? It almost seems a rite of passage into adulthood. Shakespeare continued this universal theme in *Romeo and Juliet* in 1595, capturing the whirlwind of youthful passion and the tension between sexual interest and romantic motivation on one hand, and the requisite self-regulation of adulthood on the other.

So what advice can emerge from a greater understanding of the biological fallout from puberty? What can be taken away from these effects on brain biology? What can be recommended based on recent neuroscientific insights that suggest the need for the prefrontal lobe to be pruned and refined during later teenage years? How do we as parents reconcile an engine that is ready to run with a driver that is still lacking driving skills? In researching this topic, I came upon some key messages that were distilled from a recent New York Academy of Sciences symposium on adolescent brain development. I offer them to you.

1. Much of the behavior characterizing adolescence is rooted in biology. When mixed with social influences, adolescents are more likely to conflict with their parents, take more risks, and experience wide swings in emotion.

In other word's, your teen's brain, its CEO, is under the powerful influence of forces beyond your parental control. While this is hardly a comforting thought, it does help to shift attention from expectation of full parental control to one of acceptance and greater awareness for opportunity to emerge from the "ignited passion." This is a huge shift, as any parent knows. The ability to reason with a frontal lobe that is still "pruning," that is less effective in complex social situations, and that is buffered by a storm of strong emotional motivation will not come easily. Don't take this personally. The anger, conflict, impulsivity, and reshuffling of the value pyramid is less intended to be an attack on you and more the need to transition, as all species do, from nest and full dependence to independent flight and self-care. Within the perfect storm of pubertal challenge, appreciate that your teen's brain development (which may seem conspicuously delayed at times) is working its way to full maturation.

The challenge for us as parents:

- Don't take it personally. Remember your amygdala's fight-flight button will get pushed. As your button is pushed, you'll want to fight back, get tough, and teach them a lesson. Fortunately, you have a frontal lobe that has a wealth of experience imbedded and has hopefully been nicely pruned. Consider strategies for avoiding an amygdala highjack of your own.
  - Meditation
  - Relaxation response

- Prayer
- Social support
- Counseling
- Exercise
- Music
- Pursuing recreational interests

- Be present in the moment despite a message that may imply, "No Parent Welcome." Resist the natural tendency to want to back off, withdraw, and lose interest. Be more aware of your pattern for handling conflict. Kerry and Patterson, in their book *Crucial Conversations*, make the distinction between two distinct and maladaptive styles of handling delicate situations. One is silence (avoidance, withdrawal, or masking). The other style is violence (controlling, labeling, or attacking).

  - Listen, even if it doesn't sit right with you.
  - Make eye contact and look for the subtitles of non-verbal communication.
  - Observe with interest, the behavior of your teen. Do not lose faith in finding opportunity to connect in a meaningful way.

- Stay connected. Instead of reacting to the behaviors that come as a consequence of frontal lobe "pruning," try to assist with the pruning itself. It's natural to want to avoid and distance yourself from someone who is behaving like they're radioactive. Adolescent behavior will do that. Here your frontal lobe must say, "Stay connected, stay interested, stay the course." While your teen may not leave many doors open for you to enter, it's important to be there when they do.

- Stay sane. Safeguard your own sanity in ways that model effective adult behavior.

  - Avoid shouting matches that are consuming, conflicting dead-ends.
  - Get eight hours of sleep each night.
  - Limit alcohol use in the home.
  - Get more exercise. It's a great antidote to stress, better than Prozac and with fewer side effects.
  - Meditation and the relaxation response are excellent methods to reduce the allostatic load that sometimes comes with the raising of adolescent teens.

2. The lack of synchrony between a rapidly maturing physical body and a latent-maturing brain can explain many behavioral patterns seen in teens.

Parents appreciate all too well the ease with which teenage pregnancy, STDs, and HIV can occur. Parents universally fear the consequences of their teen's sexual behavior. While education is critical, it's not going to be enough to rein in the fireworks of romantic motivation and reward seeking. While widely debated by legislators, health care professionals, educators, theologians, and social scientists, it's apparent that adolescence is a time when developmentally reward-seeking drives and romantic motivation will trump reasoning, regardless of how smart the teen is or how "solid" the family is. When it comes to adolescent sexual behavior, emotion will tend to trump logic.

> When it comes to adolescent sexual behavior, emotion will tend to trump logic.

And while I agree with promoting abstention, to "just say no" is missing the biological basis of why we behave the way we do. I'm an advocate of education, abstention, and protection. Our teens are of a generation where puberty starts earlier and their internal executive center of reasoning lags much later. I don't trust my teen's pruning frontal lobe and developing cerebellum to "just say no" when the power of the amygdala-limbic enterprise that Shakespeare and many others have written about over the centuries pushes to have the last word. These are important issues from a public health perspective. I am a proponent of sex education, birth control, and the "morning after" emergency contraception. As of this writing, the FDA has not yet approved emergency contraception despite its efficacy and safety.

3. Adolescent reward-response systems may be different from that of adults, prompting them to seek higher levels of novelty and stimulation to achieve the same feeling of pleasure.

This generalization based on current neurodevelopmental and neuroendocrine data affirm what all parents of teens know and feel all too well. The biological underpinnings of reward response and risk taking are very significant. Behavior that may seem blatantly rebellious and defiant, at least at times, expose a developmental vulnerability that teens confront in this white water rapid ride into adulthood. The vulnerability created by a reward-response system is very difficult for logical reasoning to compete with. Knowing your kid is a good kid with good moral values is great though not necessarily enough to neutralize the risk-taking allure and the uncertain ability to link choice with consequence. Good kids can drink too much. Good kids will get pregnant. Good kids can try heroin or crack just a few times and get hooked. Good kids will drive fast and experience their lives moment to moment.

When examined this way, the perpetual tension a parent feels between the need to let go for the sake of growth, learning, and independence, and the need to exert greater control is understandable. Tension. Tension. Tension. As parents know well, the domain of parental control with a teen is different from that of an eight- to ten-year-old. A prepubescent biology is much easier to exert influence over than that of a teen's pushing the limbic limit. We therefore must confront the anxiety of having to relinquish some of that control to jockeys not quite ready to ride their untamed horses. Still we can set limits. Concrete limits are very important—curfew, driving contingencies, etc. When you examine teen receptivity from the perspective of an amygdala highjack, *a specific message that links cause and effect and makes clear some expectation of accountability is likely to be more effective.* As parents, it's a good idea to set limits that are non-negotiable.

How we behave and perform as parents has the greatest influence over the behavior of our children. This is also true in every other domain of our lives—work, family, friends, community. With varying degrees of success, our behavior—what we say, how we say it, tone, choice of words, actions— will add to our teen's experiential repertoire of learning. *This is where great opportunity exists to influence the prefrontal lobe pruning process.*

The potential exists for nurture to refine what nature has given us. The perpetual challenge in raising adolescents is where the rubber of risk-taking behavior meets the road of reasoning. Here are some concluding suggestions for tailoring the parental approach to the biology you confront.

- In addressing areas of concern, focus on the behavior. Be specific. I no longer find myself focusing on issues like responsibility, respect, knowledge, or personality type. Important though these domains may be, they're inherently subjective in the criteria we choose to define them. Focusing on a specific behavior/performance issue minimizes the tendency to fall into the frustrating exchange of what it means to be responsible. It's hard for anyone to dismiss a behavior that's been observed. It is, after all, the behavior we wish to influence. Charles Dwyer, PhD, at the University of Pennsylvania, sums it up beautifully. We're more likely to influence behavioral change in anyone (friend, colleague, or teen) by addressing the individual's perceptions and values. For example: "You're an adult now, you need to be more responsible and respectful vs. please keep your room neater." Ultimately, the emphasis should shift from:

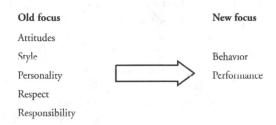

Old focus	New focus
Attitudes	
Style	Behavior
Personality	Performance
Respect	
Responsibility	

What we as parents leverage to influence behavior in our teens should also be reexamined, based on findings from current social science. For example:

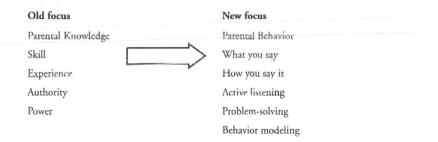

Old focus	New focus
Parental Knowledge	Parental Behavior
Skill	What you say
Experience	How you say it
Authority	Active listening
Power	Problem-solving
	Behavior modeling

- Rules and behavioral guidelines should be specific and concrete. Allowing some negotiation latitude—curfew, number of passengers allowed in the car, etc.—will leave your teen feeling more engaged and more of a negotiating partner, instead of receiving another parental mandate. The more concrete, the harder it is to impose subjective interpretation. Make sure there is clear communication and mutual understanding. A written contract can also serve to "bond" a more enduring and effective commitment.
- Apply the Ju-Jitsu approach in response to problem behaviors. This is much easier said than done. The principle, as this martial arts philosophy implores, is to "silently" absorb the energy of the circumstances, reserving the tendency to want to fight back, lash out, and punish. If both you and your teen enter the mode of an amygdala highjack, the communication is doomed. Transforming the under-

standable desire to exert parental authority to an approach that more calmly and consciously addresses options and consequences will serve you better. This approach also models a higher level of reasoning, which your teen's plastic prefrontal lobe needs to observe, experience, and absorb. *Speak when you are angry, and you will make the best speech you'll ever regret.*

- Dr. Ronald Dahl at the University of Pittsburgh refers to the adolescent "ignition of passion." The same "heat of nature" that Aristotle referred to can be harnessed for positive behaviors as well. Igniting the passion of music, generosity, theatre, literature, dance, compassion, athletics, academics, relationships, and worship can facilitate meaning, value creation, and a reward response that will reinforce positive, health-promoting, and risk-reducing behaviors.

  A study published in the *Journal of Adolescence* examined the relationship between religion and health in American youth. Religiosity, as measured by worship attendance, prayer, and the personal degree to which God was central in the lives of these youth, was linked to better decision making; increased academic and social competence; lower rates of smoking, teen pregnancy, suicidal ideation, and elicit drug use; and higher life satisfaction.

- Praise your teens! They're primed to seek and savor reward. Take every opportunity to praise and reinforce desirable behaviors and performance. Affirmation should shower your adolescent's behavioral garden.

- I offer one last opinion on assisting the teen jockey about to gallop away from the stable. While I have no direct scientific evidence for this (as I do not believe it has been well studied), I offer the following observation. You and I are well aware of the "gut feelings" that guide our thinking and behavior, sometimes in very subtle ways. The neurobiological expressions of fear, uncertainty, risk assessment, danger surveillance, etc., are deeply rooted in our midbrain where fight-flight maintains its sentry, perpetually scanning for imminent threat.

  The many mediators of the fight-flight response have been vigorously reviewed. Feeling queasy, anxious, crampy, tight, and on edge are some of the ways our gut attempts to speak to us. In this sense, the gut instincts are primed and ready for sending a warning before the prefrontal lobe can safely take over. Our gut, in essence, is an extension of our brain's communication to us.

  I recommend that you ask your teen to isolate him or herself for five minutes when confronting a decision to engage in high-risk behavior, one that may have a strong siren song of reward or the pressure to conform attached to it. Have them close their eyes, relax their breathing, and bring the current circumstances into focus. Once there, have them bring their awareness to their gut. What is their gut telling them? Is what they are about to do creating any gut anxiety, fear, or apprehension? Helping our kids (and ourselves) to become more attuned to the signals our gut sends us is like having an additional trusted friend, 24-7, guiding our choices, with or without a clear cognitive understanding. Trusting your gut is critical.

And when all is said and done as parents, we are grateful for another safe day. We pray that tomorrow will be safe as well and have faith that the right dose of guidance and understanding will lead to a smooth transition. After all, we've all been there and done that!

Chapter 17

Mindfulness Practice, Music, and a Yellow Lab

Imagine this. The Dali Lama jogging barefoot on a beach, iPod comfortably attached to his upper arm, mindful of the music, with a yellow lab running at his side. Now there's a picture of total health, ME-B³ for the Westerner. Add a colorful pair of Nikes™, and you have a pretty good marketing icon. The tagline could be . . . "Just Be It."

Surely the Dali Lama would have minimal cortisol emerging from this scenario. Wouldn't expect a great deal of adrenaline either. This would surely be fertile ground for serotonin, dopamine, opiates, GABA, and oxytocin to be dancing in harmony. Fight-flight is never on the radar screen in this scenario. Like the gazelle on the savannah, fight-flight comes and goes, transient, targeted, and efficient. Neither are there thoughts about what the future will bring. There is only the present. Reward, attachment, meaning-making, and positive emotional memories are growing and thriving in this garden. "Just Be It."

So what do the Dali Lama, a Beatles tune, and a yellow lab have in common? When it comes to enlisting the biological reserves within you to naturally promote health and healing, mindfulness practice, cuddling with your pet, and grooving to "Sgt. Pepper's Lonely Hearts Club Band" have a lot in common. I view this as an example of the awareness, reward, attachment, and positive emotional memory, or the "Fab Four," that's capable of playing inside our head.

Each of the four works well in isolation, though they inherently connect and overlap. Here's an everyday example of "mindfulness on the fly," totally transforming a health-undermining trajectory to a health-promoting trajectory—a practice that when repeated over time, pays big dividends.

As I was driving to our local library to work on this manuscript, I pulled into my favorite coffee house to satisfy an addiction, a reward-motivation response inspired behavior if ever there was one. Usually I take the route of the "drive through," but this morning something inside said, "Get out of the car. Turn off ESPN radio and interact face-to-face with another human being." As I entered, the scent of the coffee and the sight of many sweet, colorful delicacies created a beckoning dance on my limbic floor. Memories stored deep in my hippocampus of vanilla cream and chocolate reproduced the sweet taste as if actually sitting on my palate. My amygdala in its massage of these sweet memories reminded me of the deep (and very momentary) bliss that would reward the immediate consumption of these baked sirens of sucrose.

I had my work cut out for me as I have committed to cutting back on refined carbohydrates and sweets, the "white menace," as my colleague Mark Liponis would refer to them. There was a long line in front of me that was moving very slowly. I could see the store was short-staffed and the workers very busy (social awareness breeds empathy). People in front of me were ordering large numbers of coffee, donuts, and muffins. The challenge I confronted was now accentuated. I had to overcome the strong desire to purchase a donut or muffin, and I had to wait as the temptation had more time to seduce.

As I waited in line, I repeatedly looked at my watch, lamenting the time "lost" from being able to write. I found my mind racing—thinking of work, exercise, tasks, plans, strategies. I was increasingly impatient, which began to undermine the empathy I had for the workers behind the counter. It seemed the people in line in front of me were ordering every combination of coffee available, in addition to one of each of the many varieties of donuts, muffins, croissants, and breakfast sandwiches. I was fast approaching a breaking point! I began to think that any order of more than twelve items was inappropriate per family (I would consider a dozen donuts as twelve items). Yes, that's good. There should be two lines, an express line for four items or less and a line for ordering more than four. There I was, increasingly impatient and overwhelmed with temptation, all of which bubbled within as my mind raced with mindless drivel.

And then it happened.

AWARENESS

Impatience equals stress, which equals cortisol, which equals cardiovascular burden, which equals increased allostatic load. Temptation equals calories, which equals the equivalent of a five-mile run. The equivalent of a good five-mile run could be neutralized in an instant by a brief lapse of palatal indiscretion. I could sense that I had little chance against the powerful influence of the amygdala-limbic threat, particularly while my insightful prefrontal arbiter was preoccupied with total mindlessness.

RESPONSE

In line, standing, I straightened my spine and envisioned my muscles relaxing like articles of clothing hanging on a coat rack. I observed my breathing. Quietly and with every exhaled breath, I said to myself "calm-control." I brought myself to greater awareness of the people in line, the workers, the sounds, scents, and the hubbub. I attempted to observe myself, in line, aware of thoughts to which I had held firmly and slowly released. I let go of judgment. I released my thoughts of all that had passed and speculation of the future and what was to come. I entered the moment, and simply allowed it to play out around me. My breathing became more effective, my mind less distracted, my feelings more calm, and quickly I began to experience more control. In a matter of minutes I was on a different trajectory. The guy in front of me who I believed was ordering for his entire office staff, and whom I would have slapped a violation on for exceeding a reasonable limit of ingestible items, became an ambassador for those whose values for coffee and

donuts he had come to satisfy. My thoughts shifted from a scenario of judgment to a scenario that just existed without any emotion attached to it.

As I made it to the front of the line, I was calm and quick to empathize
with the obvious disparity of worker supply and customer demand. I told
myself I would get the first cup from a newly brewed pot. I stood bold and
vulnerable, face-to-face with the siren song of fresh muffins, sugary-sweet,
glazed, sprinkled, frosted, melt-in-your-mouth, perfectly displayed weapons
of mass destruction, certain that my prefrontal lobe would come out of the
bullpen in the bottom of the ninth to save the day. "Would you like any
donuts with your coffee sir?" "No thanks," I confidently replied, knowing I'd
just avoided the caloric equivalent of a forty-five minute hard run.

This is a good everyday example of the effectiveness of being more mindful and how it can quickly influence thought, feeling, and behavior. It's also
a good example for highlighting the ease and portability of mindfulness practice. After all, *mindfulness is about you becoming more aware of you.* As Jon
Kabat-Zinn, an artist and good master in mindfulness practice and application would say, "Wherever You Go, There You Are."

I've come to better understand and appreciate the importance and power of
mindfulness practice. It's always been a challenge for me to experience stillness.
My mind tends to be in many places at the same time. Sound familiar? While I
had many friends and patients who practiced meditation and yoga, I didn't feel
I could easily enter this state of being that people often shared as an essential dimension of their lives. Prior attempts to sit quietly and breathe calmly, quickly
became a struggle to ward off the thoughts that would bombard me, and respirations seemed more hyperventilation than calm spontaneity. As friends, patients, and my own self-interests inspired a better understanding of what these
practices are all about, I came to realize that I knew very little about them and
harbored many misconceptions. As a consequence,
I couldn't apply what was already within me in an
effort to realize better health. I can't help but wonder if many people, as I once did, fail to appreciate the intention, the practice, and the impact that
mindfulness practices have on every dimension of
health and healing.

I highly recommend Jon Kabat-Zinn's books
on mindfulness meditation and practice. I have

> I can't help but wonder if
> many people, as I once
> did, fail to appreciate the
> intention, the practice, and
> the impact that mindful-
> ness practices have on
> every dimension of health
> and healing.

included this and other books I've personally and professionally found helpful in the reading list at the end of this book.

Mindfulness practices like meditation, yoga, or prayer are not purposeful attempts to detach from the busy world around us. They're just the opposite, intentionally heightening awareness of each and every passing moment. While I will briefly elaborate on different types of meditation practice as an avenue to mindfulness, all mindfulness practice reaches for greater clarity as we observe who we are and how we relate to life around us. The common thread of mindfulness practice, in its many forms, is the discovery of stillness within, allowing one to see themselves, thoughts, feelings, body, and spirit as an integrated being of perfection as is, in the moment. Heightened awareness and wisdom are the by products of this practice, not drifting into never, never land.

Another misconception is that mindfulness practice has to be carried out in a silent sanctuary, with burning incense and soft background recordings of babbling brooks. Being more perpetually in the moment means cultivating an awareness of where you are, wherever you are. As the story I just shared demonstrates, simple

> Another misconception is that mindfulness practice has to be carried out in a silent sanctuary, with burning incense and soft background recordings of babbling brooks.

techniques can be applied even while standing in line in a busy public place. These are the moments in our lives that are distracting, patience-challenging, and mindless—the exact opposite of mindfulness.

Another mindfulness meditative myth is that the experience is some kind of mystical, granola-crunching, hocus pocus made possible by an individual's misguided attempt to distort reality. No. No. No. (If you feel this way, look at this as another opportunity to exercise your right to plasticity). *The whole point of this book is that mind is body.*

Mindfulness practice brings you into the control room of your body. Consider mindfulness practice as a 24/7 invitation to enter mission control, where your CEO resides. There you can directly connect with body. Nothing could be less ethereal and more earthly than mindfulness. While there's clearly a metaphysical and self-transcendental dimension to mindfulness practice, the neurobiological effects are anything but abstract. I would make the case that they are quite concrete and measurable (though we've just begun to scratch the surface using tools that enhance our meaning of these connections).

Let's first look at some easily applied mindfulness practices.

Meditation and yoga techniques have been around for thousands of years. While deeply spiritual, sacred, and mystical contexts have always existed as a cultural backdrop for these practices, anyone, anywhere can do yoga or meditate regardless of their religious, spiritual, or cultural background. A piece of music, for example, might be the "object" of awareness that enables greater clarity of being and feeling to transcend the clutter of mindlessness, without having any religious or spiritual context. Sitting in the woods, alone and still, might be a deeply moving and health-promoting context for mindfulness practice.

While there are numerous techniques and styles of mindfulness practice, Jon Kabat-Zinn makes note of the common threads that weave the many practices of mindfulness. I appreciate the importance of these threads as they each have evidence for their health-promoting biological effects. The fabric they weave becomes more glorious in scope than the sum of their individual strands. The threads of mindfulness fabric include:

- *Non-doing:* A state of just being, total acceptance, and awareness of the moment.

- *Patience:* Changing ways of being and living are journeys for a lifetime, each moment flowing from the last. Mindfulness practice requires the patience to swim against the flow of hectic daily living. There is no agenda. This will run counter to the impatience generated by an agenda perpetually unfulfilled. This is a place where I personally need more work.

- *Letting go:* . . . of the mind's "chitter-chatter." Bringing awareness to thoughts and feelings enables a perpetual scanning of that which defines your experience of life. Much of this clutter is based on fictional stories, misperceptions, learned behaviors, and emotional responses. Letting go of these patterns of living requires first an awareness that they exist. The epiphany of mindfulness in such awareness is the recognition of conscious choice and intention.

- *Non-judging:* Mindfulness practice enables a separation of what is in your life from a *perpetual opinion* about what is in your life— good, bad, deserved, fair, unfair, etc. Judgment obscures your moment's purest form. Judgment hinders the imagination. It adds a dimension to our stories of self and others that plays into the hands of the subconscious "ego-protector" that serves to undermine relationships, interpersonal effectiveness, conflict management, and emotional and behavior management, to name a few. Judgment serves our egos well. It sometimes serves our health poorly.

- **Trust:** First, you have to become comfortable getting to know yourself on the path to greater mindfulness. You must become more comfortable with vulnerability. You must trust that this is possible. You must trust the possibility that you're not fully aware of who you are. You must trust that greater self-awareness can serve you better than you're currently being served.

- **Vulnerability:** In many of the mind-body interactions I've reviewed, there is a requirement for change that exposes that which renders us vulnerable as people. Vulnerability is a fertile place in your mind's garden for grace to emerge. It is here that self-acceptance, courage, forgiveness, and gratitude emerge. It is the paradoxical willingness to allow vulnerability to emerge that enables the strength and faith to change to emerge.

- **Generosity:** Perhaps mindfulness practice is the greatest and most noble act of generosity you can give yourself. A more pristine dimension of who you are emerges, influencing your desire to give and connect with others.

SOME POPULAR FORMS OF MEDITATION

Paced Respiration

This is a practice that places attention (as all mindfulness practices do) on our breathing, the center or focal point of *prana* or energy. In paced respiration, you start by inhaling slowly. Inhalation should be deep enough to cause your belly to expand as your diaphragm pushes into your abdomen, allowing full expansion of your lungs as they slowly fill with air. As one exhales, they silently say the number "five" as air is released. This cycle is repeated at a pace that is most comfortable for the individual, counting down to one. Individuals allow themselves to simply pay attention to their breathing and how it feels as air enters and leaves the nostrils. As attention tends to wander, it is gently brought back to the process of breathing.

Relaxation Response

I have referred to this technique in other chapters. I like it because it's easy to do and enables even the most turbulent of minds to settle and calm in stillness.

While Herbert Benson, MD, popularized the relaxation response, it's a practice that many religions and cultures have practiced for thousands of years.

First, sit quietly (though sitting is not the only position this can be practiced in) with your eyes closed. Allow a wave of muscle relaxation to begin at your feet and spread to other areas of your body as a stone would set forth a ripple across the water's surface. As you bring attention to your breathing, silently express a meaningful word or phrase during exhalation. Thoughts that float inside your head are acknowledged and dismissed as you bring attention back to your breathing and your comforting word or phrase.

Body Scan

This technique enables you to focus attention on feelings or sensations such as pain, tension, or relaxation as it is being experienced in other parts of your body. In a systematic way, with breathing as a focal point, these sensations can be brought into full awareness. Thought and emotions that accompany these sensations can then be observed, embraced, and understood. Ideally, you're then better able to enter and respond to the experience with greater clarity and control.

Guided Imagery

This practice makes use of progressive relaxation and heightened awareness as influenced by a particular image that may enhance a feeling of comfort, such as sitting in a garden or on a beach. Guided imagery, for example, has helped some individuals with the common problem of irritable bowel syndrome or (IBS). With this illness, individuals often experience abdominal cramps, gas, bloating, and alteration of bowel habits ranging from constipation to frequency and urgency. Individuals who use guided imagery—coming down white-water rapids into a calm, peaceful pool of water —have demonstrated greater self-control over their symptoms.

In hypnotherapy, I've used guided imagery as a self-care technique to help others quit smoking. When the individual who smokes is under hypnosis, I ask them to imagine that their lungs are like a chimney, allowing passage of smoke and becoming black with charred toxins. This can have a powerfully inhibiting effect when the subconscious brings this image into focus during the initial act of smoking. Hypnosis, by the way, is simply a form of progressive relaxation and mindfulness that leaves individuals with heightened awareness (not a Zombie-like state as commonly depicted) as suggestions for behavioral change are introduced.

Jon Kabat-Zinn, in his book *Wherever You Go, There You Are*, offers many suggestions for how to cultivate these practices. Using imagery of mountains or lakes, for example, can initiate a process of focused attention and awareness—an entryway to mindfulness practice.

It's important to appreciate that there are no rules. There's no right or wrong way. There are varying "depths," if you will, of mindfulness that elicit a more robust neurobiological effect. However any attempt to examine your life more fully, regardless of how it's achieved, has healing value. Trust me, you don't have to be a student of Buddhist teaching or a Tibetan Monk to tap into the healing potential that is as much within you as it is anyone.

> It's important to appreciate that there are no rules. There's no right or wrong way. There are varying "depths," if you will, of mindfulness that elicit a more robust neurobiological effect.

As I mentioned, meditation, despite popular myth, does not have to be practiced while sitting in total stillness and isolation. There are a number of practices that blend spontaneous freeform or highly structured patterns of movement. Some common examples include:

Walking Meditation

This technique can be done anywhere from a wooded trail to an urban city sidewalk. Walking is slowed to allow greater awareness of the individual parts that comprise the whole of walking—raising your foot, moving your leg forward, contact of your heal to the surface, and transfer of weight from your heel to the ball of your foot, and alternating this rhythmic cycle from one leg to the other as you move forward ten to twenty feet. Walking meditation, like other forms of meditation, is not about reaching a destination like the corner or nirvana. It's about being in the moment—aware and reverent of all that makes a critical and mindless task like walking possible. Thereby, a routine and "automated" behavior becomes an object of gratitude.

Yoga

Yoga has been practiced for more than five thousand years. While there are many forms of yoga, all integrate breathing, movement, and posture to achieve full integration of mind, body, and spirit. There are thousands of postures that synchronize breathing with movement, enhancing flexibility, strength, and balance. Some have referred to yoga as "meditation in motion." I would suggest finding a videotape or CD that can serve as a guide, appropriate for your level of experience (http://www.kripalu.org/shop/shop/Video/). Classes are usually easy to find and can add the benefit of social sharing, support, and camaraderie.

Tai Chi

This form of meditation has ancient Chinese origins. Tai Chi integrates slow, gentle and deliberate circular movement with deep breathing. To an outsider, it looks like an individual is moving in ultra slow motion, having seemingly forgotten the next move. A guest staying with my wife and me was outside in our yard wearing dark clothing and practicing Tai Chi. Our neighbor called in a panic, concerned that a burglar was casing our home. Qi gong is similar to yoga and Tai Chi, integrating physical postures with breathing techniques, enhanced awareness, and focused attention. This, too, is a technique that has its origin in ancient Chinese healing practice.

While mindfulness practice has its roots in Buddhist tradition, the principles of self-care, control, and connection appear to transcend recorded time and all known cultures. These practices are gifts to all humanity.

Most experts would recommend selecting any technique that fits your lifestyle and belief system. From simple prayer to a one-hour meditation or yoga experience, an antidote to the stress-response emerges. I'd recommend starting with any technique, for any length of time that assures your success. Start five minutes each day, then aim higher—fifteen minutes twice daily. The issue again is less the amount of time and more the quality of the attention and awareness achieved. It's important to be patient and kind to yourself. Dismiss any expectation you have for how it should be done or how it should feel. True mindfulness always lives up to expectation—it is simply being. Your attention may wander. Your experience may fall short of expectation. You may wonder what the point of all of this is. Do it anyway.

> Most experts would recommend selecting any technique that fits your lifestyle and belief system. From simple prayer to a one-hour meditation or yoga experience, an antidote to the stress-response emerges.

A SUMMARY OF THE HEALTH BENEFITS
OF MINDFULNESS PRACTICE

The biological and physiological stressors (allostatic load) generated as we interpret and respond to our life experiences are the most important contributors to illness and to diminished quality and quantity of life. Mindfulness practices are the ultimate antidote to the perpetual fight-flight stress response button that is repeatedly pushed at work, at home, and sometimes at play. The scientific community has come to understand the impact that mindfulness practice has on:

- Reducing cardiovascular risk
- Reducing symptoms of anxiety and depression
- Assisting with control of chronic pain
- Enhancing comfort, quality of life, and symptom control in individuals confronting chronic illness and terminal disease
- Enhancing immune function
- Enhancing cognitive function
- Enhancing resilience

You will recall that the health benefits on this abbreviated list share, as their common salutary pathway, diminution of the stress-response and enhancement of perceptual, emotional, and behavioral plasticity that elegantly taps into our primal design to reinforce health-promoting change. The evidence is clear that:

- Prefrontal cortex and limbic system brain activity are strongly influenced in mindfulness practices.
- Diminution of sympathetic (adrenalin and norepinephrine) tone and enhancement of parasympathetic (cardiovascular-protecting) tone is seen with mindfulness practice.
- Lower levels of cortisol and inflammatory markers (like CRP and IL-6) are commonly observed in individuals cultivating these strategies for living.
- Diminished theta brain wave activity seen with mindfulness meditation represents greater clarity of thought, focus, concentration, and cognitive capacity. A Buddhist monk might say that most of us have ADD. It's a symptom of our chaotic "mindless" lives. Interestingly,

and not surprisingly, these techniques have served as useful adjuncts in the treatment of ADD.

- Symptoms of depression and anxiety have been significantly improved when these techniques are integrated with other therapies. Brain structure, function, and the neurotransmitters that are influenced by mindfulness practice are clearly connected to these important health outcomes.

- The lessening of pain and improvements in immune function and quality of life for HIV/AIDS and cancer patients are well documented. Helping an individual feel more in control of their lives at a time when many perceive all control has been taken away is a critical transformation made possible by mindfulness practice.

We understand in health care that at least 60 to 70 percent of physician visits are due to stress-related symptoms and concerns. It's intuitive that stress reduction becomes the overriding goal of self-care.

In a study of African-American adolescents with early stages of high blood pressure, transcendental meditation (when the mind is allowed to settle) practiced for fifteen minutes twice daily, significantly helped blood vessels to stretch, an important characteristic of healthy blood vessels. That function became worse in adolescents who did not meditate. Nitric oxide, a chemical produced in the body that enables this important protective response, is enhanced in meditation. Perhaps if all kids meditated (with their teachers, of course) ten to fifteen minutes once or twice each day at school, health, learning capacity, memory, and interpersonal skill development would dramatically improve.

Similar findings were noted in adults with a history of heart disease with applications of meditative techniques for thirty minutes, three times a week. Blood vessels dilated better and heart rate variability was diminished with stressful maneuvers. And here's a real surprise. Individuals also noted significant reduction in self-assessed stress levels, anxiety, and symptoms of depression.

The bottom line is that while many of these techniques may not cure disease, they can powerfully diminish the risk of acquiring disease, reduce the risk of complications of pre-existing disease, and enhance overall quality of life. No toxic pharmacology. No side effects. No financial expense. No strings. Though I'm tempted to say "no brainer," it would be more appropriate to say, "all brainer."

If you look at the concept of allostatic load as the final common pathway for illness and poor quality of life, you can appreciate the many sources of the stress response that mindfulness practice can positively influence (See figure 17.1).

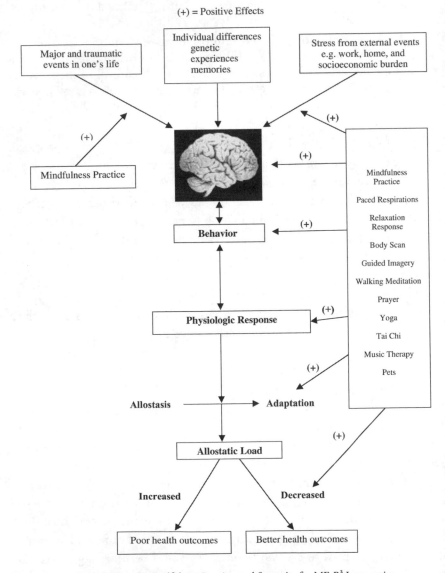

Figure 17.1   Allostatic Load, Mindfulness Practice, and Strategies for ME-B³ Intervention

MUSIC: WHAT'S ON YOUR iPOD?

If the soul had an appetite, music would likely be its entrée of choice. For as long as recorded time, there's evidence that humans cultivated rituals of rhythm. Music has been recognized to restore, maintain, and improve physical, emotional, and spiritual health and well-being. Music is a powerful portal of entry to stored memories and the emotional and the experiential context they were created in. No doubt, you've heard a song on the radio that immediately rekindled a forgotten memory and how good or perhaps how melancholy you felt in the place and time of your memory's origin.

> Music has been recognized to restore, maintain, and improve physical, emotional, and spiritual health and well-being.

There's been growing recognition in traditional models of biomedical medicine of the importance of integrating music into the delivery of care, particularly in the hospital setting. Many patients and families are encouraged to bring music to be played in their hospital rooms. Many hospitals now have mobile libraries of music (as well as videos and books) that allow patients to select what would be comforting and of pleasure to them. The portable nature of music via CDs and MP3s allows music to "follow the patient" as they go for a biopsy or fMRI. Music serves as a soothing distraction to the anticipatory thoughts of such anxiety-provoking tests and interventions.

Coincident with a trend toward more "patient-centered" integrated approaches to health care, a growing number of clinical studies support music as a valid therapeutic intervention. Music has been shown to reduce feelings of anxiety, particularly in anticipation of a stress-inducing diagnostic test or treatment. There's speculation that music may have a beneficial effect on the cognitive component of the stress response, which involves thought processes linked with the stress response—anticipating pain, fear, side effects, knowledge of risk, etc.

Active participation in musical activity such as singing with a group has been shown to increase antibody production in the respiratory tract called IgA. Other possible beneficial effects on immune function and stress hormone levels have been demonstrated. Music can also be the core object of meditation and mindfulness practice. Improvements in self-esteem and in symptoms of depression and anxiety have been reported when an active music program was added to conventional treatment in individuals with multiple sclerosis.

In patients diagnosed with terminal cancer, music therapy improved quality of life and was a source of comfort in symptom management. Music has been employed as an adjunct to other treatments in individuals with behavioral health problems like depression and psychosis.

When studying musicians and the effect that learning to play an instrument has on brain development, some interesting findings emerge. Enhanced activity is seen in the brain regions that involve hearing but also in areas that involve higher levels of cognition and reasoning. For example, musically trained adults perform better on word memory tests than other adults. Preschoolers taking piano lessons perform better on word puzzles and scored higher on math proficiency. Playing an instrument seems to significantly "boost" the effects on brain structure and function that listening alone does not. I should never have given up the clarinet in elementary school.

Music therapy is now considered, in some instances, a routine part of the treatment plan for a host of medical problems. As a therapeutic tool, it can help to improve physical and mental functioning through carefully structured activities. Examples include singing, listening, moving to music, playing instruments, and imagery exercises.

Dancing

Perhaps one of the greatest assets of music in the promotion of health and healing is its natural connection with movement. You know that tendency to start tapping your foot to a particular tune? Music has a way of lowering the threshold to move and when people move to music they tend to feel better than when they move in the absence of music. Can you imagine an aerobic or spinning class without music? From cardiac rehabilitation clinics to physical and occupational therapy to substance abuse treatments, movement to music and rhythm-related activity induces a clear short-term reward, characterized by enhanced mood, reduction in pain, and improved mobility and performance capacity.

While I have not shared this secret with many people, for the last five years I've adopted a wonderful habit of music mindfulness meditation. It's a good example of how meditation can be practiced without sitting still and being quiet. Recall that mindfulness practice is about heightened awareness and greater attention to the moment you're in, mind uncluttered and emotions freely flowing without effect. My technique involves finding a place where I can be alone and undisturbed. A small space is cleared on the floor. A portable music player is used with headphones. Songs are specifically selected if they meet my therapeutic criteria (I'll elaborate on these criteria in a moment). Not any tune will do. Then, in total darkness, I play music for twenty minutes and dance (move might be a more apt verb to describe my activity) to my heart's content.

One reason for the total darkness is my self-conscious insecurity with how I dance, a slight notch above Elaine, the character on *Seinfeld* whose dancing style could best be described as spastic. I also like total darkness as visual stimulation is diminished, more fully allowing images I relate to the music to emerge. In addition, there's a wonderful reinforcement of balance and trust that's engendered by movement in the dark. Clearing the dance area of dangerous items like furnishings with sharp edges will further promote trust as you move in total darkness. This has been a wonderful intervention for mind, emotion, and movement that clears my cluttered thoughts and enhances my mood, with the added benefit of burning some calories. Try this "dancing in the dark" mindfulness movement each day for fifteen to twenty minutes, increasing your time as desired. It's important that this be your undivided time.

Music as a Companion

There's been a revolution in the digitalization and portability of music. The MP3 player like Apple's signature industry-standard, the iPod, has made it possible to access and transport tremendous numbers of tunes. I like to think of it as **MP3 for ME-B³**.

While listening to music you love and enjoy is therapeutic in and of itself, it's a great tool to transform sedentary inertia into movement and activity. Many people walk, jog, and exercise to music, and health clubs have cardiovascular aerobic equipment that allows you to plug in to music. If you're using stationary equipment, concerts on DVDs are particularly effective given their multi-dimensional stimulatory effect (sight, sound, action, and energy). A friend recently gave me a U-2 concert on DVD. It complements exercise like a nice Merlot complements a handful of walnuts.

I like to run outdoors whenever possible because of the natural element's "call to move." Running without my iPod, however, would be tantamount to leaving a trusted friend behind. There is, by the way, no substitute for running with a friend. Exercise, conversation, and connection do wonders for mind-emotion-brain-body-behavior as you now appreciate. Any residual fight-flight activity from earlier in the day dissipates. Nothing the FDA has approved, to my knowledge, can reproduce these effects.

Music, like running with a friend, takes the experience of exercise to another level. When you reach the point of working your joints, muscles, and cardiovascular system, and you're enjoying it (thank you biological bliss), you're likely to be motivated to again seek the reward.

So what is on my iPod? I carefully select the music, then play it in a particular order with variable and well-choreographed volume adjustments. I choose my music as thoughtfully as I choose an antibiotic for a patient I'm treating with a bacterial infection. We're talking music therapy here! I desire the best therapy available for me! So what are the criteria that become the basis for a handpicked tune ending up on my iPod?

- I have to really *love* the song (note the use of the word love, not like).
- The rhythm/beat should resonate with the rhythm of the activity.
- The song cannot exceed five minutes.
- The song should have a strongly positive emotional and experiential context attached to it, a memory or image that *ignites meaning* in your life.

While the tunes on my iPod meet each of these criteria with variable success, *all criteria are met.* The endpoint is to make the activity as mindful as possible, conducting the orchestra with passionate zeal, and purposefully lighting up brain regions that foster reward, motivation, and the ultimate positive emotional state. Usually when I start to run, I hurt in multiple places. My breathing is not efficient and well synchronized. By choosing tunes I really love, I become more mindful of the music, then the pain I'm experiencing, though present, is just co-existing. It's not the center of my attention. The music guides me to a pace and rhythm that has worked well for me (this will and should change as your performance capacity changes). For example, I have carefully placed Sugarloaf's *Green Eyed Lady* as my third tune. The beat in this tune becomes my guide to the pace I should be moving at, and the song comes on at minute eight of a forty-five-minute routine. I prefer to keep the tunes under five minutes as each tune elicits a unique and complementary effect. I would rather experience the variety of ten changing venues than I would three or four ten-minute riffs.

The piece de résistance is having a positive emotional context that comes to life as you experience the tune. For example, Steely Dan's "Bodhisattva" (live version), in addition to meeting all criteria, immediately conjures up fond memories of college in Boston, friends from the mid-seventies, and the sights and sounds of Beantown I experienced as a young adult. All of which translates to total contentment.

We store so much more than just the lyrics, the tunes, and the picture on the album cover. We store a recording of life, an experience that is reawakened and replayed. You can choose to rekindle such an experience purposefully and consciously that leaves you detached from the work of exercise. When Earth Wind & Fire's "House of Fire" resonates between my eardrums, I'm less mindful of the track I'm running on and the effort involved. Instead, I'm in Newport, Rhode Island, experiencing the bliss of another summer night in an oceanfront town. I sense the sounds, smells, lights, and salt air with vivid recall and deep contentment. When Toto's "Roseanna" resonates in my brain, I'm running on a baseball field certain of making an improbable catch.

Thirty-five minutes into the routine, I usually feel ready to "wean down." Weaning is important as you transition from this biological symphony of ME-B^3. But wait a minute. As my thoughts shift to weaning, the encore tune begins to play on my iPod. This, too, is a strategically placed tune, targeted to fuel a fire about to extinguish. It's at this point in my routine that my legs and back would welcome rest. It's at this point that my lungs feel they've moved enough oxygen and that my heart has pumped enough blood. My motivation to move is starting to wane, as I knew it would. That, however, was a moment ago. Now I'm in the moment of U-2's "With or Without You." Soon, and to my stunning amazement, I'm moving faster, my breathing is deep and coordinated, and my arms and legs are moving in total synchronicity. No longer am I a pigeon-toed, middle-aged man about to fold. Instead, I'm a pigeon-toed, middle-aged man catapulted into a new orbit. Arms pumping, heart pounding, sweat pouring, oxygen burning, I'm back out on stage for my encore performance. I'm "giving myself away." I'm mindful of only the rhythm of the percussions as the song beautifully proceeds. A bright neon orange light in my brain is now flashing: "*Entering Flow State.*" Put me in a PET scanner now! This is what I want my brain to look like at least once per day. Thought, emotion, reward, brain, behavior, body, all the beneficiaries of music's effects—an enormously important health-promoting behavior that I'm addicted to.

PETS AND PEOPLE

When it comes to loving, nonjudgmental, and steadfast companionship, pets rule! I must say I have a bias as a longtime dog lover. I've cared for many patients whose pets were the most important living souls in their lives, and I've heard the same sentiments: "My pet knows when something isn't right with me." "My pet is so comforting to me." "When I walk through the door it's like she hasn't seen me in years." "I feel so good when I'm holding my pet."

Some hospitals and clinics are beginning to use pets in a therapeutic capacity. Pet therapy, as it is referred to, attempts to facilitate healing by bringing specially trained dogs into hospital settings. I know I've always enjoyed seeing these animals walking in our hospital hallways. Given the lift in spirits many patients and staff receive from therapeutic pets, I'm convinced that pets connect with us on an "energy level" that cannot be seen, though definitely felt. They are extremely sensitive to human moods. Some dogs can even sense seizures before they occur in their owners.

Pets are a buffer to isolation and loneliness. I'm certain that my mother's dog did much more for her mood than her Zoloft ever did. They never hold a grudge. They don't attach contingencies to the emotions they express. Perhaps they are trying to tell us something. Animals are increasingly recognized as allies in health as people deal with acute or chronic illness. They provide valuable attachment and bonding rewards—and as we know, the neurobiological footprints of meaningful relationships, animal or human, have positive effects on mood, thought, health, and behavior. While studies are limited, they support what any pet owner knows—pets leave you feeling good! Pet ownership has been associated with:

- Lower blood pressure and triglyceride levels
- Increases in oxytocin, an important neurohormone in bonding and attachment
- Increase in endorphins
- Decreases in subjective levels of stress and anxiety

- Improvements in rehabilitation after a stroke
- Improved behavioral health outcomes
- Improved social functioning and impulse control
- Enhanced self-worth
- Reduction in measurements of anger, hostility, tension, and anxiety after as little as ten minutes of cuddling with a pet.

For many people who live without human companionship, pets fill an enormous void. The relationships between some of my patients and their pets are sometimes much deeper than those shared between people. Humans tend to hold grudges. Pets do not. Humans tend to get mired down in cluttered and distracted thought. Pets are perpetually in the moment. Many of my patients have been quick to comment on how they can just be themselves around their pets. People feel better around their animals because of the power of attachment, bonding, relationship, and reward. These positive emotional byproducts are a logical consequence of meaning-making, bliss, and contentment. Thoughts like, "I have to get better quickly to care for my pet," dominate a mind that could just as easily be thinking, "No one cares about me, so why bother?" Pets are a major source of purpose to rally around when we confront setbacks in life. Pets need us to care for them and reward us for our love. Behaviors critical to self-care-movement and daily purposeful activities are more likely to emerge when life revolves around a pet that depends on us for nurturing.

When confronting a mental task like solving a puzzle or memorizing a list of objects, people performing with their animal pals did better than with a spouse or when alone. Changes in heart rate and blood pressure were less pronounced and returned to baseline more quickly in the presence of a pet when confronting a challenging mental task. People with high stress jobs and high blood pressure showed improvements in mental tasks and blood pressure readings six months after adopting a pet. People often do more, eat less, and manage their weight more effectively when they own pets.

In a world replete with lonely, isolated people and a multitude of pets in need of loving, nurturing homes, it seems a wonderful public health opportunity exists to fill a mutual void.

Chapter 18

Resilience: Keeping Your Eyes on the Horizon

> ". . . everything can be taken from a man but one thing: the last of the human freedoms . . . to choose one's attitude in any given set of circumstances, to choose one's own way."
>
> Viktor Frankl

As certain as taxes and death, we can anticipate adversity in our lives. No one is sheltered from the vulnerability of being human. Resilience is the process of adapting well in the face of such adversity.

William Ochan Levi grew up in Sudan on the banks of the Kulo-jobi River. He and his family fled persecution in Southern Sudan in 1987 as people were viciously slaughtered and villages burned to the ground by tribal jihad soldiers. Religious persecution of Christians by the Islamic Jihad forced hundreds of thousands of Sudan refugees into Uganda and Kenya. Children wandered, struggling to survive another day without starvation and dehydration. They were orphaned, lost, and swept into a tumultuous and confusing dark cloud of human tragedy.

Levi, a Messianic believer from an African Hebrew tribal group, grew up as a refugee in the wilderness of Uganda. As a teen, he returned to his homeland, only to face persecution, arrest, and torture. His miraculous escape from jihad forces was the first step in an odyssey that ultimately led to a new life in the U.S. He went on to found Operation Nehemiah Missions International. In recent years, he's been working on a project to build a medical treatment facility that could address the profound burden of disease and plight in the thousands of refugees in the region.

His story as told in *The Bible or the Axe* is a story of profound courage, strength, mission, and purpose, all inspired by a life characterized by profound resilience.

When I first looked into Levi's sincere and embracing eyes and asked what he and millions of other Sudanese refugees relied on to survive another day, his answer without hesitation was love, purpose, and a very strong faith. While every conceivable gift of life seemed stripped away, the souls of the Southern Sudanese who continued to move forward regardless, did so because of the gifts of love, purpose, and faith that remained in their hearts and on their horizon. As author, psychiatrist, and Holocaust survivor Viktor Frankl courageously expressed, no one can take away that which lives deep in our souls.

Levi has raised the money needed to obtain supplies, a generator, an irrigation/water system, and medications. With the courageous efforts of many, he will soon see this project come to life as a small hospital-clinic that will be a Godsend in the midst of chaos, made possible by the collective resilience of the human spirit.

Research has shown that resilience is ordinary not extraordinary, meaning that people commonly demonstrate the capacity for resilience. This has been my own experience, that of family and friends, and the experience of many of my patients and their families as we confront major setbacks in our lives. While our setbacks may not be as traumatic as that which Levi has witnessed and experienced, we all experience pain and adversity in our lives—losing a loved one or suffering a divorce. We also experience a host of less traumatic setbacks in our lives like losing a job, struggling to make ends meet financially, maintaining our relationships, and dealing with health issues. How we "bounce back" in response to the difficult experiences in our lives is what resilience is all about.

So why is it that some people just seem to cope better in response to life's obstacles? Is resilience a trait you're either born with or without? Can resilience be cultivated? What do we currently understand about the nature and nurture contribution in connection to the capacity for resilience? What do we understand about the biological underpinnings that distinguish vulnerability from resilience? Lastly, can resilience be taught, and if so, what are some paths to getting there?

I will address these questions with an emphasis on the implication for health, healing, allostatic load, and surviving well. Consistent with the other critical health and healing dimensions of self-care I've discussed thus far, resilience is influenced more by nurture than it is by nature. Resilience involves behaviors, skills, and perceptions that can be learned and developed by anyone. While an individual may have a genetic predisposition for depression or bipolar disease that might undermine their capacity for resilience, evidence nevertheless suggests that our capacity for resilience is strongly influenced by experience, environment, and interpersonal support.

Evidence also suggests that children begin to learn and develop resiliency skills at a young age. Emmy Werner, a professor of human development at the University of California at Davis, has researched resilience in children and has found that the strength of the parental bond, particularly in those pre-K years, is a crucial determinant of effective adult adaptation. Developing capacity around a particular strength like reading or drawing assists children with a foundation to build upon and to fall back on when confronting increased stress. Belief in something seen on the horizon with personal meaning attached, for example, "becoming an artist or an author one day" or being part of a belief system like a faith community, serves as a rudder when the water gets choppy and the winds unpredictable. Not surprisingly, childhood and adult experiences of violence, abuse, exposure to drug and alcohol abuse, and dysfunctional families weaken resilience.

The abundance of available research that informs our understanding of resilience using tools to measure resilience capacity, the relationship between resilience capacity and health outcomes, and the human attributes that are most consistently associated with resilience demonstrates the following:

- **Relationships** are a critical dimension woven throughout the fabric of a resilient individual's life. Having caring and supportive relationships at home, work, and play is an important factor. Relationships defined by love, trust, encouragement, and support foster an individual's capacity for resilience. In Chapter 14, we examined the overall health importance of social attachment and the positive biological effects associated with interpersonal connection. It's not surprising that supportive interpersonal connection is one of the "nurturing" dimensions to resilience.

- **Meaning matters.** Much has been said about the healing potential unleashed with purposeful pursuit of meaning in love, work, and play. Individuals who identify and develop such areas in their lives naturally cultivate a lush garden of personal meaning to fall back on as a source of strength and optimism. These characteristics are essential in the development of resilience. In the same way, values like friendship and academic and athletic skills become motivators with the reward in the satisfaction of those values. For resilient individuals, sources of meaning and personal strength serve as a beacon guiding them through the most challenging storms.

In 1942, a young Austrian physician named Viktor Frankl, his new bride, parents, and brother were arrested and taken to a concentration camp in Bohemia. While locked inside a Nazi concentration camp as prisoner "119, 104," Viktor Frankl would realize the significance of meaning as a lifeline amidst a dark sea of human sadness and unimaginable human suffering. Frankl's father died of starvation and his mother and brother were killed in Auschwitz in 1944. His life's work up to that point—a manuscript for *The Doctor and the Soul*, which he had attached to the lining of his overcoat—was destroyed. He nearly died of typhoid fever, keeping himself awake and alive by reconstructing his manuscript on stolen slips of paper.

Frankl was interested in observing who survived and who didn't, assuming of course, an opportunity to survive, which did not exist for millions of Jews. He observed what philosopher Friedrich Nietzsche had noted previously, "He who has a why to live for can bear with almost any how."

> "He who has a why to live for can bear with almost any how."

People, he observed, who had unfinished stories, who believed and expected to be reunited with loved ones, or who had great faith and sources of meaning in their lives had a better chance of survival than those who lost hope. Striving toward a worthy goal distinguished those who would make it through another day from those who would not. Frankl saw the project of meaning-making as a human gift. ". . . like faith, hope and love, meaning

> ". . . like faith, hope and love, meaning could not be willed but could only emerge from experience, discovery, and greater self awareness."

could not be willed but could only emerge from experience, discovery, and greater self awareness."

Frankl suggested three approaches to finding meaning in life:

- **Experiential value:** This implies experiencing something or someone we value, i.e., another person, piece of art, music, nature, etc. Developing and pursuing that which we experience as valuable enhances meaning in our lives.

- **Creative values:** This refers to "doing a deed," as Frankl phrased it. Creativity here implies acting/behaving/performing in ways that are aligned with the pursuit of what we value such as becoming more involved with life or showing acts of benevolence toward others. We can passively experience or actively create experience that fills this reservoir of purpose.

- **Attitudinal value:** To Frankl, attitudinal value referred to virtues like compassion, bravery, or a good sense of humor. Suffering, as Frankl experienced and reflected, could be endured with dignity when meaning could emerge from it, just as grief is sometimes the price we pay for love. Compassion, gratitude, and generosity are not fully realized without the experience of suffering, loss, and deprivation. Suffering, in this context, serves as fertile ground for life sustaining "attitudes" to emerge.

Frankl's experience resonates with the resilience I've observed in people "suffering" with kidney disease. Love, experiential values, meaning, and purpose allow people to persevere in remarkable ways. Meaning and the opportunity to complete a dying person's life story are vital dimensions to end-of-life care that are often incompletely addressed by family, friends, and our system of health care.

Resilience research suggests the following strengths as critical to the capacity to bounce back from adversity:

- **Self-awareness.** Individuals who demonstrate greater capacity for resilience in their lives have developed a strong sense of who they are and greater confidence in their strengths and abilities. Kids, for example, who find something they can do better than anyone else are more likely to transcend obstacles in life. Adults who can "read their gut" are better able to link behavioral choices with consequences, are more mindful of their inner compass, and are more likely to bounce back. Developing a sense of self-worth is a vital dimension to this perceptual awareness.

- **Emotional Management:** Resilience requires the skills and capacity to manage strong feelings and impulses. I've been strongly influenced in my own "resilience development" endeavors by the work of Daniel Goleman and others in the field of emotional intelligence. These critical competencies are skills that enable resilience in every aspect of life. In addition to self-awareness, self-management competencies are very important. Goleman elaborates on skill development in areas of:
  - Emotional self-control—keeping disruptive impulses under control
  - Transparency—displaying honesty and trustworthiness
  - Adaptability
  - Initiative—readiness to mobilize the courage to act and seize opportunities
  - Achievement—the desire to satisfy values
  - Optimism—developing positive perceptual frames for examining circumstances.

- **Selfless Acts:** Children and adults who are more likely to rebound have had experiences of helping others in need. Serving others enhances one's capacity when confronting a crisis to better serve one's self. Our own experiences are placed in a broader context when we're aware of the needs of others and that we're not alone in our vulnerability. Virtues of generosity, gratitude, empathy, forgiveness, and altruism are commonly seen in people who exemplify resilience. A conversation with William Levi affirms this observation.

- **Skills in Communication and Problem Solving:** Awareness and communication of needs, beliefs, and expectations are necessary skills as you navigate your lifeboat of resilience through choppy seas. Developing skills in conflict management and problem solving add substantial buoyancy to the vessel you're navigating. Many of the setbacks we confront in our lives center on interpersonal conflict. The stakes are often high with respect to the quality of our lives. Resilient individuals understand that survival, at some level, requires preservation of vital relationships and an ability to communicate and work through differences.

- **Good Health:** Individuals who enjoy better health are more likely to bounce back from adversity. While good health alone is not a guarantee for resilience, individuals with poor health are more likely to be rendered vulnerable in response to stressful setbacks. You'll also note that the characteristics that form a foundation for resilience are, in themselves, health promoting! This is another good example of the inherent positive reinforcement of mind, emotion, behavior, and health.

THE NEUROBIOLOGY OF RESILIENCE

When we reflect on what we currently understand about the neurobiological underpinnings of the reward-motivation response, social connection and attachment, and the fight-flight stress response, we see considerable overlap in brain structure, neurotransmitter messengers, and integrated pathways. For example, it doesn't appear to be a coincidence that the pathways that foster social bonding are linked to the pathways for reward-motivation. When in sync and working well, social connection creates a strong feeling of reward-motivation and powerfully neutralizes the effects of fight-flight and the stress response. Any disruption in this delicate balance or homeostasis can alter the landscape, influencing how we interpret and respond to our experiences.

For example an individual who is feeling depressed may not have the same feeling of social reward around other people as an individual who is happy. The fight-flight stress response meter will likely be on high in the former scenario and well constrained in the latter. A person in response to an emotional setback such as a major conflict with an office colleague may experience a stronger sense of reward after a carbohydrate binge than someone better able to manage their interpersonal connections. While a carbohydrate binge will still feel good for the latter person in the example, the reward of conflict reconciliation and the implications for trust and capacity development will feel even better and be more sustained. The neurobiological line between vulnerability and resilience appears to be a fine one.

The characteristics of resilience like solid analytical functioning, emotional intelligence, a positive self-concept, altruism, optimism, and learned helpfulness have neurobiological correlates in our regulation of reward-motivation, fear conditioning, and social attachment. How an individual responds to extreme stress is, at least in part, a function of how effectively these systems interact.

The resilience research on children, adolescents, and adults in a variety of settings—war, family violence, poverty, and natural disasters—reveal consistent patterns of individual characteristics associated with adaptation. Based on resilience research, to develop resiliency, it's critical to build a capacity to more effectively manage the following:

- **Reward and Motivation:** To develop resiliency, seek out positive pleasures at home, work, and play; find meaning and value satisfactions that positively reward such resiliency skills as problem solving, exercise, and mindfulness practice; and work on positive emotions like optimism.

- **Learned Helpfulness:** Individuals who have had prior experiences that led to positive responses and adaptation to severe stress are more likely to positively reinforce *learned helpfulness* in response to future setbacks. Social cooperation or "reciprocal altruism" is a core behavioral principle of human social life and has been linked to resilience. Studies have revealed a link between mutual cooperation and activation of reward processing in the brain. This reward system helps people to help others, and in turn, reciprocity is facilitated. It is a beautiful and positively reinforcing interpersonal design that has clear survival advantages.

- **Conditional Fear:** It's important to become aware of how specific experiences and memories—those that are encoded with stress-fear responses and associated with negative emotional states—become relived patterns when confronting subsequent setbacks. These conditional fear responses tend to "spill over" into other experiences that share similar conditioned stimuli—person, place, scenario—and undermine the capacity to foster effective emotional, perceptual, and behavioral responses. We need to reconfigure these conditioned fear responses and learn healthier ones. For example, conditioned fear, sadness, and emotional paralysis can be transformed into learned helpfulness, i.e., instead of automatically hating a particular individual, you could work on ways to help them.

- **Adaptive Social Behavior:** The ultimate trump card, individuals who cultivate social connection are more likely to develop virtues of empathy, altruism, and teamwork. Daniel Goleman would categorize these skills as social-management emotional-intelligence skills. In the challenging, capricious, and complex organizational health care culture I work in, adaptive social behavior has allowed me to maintain my balance and buoyancy with patients and colleagues. Individuals whose skills are lacking, usually associated with a diminished awareness of the deficiencies, perpetually struggle to serve their own values and the values of those they serve.

I have adapted a summary table from Dennis Charney, MD, (*American Journal of Psychiatry,* 2004) of important brain structures and neurotransmitters known to be important in facilitating resilience or, when disrupted, predispose states of vulnerability (Table 1).

Table 1. Brain Mechanisms Related to Resilience

Response	Neurochemical Systems	Brain Regions	Association with Resilience
Reward-Motivation	Dopamine, endorphins Glutamate, NMDA	Medial prefrontal cortex Nucleus accumbens Amygdala, hippocampus	Diminished fight-flight response. Enables a reward experience in the midst of stressful setbacks.
Fear-Conditioning	Glutamate, CRH, cortisol NMDA	Medial prefrontal cortex Sensory cortex Anterior cingulate gyrus Thalamus, amygdala	Adapt to prior experiences of fear in positive, health-promoting ways. Learned helpfulness.
Inhibitory Avoidance	Adrenalin/norepinephrine CRH, GABA, endorphins	Medial prefrontal cortex Amygdala Hippocampus	Reduced stress response. Better ability to perceive and avoid risk. Adapting to behave more effectively based on a more accurate perception of social and experiential context.
Memory Reconsolidation	Glutamate, NMDA Norepinephrine	Amygdala Hippocampus	Enables more effective reorganization of the original memory/experience. More effective behavioral responses and symptom management emerge.
Social Attachment	Dopamine, endorphins Oxytocin, NMDA	Prefrontal cortex Nucleus accumbens Pituitary Locus coeruleus Caudate nucleus	Bonding and attachment. Supportive social networks refostered. Diminished stress response. Enhanced meaning.

In studies of men in combat and those in other stressful occupations—medical professionals, police men and women, firefighters, astronauts—effective action under stress was made more likely when a group was bonded in shared purpose and altruism. With these two characteristics, the ability to transcend fear en route to maximal performance was more likely to be realized. Resilient individuals are hardly without fear. The difference is that they're able to co-exist with fear, keeping the stress response in check and garnering their available resources to maintain cognition clarity, emotional control, and interpersonal connection.

Acts of resilience beget acts of resilience as the neural mechanisms of overwhelming fear that may have once accompanied an experience (e.g., returning to work after a long absence) become extinct as our "fear-constraining" support responses are cultivated. In the professions noted above, the ability to extinguish paralyzing fear is necessary to perform such tasks as entering a burning building, confronting hostile gunfire, or delicately navigating a scalpel.

Research suggests our medial prefrontal cortex is an important interpreter of an emotionally generated fear response. It is in this region where a range of outcomes related to reward or punishment are assessed, driving subsequent behaviors accordingly. An inability to link reward with resilience-building capacity will enable fear and health-undermining behaviors to sustain themselves. Empathy and altruism, critical stress adapting skills, also appear to be associated with activity in this region of the brain.

Greater understanding of these complex mechanisms enables paths to more effective resilience, reduction in allostatic load, and better health. This is another example of the potential made possible by neural plasticity or the capacity to reconfigure the symphony of fear, reward-motivation, and social connection.

RESILIENCE, ME-B^3, AND ALLOSTATIC LOAD

Resilient individuals are able to interpret and respond to traumatic and stressful life events in a manner that fosters growth, interpersonal connection, and more effective service to self and others. These perceptual, emotional, and behavioral adaptations have the collective effect of "reeling in" the multiple adverse health effects of fight-flight stress responses, while enhancing the response of reward-motivation and connection. This all adds up to a reduction in allostatic load, improved quality of life, and more effective aging. While the nurturing experiences in our lives and our response to them are significant determinants of our capacity for resilience or vulnerability, the primal capacity for resilience is already within us. We are designed for resilience. We would not have survived as long as we have

> Resilient individuals are able to interpret and respond to traumatic and stressful life events in a manner that fosters growth, interpersonal connection, and more effective service to self and others.

without this capacity. What a gift! Our resilience is really more ordinary than extraordinary and amenable to development, strengthening, and sustaining as you discover possibility in each moment of your life.

SUMMARY: STRATEGIES FOR BUILDING RESILIENCE

We've examined resilience as a set of cognitive, emotional, and behavioral skills that are capable of being developed and cultivated. Resilient individuals are more likely to feel in control of their lives. This is a major asset in transcending the traumatic and recurrent stress we can all expect to experience. Resilient individuals will tend to rate their quality of life more highly than less resilient individuals, age more gracefully, and, in some instances, live longer. Resilience is about surviving and surviving well.

> Resilient individuals will tend to rate their quality of life more highly than less resilient individuals, age more gracefully, and, in some instances, live longer. Resilience is about surviving and surviving well.

The American Psychological Association (www.helping.apa.org) has an informative website that offers **"10 Ways to Build Resilience."** I have elaborated on most of them and include them here with strategies for cultivating them. The overlap of the neurobiological underpinnings of resilience and their implication for reduction in allostatic load and health and healing—combined with effective conflict management, social connection, regular exercise, nutrition, forgiveness, and mindfulness practice—is no coincidence.

The mutual effect of each of these domains on optimal health and quality of life speaks to their elegant interconnection. This positively reinforcing cycle of thought, emotion, behavior, and health rewards in a cumulative fashion.

The power is within you. You're not alone. When you begin to see your life as a discovery made possible in each and every moment, you will become addicted to health, a healer of self, and a healer of others.

- Make connections
  - Invest in friendships
  - Social recreation/play
  - Faith communities
  - Volunteerism
- Seek health promoting rewards
  - Music/art
  - Dance
  - Exercise aerobic/resistance
  - Make a small and positive nutritional change
- Self-care
  - Mindfulness practice
  - Prayer
  - Better eating habits
    Regular activity
- Acts of non-self
  - Volunteerism
  - Generosity
  - Gratitude
  - Altruism
- Learn from the past and live for the present
- Develop conflict management skills

Chapter 19

Habits for Surviving Well

> "Learning is not compulsory . . . neither is survival."
>
> W. Edwards Deming

In my book, *The Savvy Patient*, I ended with a chapter entitled, "Parting Wisdom: The Best Medical Advice I Have to Give." In concluding this book, I'd like to summarize what I believe to be the seven most important health-promoting behaviors. It's an integration of advice from *It's All in Your Head* and *The Savvy Patient*. This advice, along with a summary of care and resources available, will help you to achieve the best quantity and quality of life. It embodies the best of what is possible both by partnering with our system of health care and by becoming a more effective steward of self-care.

1. MAKE AS MANY FRIENDS AS YOU CAN

To love and to be loved is perhaps the ultimate promoter of health and healing. The more connected you are with others you care about and who care about you, the better off you'll be. I know there are people who may prefer to be left alone. That is a choice, and we have many reasons for the choices we make. There are people, however, who find themselves isolated and alone who get lost in the busy background of life. The reasons for this isolation may be less conscious choosing and more loss of control — mental illness, developmental disabilities, chronic medical problems, substance abuse, or lack of awareness by friends and family.

If you have a loved one you are distant from (geographically speaking), appreciate that the occasional reassuring phone conversation may not reflect accurately what is happening behind the scenes. Many people who experience a decline in functional capacity and safe independence may not reveal their vulnerability for fear that they may worry others, be forced into a nursing home, or otherwise lose their independence. For some lonely people, feelings of shame or embarrassment may make reaching out to others for help more difficult.

Despite the challenges, the evidence is clear. There is no capital more liquid than relationship capital. In our most important relationships, those that best serve our values, we should aim for trust, bonding, pleasure, and reward, a sort of interpersonal oxycontin effect, if you will.

> In our most important relationships, those that best serve our values, we should aim for trust, bonding, pleasure, and reward, a sort of interpersonal oxycontin effect, if you will.

2. WASH YOUR HANDS

If God spoke to me by saying, "Mark, you're down to your last three words, what do you want to say to your fellow humans that would have the most profound impact on life here on earth?" It would be a close call between "love thy neighbor" and "wash your hands." A close third would be "move, move, move." All would have a profound impact on the quality of human life.

From a mind-body-behavior perspective, washing your hands falls into the category of one of the more important behaviors. You will notice a dramatic decrease in communicable illness (most of what we commonly confront by way of infections). Though some of my friends think I'm a bit of a neurotic nut, I usually keep one of the waterless hand antiseptics nearby for use, particularly if I know I'll be shaking a lot of hands.

3. LAUGHTER

Not many things out there feel as good as a deep belly laugh. They're the best. Humor is definitely therapeutic and as a health tool, woefully underutilized.

In the midst of a painful time, people sometimes are able to see a biting absurdity in their reality or in the responses of the people around them. A patient once said: "Here's the kidney stone you asked for Dr. Pettus. While doing the Hell Dance, this popped out of my penis! You can add it to your rock collection." Now I thought this was a pretty witty way of expressing an awful experience with therapeutic humor.

Another patient of mine who'd recently had his leg amputated had just received a new prosthesis. When doing my rounds, I stopped by and asked him if he had any plans for the weekend. He looked at me and smiled. "I'm thinking of taking my wife dancing, but I'm afraid of what might happen if I shake a leg." We shared a great laugh, one that connected us. I've always admired and been intrigued by people who are capable of transcending painful and difficult circumstances with a smile or expression of humor.

Humor is a main ingredient in all aspects of health promotion, self-care, and resilience. Laughter, for instance, occurs much more commonly in social situations, spreading quickly through the brains of those engaged in the "joke." It's an excellent communication tool, disarming any tension that may exist between people, and when reciprocated, it's a signal of meaningful connection. It's also an excellent tool for coping, and when cultivated, enhances mood and reduces symptoms of anxiety. Norman Cousins brought this connection to light by sharing his personal story of illness, fear, and the transforming power of humor in his book *Anatomy of an Illness*. When it comes to coping with illness, surround yourself with loving, compassionate, and empathic people who possess a good sense of humor.

> Humor is a main ingredient in all aspects of health promotion, self-care, and resilience.

Humor and laughter have been shown to enhance immune function and antibody production and lower cortisol levels. Individuals participating in a cardiac rehabilitation program that integrated thirty minutes of funny video recordings each day had significant lowering of cortisol levels after one year, compared to their counterparts. They also had lower blood pressure, fewer episodes of irregular heart rhythms, and fewer repeat heart attacks.

Humor is also useful tool for enhancing trusting partnerships between clinicians and their patients. Dr. Michael Miller, of the University of Maryland School of Medicine, found that watching a funny movie for fifteen minutes relaxed people's arteries, enhancing blood flow or circulation. This effect was seen for up to forty-five minutes after the induced laughter, an effect not unlike aerobic exercise.

I have found a good sense of humor to be an effective icebreaker when dealing with conflict, tense circumstances, and overwhelming stress. Laughter is perhaps one of the more formidable antidotes to the stress response and allostatic burden. In the legacy of Norman Cousins, I integrate humor therapy as part of my bedtime ritual (another private secret exposed). DVD technology makes it so much easier. I have a mini-library of very funny DVDs, including the *Dick Van Dyke Show, I Love Lucy, Taxi, Cheers,* and *Saturday Night Live.* The giggles soon take over and any mindless drivel that is still squeezing cortisol from my adrenal glands soon begins to wane. Very effective stuff this humor.

A smile is also a powerful mood enhancer. From infancy we are rewarded deeply for the giggles and smiles we share. No parent ever forgets the feeling they have when their baby's first smile lights up the room. Smiles like laughter are very contagious and will tend to transcend the most suspicious and distrusting of individuals. We're innately rewarded for receiving and sharing a smile or chuckle.

If you examine a smile that's a gesture of politeness—with or without an element of sincerity behind it but not associated with deep happiness—you'll see only the corners of the mouth turning upward. On the other hand, the "Duchenne smile," named for the eighteenth-century French physiologist who first described it, involves the involuntary contraction of the muscles around the eye. The eyebrows are pulled downward as if to stretch closer to the mouth turning upward. This is a smile with genuine happiness attached to it.

Activity in the nucleus accumbens of the prefrontal lobe appears connected to the positive emotions experienced with the smile. This area of the brain, particularly in the left hemisphere, has also been associated with the reward response. No wonder laughter feels so good and is so good for you. By smiling or laughing, you've engaged a reward response, a context of social attachment, and a constraint of the stress response. So if you're wondering how sincere the smile you are receiving is, look into the eyes of the person smiling at you. If their eyes are without expression, tell them a good joke. You'll both benefit from the health dividend.

4. DANCE TO THE MUSIC

If you're looking for something fun and effective, I'd highly recommend dancing. The benefits are many and include improved musculoskeletal flexibility, enhanced mood, caloric expenditure, and a boost to your reward system. I do it alone, sometimes in the dark, and select tunes based on the fond memories they inspire. I like to think of them as "designer tunes." For example, I can predict that about thirty minutes into a forty-five minute run, I'll begin to feel fatigued and think about the need to wind down. Then just when I thought I was at the point of maximal return, I hear the slow and gradually louder intro to U-2's "With or Without You," and within seconds, I'm moving faster, legs and arms pumping harder, heart and pulse beating more vigorously. I'm less cognizant of the fatigue and resignation that had just washed over me. I'm in total mind-body-behavior synchronicity, a wave of human protoplasm flowing in self-transcendence. I am in maximal effort, but it feels effortless. The bell inside my limbic system is ringing to the sound of flow-state as the instrumental conclusion to "With or Without You" plays before my mind's eye. Total awareness. Just the percussion and nothing else . . . resonating with my cardiac output brings me home to the promised land.

5. CULTIVATE YOUR MOJO

While Austin Powers' mojo was more a source of sensual energy (indeed very important), here I'm referring to mojo as your personal energy source for all that brings joy, meaning, and value satisfaction to your life.

As the market for your energy becomes more competitive, demand has a good shot at outpacing supply. When it comes to your precious energy, it's important not to lose track of the supply-demand balance. Distraction and diversion make it hard to track the needle on the mojo tank. It can insidiously begin to tilt with subtle and certain implications for change in mood, concentration, confidence, pain threshold, and performance. Greater mindfulness of the importance of this balance in your life coupled with the awareness of the need to adapt when time demands get excessive makes possible your potential to sail smoothly under the toughest of circumstances. Transcending these challenges may seem impossible as the perceptions that frame our circumstances create "deflated expectations" of our ability to move forward. We believe we are capable of less than we really are and thus set expectations accordingly. Ask yourself this: Could you limbo beneath the bar at the expectation level you've set for yourself?

6. CUDDLE WITH SOMEONE YOU CARE ABOUT, AT A MINIMUM, TEN MINUTES PER DAY

I know what you're thinking. Cuddle? Does Dr. Pettus think I'm in preschool? Has he become Dr. Barney, the purple health care professional? We mammals were born to cuddle. Holding someone close, feeling the air moving in and out of their lungs, and feeling their hearts beating inside their chests (or saliva on your skin if you're cuddling with a dog) will unleash within you a surge of oxytocin-dopamine-endorphin induced bliss and satisfaction (you also help release this in the person you are cuddling with). As the biological effects may begin to wane within hours, I'd suggest cuddling more often—two to three times per day. Don't take this incredible gift for granted.

7. LOOK BENEATH THE SURFACE: HEALTH PROMOTION, DISEASE SCREENING, AND DISEASE PREVENTION

Feeling well does not equal good health. Look beneath the hood even if your car seems to be running well. Here are a few basic pearls for some common health issues with vital implications for screening, early recognition, and integrated approaches to treatment.

Diabetes
The number of people with diabetes in America is rising at an alarming rate; it is triple what it was some thirty years ago! There's been a comparable rise in individuals with pre-diabetes, many of whom will develop diabetes over time. The statistics are disturbing. There's a clear connection between the growing prevalence of diabetes and pre-diabetes with the epidemic of obesity in the U.S. The overwhelming majority of people who are at risk or who develop diabetes are overweight, make poor nutritional choices, and lead sedentary lives. We now recognize this risk can appear in adolescence and early adulthood. The risk rises further as people age. And while there may be a ge-

netic predisposition for diabetes, it's possible to prevent and reverse many of the genetic expressions of diabetes with lifestyle and behavioral change. Evidence has shown that people who are at high risk for diabetes, when able to lose 5 to 7 percent of their current weight and who walk 150 minutes per week can substantially reduce their risk of becoming a diabetic. Diabetes is associated with the following conditions, among others:

- Kidney failure: Diabetes is the number one cause of kidney failure requiring dialysis and kidney transplantation in the U.S.
- Increased risk of cardiovascular morbidity and mortality, e.g., stroke, heart attack, poor circulation, and death
- Vision loss: Diabetes is the number one cause of loss of vision in the U.S.
- A major risk factor for amputation
- A higher prevalence of depression
- Early death from all causes

How do you know if you are at risk for diabetes? Here are some risk factors that should prompt screening. Remember, most people with diabetes have no symptoms that would point to a problem in the first place.

- Positive family history of diabetes
- Risks for "lifestyle syndrome"
  - Body mass index greater than 30 (refer to the BMI table in Chapter 8: Lifestyle and Behavioral Change)
  - Waist-to-hip ratio greater than 9 for men, greater than 8.5 for women
  - High Blood Pressure or "pre high blood pressure" (BP > 130/85)
  - Waist circumference (based on data from Caucasians, smaller for Asian Americans)
    - Greater than 35 inches in women
    - Greater than 38 inches in men
  - High triglyceride blood levels (>150)
  - Low HDL cholesterol levels
    - Less than 50 in women
    - Less than 40 in men

In 2004, the American Diabetes Association updated guidelines for defining diabetes and just as important, pre-diabetes. *Know these numbers.*

Blood sugar	Normal	Pre-diabetic	Diabetic
Fasting	Under 100	100–125	126 or higher
2 hours after eating	Under 140	140–199	200 or more

As I noted earlier, a disturbing 10–12 percent of Americans fall into the pre-diabetic range. Diverse, silent changes in health begin in this stage and many people will progress to full diabetes. If you're in this category and can walk 150 minutes per week and lose 5–7 percent of your current weight, you can reduce your risk of progressing to full diabetes by 50 percent! No drug is known to be that effective.

BLOOD PRESSURE—GET IT CHECKED!

More than forty million Americans have high blood pressure. Most people recognize that high blood pressure (HBP) is a significant risk factor for heart disease and stroke. Did you know that HBP is a leading cause, like diabetes, of progressive kidney failure requiring dialysis or transplantation? Did you know the HBP could lead to heart failure, a problem of the heart not relaxing and contracting properly? Did you know that HBP could increase the risk of death from cardiovascular causes such as heart attacks, heart failure, and stroke?

HBP, like so many chronic health problems, is deceptively silent until the volcano erupts or until the lights of the oncoming train appear. Headaches, by the way, are usually not related to HBP. The overwhelming majority of individuals with headaches, even if they have HBP, will have other causes for their symptoms. The take home message here is don't wait for a headache to be concerned about your blood pressure.

I see people all the time with milder, progressive problems because of blood pressures that are not where they need to be. Here are some words of wisdom as they relate to HBP and, as you will see, some familiar themes as they relate to health maintenance and disease prevention.

- Have your blood pressure taken during adolescence, particularly if your parents have a history of HBP or if you're overweight.

- Have your blood pressure taken annually as a minimum screen. This will take five minutes out of 525,600 minutes a year. There's simply no excuse for not having your BP checked. This can be done at your physician's office, through various free community screening offerings, or by friends or family members who can measure your pressure. The UPSTF strongly recommends screening by age eighteen at the oldest.

- If your blood pressure is "borderline," e.g., 126–140 systolic and/or 76–90 diastolic, have it repeated periodically, at least every month for the next three months to establish a consistent pattern. Remember, do not minimize the importance of your readings being referred to as "borderline."

- You may come across the expression "white coat hypertension." This refers to the phenomenon of readings in a medical office setting being higher than outside the medical office setting. Though sometimes dismissed as an insignificant concern, white coat hypertension may reflect true hypertension. While it may be milder in its severity, an increased risk of complications over time may exist. My best advice? If you're labeled with white coat hypertension, have frequent readings taken and documented both outside and in medical office settings. I would strongly consider treatment if consistently higher than normal readings occur, regardless of what setting they're taken in.

- Recent published guidelines make note that some individuals with a top number (systolic) between 120–130 and a bottom (diastolic) between 80–85 may be at increased risk for developing high blood pressure in the future. There's some controversy about this among experts in the field. If your BP is in this range, particularly if your parents have HBP, if you are overweight, or if you have another risk factor for heart disease such as high cholesterol, have your pressure checked regularly, at least once a year, as a matter of routine.

- Under any circumstances, losing as little as 5 percent of your current weight, if overweight, with regular activity such as walking 150 minutes a week (sound familiar?) and for some people, moderating salt in your diet, could be the difference between needing medication and not needing medication.

TAKE SMALL STEPS, FOLLOW THE PLAN!

A healthy prognosis for the planet requires the collective energy and positive emotions of people everywhere. The reflections I've shared are both simple and challenging. It's important before you move forward to dispel the notion that simple is easy. How easy something is to understand says little about the degree of difficulty involved in its effective execution. You'll also be tempted to say, "Sure Pettus, this is not rocket science . . . how effective can this be?" Or perhaps, "I've heard this a million times before. I can't believe it could possibly change the way I feel right now."

The take home message is that how you think and how you feel are powerful determinants of our biology and therefore our health and wellness. Positive thinking trumps negative thinking every time, and gratitude, hope, compassion, and empathy trumps anger, distrust, and fear every time. So here are some simple behaviors to consider that will surely enhance the quality of your life. It's not magic. Remember, it's a biological state you're capable of producing! It's your mojo. The planet is depending on it.

> The take home message is that how you think and how you feel are powerful determinants of our biology and therefore our health and wellness.

- Exercise five days per week. Start with what's doable and do it. In two to three weeks, you'll want to do more. Plan for success.
- Experience nature each day. Outdoor walks are the best.
- Nurture an important relationship (one with deeper meaning). This might include making time to talk, socialize, and connect. Consider writing a note (written words are powerful) to someone you need to be in closer touch with.
- Volunteer your time to a cause, person, or activity that means something to you. The best service to self is service to others.
- Find a quiet spot to practice relaxation breathing exercises or meditation for ten minutes twice daily. The benefits here are immediate.
- Cut out one snack per day. Imagine 250 calories less per day, f-o-r-e-v-e-r.
- Follow the **Four Week Addicted-to-Health Program** in Chapter 2. It will help you take small, doable steps to a healthier you.

I welcome your feedback, comments, and suggestions regarding the contents of *It's All in Your Head*. If you're interested in an insider's perspective on how to more effectively navigate our complex system of health care and how you can more effectively partner with it, feel free to check out *The Savvy Patient: The Ultimate Advocate for Quality Health Care.*

Peace to you on your journey of health. Embrace life. Live well.

markpettus@savvypatient.com

Suggested Reading

Benson, Herbert, MD, and Miriam Klipper. *The Relaxation Response*. Reissue ed. HarperTorch. 1976.

Collins, Jim. *Good to Great: Why Some Companies Make the Leap . . . and Others Don't*. Collins. 2001.

Dalai Lama and Howard Cutler. *The Art of Happiness: A Handbook for Living*. Riverhead. 1998.

Fisher, Roger, William Ury, and Bruce Patton. *Getting to Yes: Negotiating Agreement Without Giving In*. 2nd ed. Penguin. 1991.

Frankl, Viktor. *Man's Search For Meaning*. Revised and updated ed. Pocket.1997.

Goleman, Daniel. *Emotional Intelligence: Why It Can Matter More Than IQ*. Bantam. 1997.

Goleman, Daniel. *Primal Leadership: Realizing the Power of Emotional Intelligence*. Harvard Business School Press. 2002.

Johnson, Steven. *Mind Wide Open: Your Brain and the Neuroscience of Everyday Life*. Scribner. 2005.

Kabot-Zinn, Jon. *Wherever You Go, There You Are: Mindfulness Meditation in Everyday Life*. 10th anniversary ed. Hyperion. 2005.

Kurzweil, Ray and Terry Grossman. *Fantastic Voyage*. Penguin Books. 2004.

Lappé, Frances and Jeffrey Perkins. *You Have the Power: Choosing Courage in a Culture of Fear*. Tarcher/Penguin. 2004.

Luskin, Frederic. *Forgive for Good: A Proven Prescription for Health and Happiness*. Harper. 2001.

McEwen, Bruce and Elizabeth Lasley. *The End of Stress As We Know It*. National Academies Press. 2002.

Patterson, Kerry Grenney, Joseph McMillan, and Ron and Al Switzler. *Crucial Conversations: Tools for Talking When Stakes are High*. McGraw-Hill. 2002.

Perlmutter, David and Carol Colman. *The Better Brain Book: The Best Tools for Improving Memory and Sharpness and for Preventing Aging of the Brain*. Riverhead Books. 2004.

Pettus, Mark. *The Savvy Patient: The Ultimate Advocate for Quality Health Care*. Capital Books. 2004.

Sabo, Alex. "The Neuroscience of Stress, Reward and Attachment: How to Use It to Improve Your Health." From The Healthier Berkshire Conference, Hancock, Massachusetts. May 2004.

Sabo, Alex. "The Stress Response and the Separation Cry in Medical and Psychiatric Illness." *Berkshire Medical Journal.* 1997; (4): 5-10.

Sapolsky, Robert. *Why Zebras Don't Get Ulcers.* 3rd ed. Owl Books. 2004.

Schlitz, Marilyn, Tina Amorok, and Marc Micozzi. *Consciousness and Healing: Integral Approaches To Mind-body Medicine.* C.V. Mosby; Bk & DVD edition. 2004.

Seligman, Martin. *Learned Optimism: How to Change Your Mind and Your Life.* Free Press. 1998.

Weil, Andrew. *Healthy Aging: A Lifelong Guide to Your Physical and Spiritual Well-Being.* Knopf. 2005.

Weil, Andrew. *Natural Health, Natural Medicine: The Complete Guide to Wellness and Self-Care for Optimum Health.* Rev. ed. Houghton Mifflin. 2004.

About the Author

Dr. Mark Pettus is a board certified Internist and Nephrologist practicing for over 20 years. He received his A.B. from Boston University and his M.D. from the University of Massachusetts Medical School. His postdoctoral training was at Harvard Medical School. He is a fellow of the American College of Physicians. He is an alumnus of the Harvard School of Public Health's Advanced Program on Conflict Resolution, Negotiation, and Mediation. He is certified as an Age Management specialist. He is a sought after speaker and has lectured extensively on regional and national level and has a special interest in the spiritual-health connection.

His first book, "*The Savvy Patient: The Ultimate Advocate for Quality Health Care* (Capital Books, 2004) has been well received. He has appeared on radio stations nationwide and featured on several TV programs including *New England Newsmakers, Living the Life, The 700 Club, Geraldo Rivera At Large* and *Good Day NY*. He has been featured in *Newsweek, Reader's Digest, Women's Day* and a host of other journals and magazines. Dr. Pettus is also a regular guest on NPR radio. Dr. Pettus is the Medical Director of the Institute for Age Management Medicine. He lives with his wife Lee Ann and two children Anna and Alex in Dalton, Massachusetts. Visit his web site at www.savvypatient.com.

Index